DIAGNOSTICS FOR STRATEGIC DECISION-MAKING

This book develops a comprehensive understanding of diagnostics for strategic decision-making through a model called Rapid Due Diligence. This method draws on academic rigor, critical thinking, systems dynamics, and advanced practicum to provide a compelling solution to the need for effective diagnostics that enable sound strategic decision-making.

Guiding the reader through the six stages of the process from discovery, through analysis, synthesis, and interpretation, Thompsen rigorously and rapidly engages all typical postgraduate disciplines in producing insights for practical application. Drawing on similarities with applied social science research, the Rapid Due Diligence method is supported with scores of techniques, tools, instructions, guidelines, practical advice, and examples. Detailed cases and abbreviated examples of a variety of real strategic situations are provided from organizations operating in North America, Europe, Asia, India, and Australia.

Ideal for graduate students, organizational leaders, and decision makers with a diagnostic method for building a strategic plan, this book is designed to invite deeper understanding and practical application of a strategic diagnostic process that discovers insights for achieving positive results.

Joyce A. Thompsen is the founder and principal of Thompsen Consulting, USA, where she has worked with a host of high profile clients, including Samsung and MassMutual.

Joyce Thompsen's Rapid Due Diligence process works! I experienced the benefits of this practical approach first-hand during the implementation of a large scale strategic initiative. Get ready to deliver meaningful progress in a short period of time, building credibility and momentum quickly. The structured yet flexible framework and tools also provide the benefit of constant consideration to cultural needs, norms and brand alignment! This book will stimulate powerful, high-level thinking for students and leaders regardless of their field.

Julianne McAndrew, *2nd Vice President, Training & Development, Travelers, USA*

DIAGNOSTICS FOR STRATEGIC DECISION-MAKING

The Rapid Due Diligence Model

Joyce A. Thompsen

NEW YORK AND LONDON

First published 2017
by Routledge
711 Third Avenue, New York, NY 10017

and by Routledge
2 Park Square, Milton Park, Abingdon, Oxon OX14 4RN

Routledge is an imprint of the Taylor & Francis Group, an informa business

© 2017 Taylor & Francis

The right of Joyce A. Thompsen to be identified as author of this work has been asserted by her in accordance with sections 77 and 78 of the Copyright, Designs and Patents Act 1988.

All rights reserved. No part of this book may be reprinted or reproduced or utilised in any form or by any electronic, mechanical, or other means, now known or hereafter invented, including photocopying and recording, or in any information storage or retrieval system, without permission in writing from the publishers.

Trademark notice: Product or corporate names may be trademarks or registered trademarks, and are used only for identification and explanation without intent to infringe.

Library of Congress Cataloging in Publication Data
A catalog record for this book has been requested

ISBN: 978-1-138-20220-7 (hbk)
ISBN: 978-1-138-20222-1 (pbk)
ISBN: 978-1-315-47449-6 (ebk)

Typeset in Bembo Std
by codeMantra

To my husband, John R. Wright, Jr., and my sons,
James and Matthew Thompsen

CONTENTS

List of Figures	viii
List of Tables	ix
List of Boxes	xi

1	Introduction	1
2	Definition of Rapid Due Diligence	7
3	Stage One – Scope of the Inquiry	19
4	Stage Two – Preparatory Investigation	30
5	Stage Three – On-Site Discovery	42
6	Stage Four – Analysis and Observation Development	54
7	Stage Five – Synthesis and Formulation of Recommendations	135
8	Stage Six – Delivery of Process Results	180
9	Impact of Rapid Due Diligence	201
10	Case Studies	211
11	For Further Consideration	313

Index	319

LIST OF FIGURES

2.1	The Triple Win	8
6.1	Continuum of Strategic Fit	62
6.2	Flow Network Diagram	67
6.3	Achieving Syzygy within Organizational Performance	74
6.4	Barriers to Effective Strategy Execution	82
6.5	Performance Management Cycle	84
6.6	Establishing Objectives Aligned to the Business	85
6.7	Examples of Performance Management Competencies	87
6.8	Employee Evaluation Form	88
6.9	Drivers of Performance	118
6.10	Value of Loyalty	118
6.11	Potential Trigger Points in Customer Choice Analytics	119
7.1	Sample Causal Loop Diagram	137
7.2	The Triple Win	163
8.1	Slide Deck for a Rapid Due Diligence Discussion	187
8.2	Comparative Course of Action	191
8.3	Snapshot of Change Capability	199
10.1	Strategic Dimensions Status	212
10.2	Causal Loop Diagram of Service	222
10.3	Continuum of Management Support	224
10.4	Customer Service Culture Change	257

LIST OF TABLES

2.1	Rapid Due Diligence Method of Diagnostics	10
3.1	Rapid Due Diligence Method of Diagnostics: Stage One – Scope of the Inquiry	19
3.2	Sources of Rapid Due Diligence Evidence	26
4.1	Rapid Due Diligence Method of Diagnostics: Stage Two – Preparatory Investigation	30
4.2	Strategic Dimensions of an Organization	31
5.1	Rapid Due Diligence Method of Diagnostics: Stage Three – On-Site Discovery	42
6.1	Rapid Due Diligence Method of Diagnostics: Stage Four – Analysis and Observation Development	54
6.2	Code List for Analysis Operations	55
6.3	On-Site Discovery: Interview Content and Analysis Notations	56
6.4	On-Site Discovery: Panel Interview Content and Analysis Notations	57
6.5	Analysis Operation: Readying Data for Analysis	57
6.6	Analysis Operation: Coding for Drawing Conclusions	58
6.7	Strategic Dimensions of an Organization	60
6.8	Integrated Strategic Focus and Potential for Impact	65
6.9	Situation Worksheet with Strategic Thinking Questions	66
6.10	List of Commonly Used Ratios	69
6.11	Components of Measurable Targets	73
6.12	Sample Competencies by Job Family	86
6.13	Potential Critical Knowledge Areas©	93
6.14	Potential Critical Talent Profile To Effectively Activate Critical Knowledge Areas©	93
6.15	Elements Contributing to an Employee Value Proposition	95
6.16	Integrated Strategic Human Capital Alignment Framework	99

x List of Tables

6.17	Factors Interfering with Change Initiatives	107
6.18	Enterprise-Wide Business Development Process	123
7.1	Rapid Due Diligence Method of Diagnostics: Stage Five – Synthesis and Formulation of Recommendations	135
7.2	Discovery Tool: Leadership from a Distance	151
7.3	Principal Themes from Commentary	160
7.4	Implementation Options	167
8.1	Rapid Due Diligence Method of Diagnostics: Stage Six – Delivery of Process Results	180
8.2	Project Map Template	185
8.3	Sample Project Map	186
8.4	Sample Implementation Chart	188
8.5	Potential Cost of Employee Turnover	192
8.6	Sample RACI Chart	193
8.7	Sample Communication Plans	194
8.8	Managing Matrix Intersections	198
8.9	Mutual Expectations for Performance with Major Customers	199
10.1	Business Development Process	216
10.2	Lean Six Sigma Rapid Improvement Event Structured Observations Grid	228
10.3	Integrated Strategic Human Capital Alignment Framework	247
10.4	Mission Planning with Congregation Council	289
10.5	Congregation and Leader Goals	294
10.6	Key Areas of Mission and Ministry Worksheet	297
10.7	Strategic Fulfillment Map	298
10.8	Strategy Fulfillment Scorecard	300

LIST OF BOXES

3.1	Draft Investigative Research Design	26
3.2	Example of Scope of Inquiry	28
4.1	Document Review Notes	32
4.2	Document Review Summary	33
4.3	Sample of Multiple Discovery Methods	36
4.4	Sample Interview Guide	37
5.1	Conducting a Variety of Discovery Techniques	46
5.2	Discovery Techniques in Production Operations	48
5.3	Customer Site Visits	50
6.1	Mapping Strategic Drivers to Sales Performance Metrics	70
6.2	Measuring the Effectiveness and Impact of a Learning Strategy	75
6.3	Development of an Employee Value Proposition	96
6.4	Building Organizational Capacity for Change Integration	108
6.5	Insights on Customer Preferences	119
6.6	Multinational Business Development Process	122
6.7	Seeking Product Development Improvements	125
6.8	Improving Operational Quality and Efficiency	128
7.1	Effects of Hidden Disagreement	140
7.2	Example of Integrating Differing Geographic Cultures	143
7.3	Sample of Preliminary Observations	160
7.4	External Research Comparison	161
7.5	Partial Set of Sample Recommendations	176
10.1	Corporate University Launch Announcement: Key Talking Points and Process	274
10.2	Mission Planning Charts	291
10.3	Strategic Planning Map	299
10.4	Competencies for Business Development Professionals and Managers	306

1
INTRODUCTION

Learning Objectives

- To understand the need for diagnostics for strategic decision-making.
- To identify potential issues that can signal the need for diagnostics.

The purpose of this book is to develop a comprehensive understanding of diagnostics for strategic decision-making, with a focus upon a method entitled Rapid Due Diligence. Diagnostics are defined as the practice of critical organizational analysis and identification of opinions, conclusions, and supporting evidence for strategic decision-making. The Rapid Due Diligence diagnostic method is an intense, complex, strategic process of investigative discovery, analysis, synthesis, and interpretation that engages all of the typical postgraduate disciplines in producing insights within a short period of time for decision-making and practical application.

The Need for Diagnostics for Strategic Decision-Making

Organizations of all types around the world are continuously searching for new insights that can enable realization of greater results and impact. This phenomenon gives rise to a compelling need for effective diagnostics which draw upon academic rigor, critical thinking, and advanced practicum of an integrated set of postgraduate disciplines to enable sound strategic decision-making.

A number of issues can signal the need to engage in diagnostics for strategic decision-making. Following are several examples of such issues:

- An organization has recently forged a new business model or grand aspiration, with or without the assistance of an outside strategy consulting resource.

2 Introduction

The granularity of the execution plan for realization of the targeted results is incomplete. The capability and capacity of the organization to fulfill the plan are unclear, uncertain, or unknown.

- A strategy is already underway, and it is losing momentum or not producing sufficiently favorable early trends or impact. A recovery or modification is needed mid-stream.
- Current organizational practices appear to have stalled or impeded the full realizable results of a new strategy. Considerable clarity, redirection, and perhaps transformation are required for successful execution of the initiative. A deep examination of the organization is needed.
- There are market demands for significant improvement in any of a number of dimensions, for example, product quality, customer attention, delivery time, technical product installation, after-market service, or measurable impact. These demands are perceived to stretch the organization beyond its current limits, and insightful innovations are required.
- A new brand is planned for introduction to the marketplace, and the organization cannot afford to fail to deliver as promised in order to stay competitive. All aspects for the communication and delivery of the new brand need to be thoroughly examined and precisely aligned to effectively achieve the full value and competitive preference in the minds of the targeted market's customers.
- A merger or acquisition has been announced, and a strategic approach is required to ensure the right combination of talent is on board to deliver the Return on Merger or financial and market positioning results promised to shareholders. Diagnostics are needed to identify, compare, contrast, align, and place the talent, knowledge, and experience of the respective employees of the participating organizations within the requirements of the overarching strategy.
- An organization aspires to undertake a strategic move of great significance to its future financial sustainability. Similar attempts in the past have been seriously disappointing or outright failures, and there is insufficient understanding of why those results occurred. These situations require examination to illuminate potential patterns that need to change and to identify effective alternatives.
- Targeted results of a new strategy require at least a double-digit percentage change from the current run-rate of a critical metric. A significant change is necessary in one or more major processes or how the organization does business. Greater clarity is required to guide any degree of change or transformation.
- A strategy carries greater risk than normal to a work group, business unit, or an entire enterprise. Key owners of the strategy are seeking greater certainty in attaining the targeted results.

Introduction **3**

- An organization identifies a new competitive opportunity to advance its stature in a specific market segment, and failure is not an option. Diagnostics are required to ensure sound strategic decision-making in all dimensions of this undertaking.
- A number of strategic initiatives are simultaneously underway within an organization. These initiatives may compete for resources and mindshare and require greater clarity and intentional integration.
- A new market category or business opportunity has been identified, and there is uncertainty about how to best capitalize on the situation in a timely manner.
- The customer value proposition has been compromised, and the organization's responsive strategy must be on target to invite customers and stimulate loyalty. More precise information is required to match the distinctiveness of the value proposition with the organization's capability, processes, and practices in delivering on the promise.
- A not-for-profit organization is losing appeal to its members and donors, and its financial viability is languishing. Diagnostics are needed to pinpoint specific causes for this unintended diminution and to provide alternative strategies aligned with its unique mission and values.
- An organization has experienced a change in its senior leadership, and all key initiatives and strategies are subject to review. The rigor of diagnostics for strategic decision-making is required to achieve a more thorough examination of current and potential strategies.
- An outside auditing firm or regulatory agency has identified an item of material and potentially deleterious impact. Immediate remedial action is warranted, and the process is being vigilantly observed.
- A competitor has made a surprise announcement that represents a stark disruption to the organization's position within its market space. Diagnostics are needed to ensure a precise review of the situation and to formulate innovative options for effective strategic decision-making.

These situations with sudden or unexpected competitive disruption, strategic failures, dislocations, or fleeting opportunities fuel an organization's drive to find new insights with accompanying promises of preferred outcomes. In all cases, sound diagnostics are required for strategic decision-making. These are situations that warrant the academic rigor, critical thinking, and advanced practicum of an integrated set of postgraduate disciplines. Further, the urgency of such situations requires a more rapid execution of the diagnostic process. Deeper levels of critical analysis and information are required to provide greater clarity, identify opportunities to crystallize or reset direction, discover alternative approaches, expose weaknesses in operational execution, reveal potential adverse consequences, align resources more effectively, gauge

4 Introduction

results more accurately, and provide new supporting evidence to strategic decision-making.

All too frequently, the typical responses in such situations can be delayed, costly, time-consuming, bias-laden, and inadequate to comprehensively address the core issues or enable effective decision-making. For example, there may be slow realization of the need or even unwillingness by executives or managers to evaluate the efficacy of current strategies or conduct post-mortem analyses on disappointing results. These decision-makers may be encumbered by overconfidence evoked by memories of the organization's historical performance and blinded to the need for any diagnostics or potential changes. Furthermore, employees may exercise self-preserving caution in choosing to remain inert or silent when strategies appear to be off-course or producing insufficient results; therefore, key decision-makers may not know that a strategy is about to fail.

There is a broad need for an objective, strategic, rapidly executable, organizational diagnostic method that draws upon both academic rigor and experiential practicum from an integrated set of disciplines. Such a diagnostic method requires access to decision-makers and performers at all levels of responsibility and productivity. This method also requires researchers to have the disciplined capability and capacity to rapidly conduct sufficient inquiry, critical analysis, and synthesis in order to produce reliable observations, fresh insights, and potential remedies with sound supporting evidence. It is essential for postgraduate students, management professionals, and decision-makers to understand why this capability is so necessary for organizational success and how to equip themselves to perform such a diagnostic method with integrity.

Outline of the Book

The book aspires to develop a deeper understanding of diagnostics for strategic decision-making, with a focus upon the Rapid Due Diligence method. A core assumption is that postgraduate students already possess a sound grasp of master's level disciplines of business management. The nature of the Rapid Due Diligence diagnostic method produces continuous and time-sensitive interactions with a host of data, models, concepts, and frameworks which place great demands on the intellectual capabilities and maturity of the diagnostic researcher. This method also draws upon the rigor of applied social science research.

The book is organized to establish the need for diagnostics for strategic decision-making and the distinctive characteristics of the Rapid Due Diligence method of strategic organizational diagnosis. The method is defined and described in several stages, supported by a variety of constructs, models, and perspectives. Illustrative examples of applications are drawn from several case studies of organizations operating in North America, Europe, Asia, and Australia. Discussion questions accompany each chapter. Selected bibliographies for further reading are provided in several chapters. The outline of the remainder of the book is as follows:

1. Chapter Two defines the Rapid Due Diligence method as a unique form of strategic organizational diagnosis. Its distinctive differentiation from other forms of diagnosis is described. The overall method with its six progressive stages is introduced. Similarities between the Rapid Due Diligence method and applied social science research methodology are explored.
2. Chapter Three describes the scope of the inquiry, the first of the six stages of the Rapid Due Diligence diagnostic method. Each stage sets forth the roles of principal players, process steps, expected outcomes, and projected duration. Guidelines are provided for preparing an effective investigative research and diagnostic design or plan.
3. Chapter Four describes how to refine the final investigative research and diagnostic design or plan. This design defines the types of evidence to seek and how to conduct the initial background investigatory research in order to secure further clarity into the central issue.
4. Chapter Five provides instructions and protocol guidelines for conducting a number of forms of on-site discovery with subject matter experts. The investigative research and diagnostic design also provides instructions for preparing, organizing, and managing evidence.
5. Chapter Six explores a variety of analytical techniques and how to apply multiple filters to all forms of evidence. A series and sequence of specific analytical techniques, models, or constructs are applied to address the central issue in a direct, effective, and efficient manner.
6. Chapter Seven describes how to choose and apply more complex types of analysis and integrative synthesis to the various forms of evidence and any preliminary findings. Techniques are included for formulating conclusions about the evidence, estimating implications for potential impact, and creating recommendations for strategic decision-making.
7. Chapter Eight describes how to prepare the findings, observations, conclusions, and recommendations for action in appropriate and effective frameworks for strategic decision-making and potential action. Guidelines are included for facilitating discussions of results from the Rapid Due Diligence diagnostic method with key decision makers.
8. Chapter Nine provides specific examples of results achieved in real case studies where recommendations from the Rapid Due Diligence diagnostic method were accepted and applied.
9. Chapter Ten provides full descriptions of several case studies of a variety of strategic situations, drawn from organizations operating in North America, Europe, Asia, and Australia.
10. Chapter Eleven frames questions and ideas for further research and discovery to enhance the Rapid Due Diligence diagnostic method.

6 Introduction

Discussion Questions

- Why are effective diagnostics important for strategic decision-making?
- What are the risks or rewards that can flow from the various ways of responding to strategic issues?
- What are the specific disciplinary perspectives that should be incorporated in the diagnostic method for the situational examples noted in this chapter?

2
DEFINITION OF RAPID DUE DILIGENCE

Learning Objectives

- To define the Rapid Due Diligence diagnostic method and its six progressive stages.
- To understand the similarities and differences between Rapid Due Diligence and applied social science research methodology.

The Rapid Due Diligence method is a unique form of strategic organizational diagnosis. Whereas it is a practice of critical organizational analysis and identification of opinions, conclusions, and supporting evidence for strategic decision-making, it embodies a level of intensity and complexity that engages all of the typical postgraduate business management disciplines as well as certain aspects of applied social science research methodology within a short period of time.

The reason this method is described as rapid is that the entire body of work is typically completed within thirty days or less, depending upon the scope and complexity of the situation. Where there has been considerable urgency, the process has been completed within ten or fewer days.

Comparison of Diagnostic Methods

Some typical attempts to conduct diagnostic analysis can fail to deliver fully effective results for sound strategic decision-making. For example, some resources may choose to apply their own complex algorithms to customer or market analytics, financial formulas, or other models, then to make high-level strategic recommendations without practical assistance to the organization on how to execute any necessary changes. Others may choose to pursue singular, purely theoretical models in their diagnostic processes which often stand disconnected and in relative isolation from the complex realities of practical strategy formulation and execution. Still others may search for predetermined conditions that are designed to make their own, often overly simplistic, prepackaged solutions attractive while not necessarily solving real or core issues. These approaches tend to deliver incomplete, potentially biased, or inaccurate portrayals of the core situation and potential remedies.

By contrast, there are several areas of balanced focus for the Rapid Due Diligence method of diagnostics. The initial focus is on the current business situation or presenting symptoms, the degree of clarity and execution of an existing or proposed strategy, the integration of multiple strategic initiatives, and appropriate measurement of impact across the broad scope of the business, including the status of critical business management or financial ratios. The area of inquiry can include an entire enterprise, a large business division, specific geographic locations, singular production facility, or market category. This applies to either a for-profit or not-for-profit organization. Another swath of inquiry is on the organization's verifiable capability, capacity, and cultural will to deliver on the desired strategy to achieve the targeted results. A third broad category of attention lies in the field of behavioral economics, customer interests, and market potential or actual response to the strategy. This method does not rely on a singular model to illuminate what is often a multi-layered labyrinth with interrelated intersections and interstitial areas of influence or execution.

The Rapid Due Diligence method of diagnostics is undertaken with a distinctive point of view to seek and position the potential for a balanced Triple Win with the acceptance and implementation of any recommendations for strategic consideration. Upon realization, the Triple Win (Figure 2.1) means substantial benefits will be derived by an organization in its business health and viability, by its customers in their degree of satisfaction with products and services, and by employees who engage the strategy and bear the tasks of delivering those products and services.[1]

FIGURE 2.1 The Triple Win.

By comparison, a host of other diagnostic methods tend to lean toward delivery of benefits primarily to the financial or competitive well-being of the organization alone. Perhaps as an ancillary or secondary benefit, the customers may experience greater satisfaction with the products and services. Employees are often left to be content with, at best, the potential for increased job security.

The Rapid Due Diligence diagnostic method is intentional in its discovery, analysis, synthesis, and interpretation of findings to seek benefits for all three perspectives in the context of a Triple Win. For this reason, the investigative research and diagnostic design or plan for the Rapid Due Diligence diagnostic method deliberately includes a balance of discovery in areas of related business and financial factors, satisfaction and loyalty ratings of customers as they do business with an organization, and the degree of engagement of all contributing employees with their talent, skills, abilities, knowledge, and motivations. More complex analysis and synthesis techniques are also applied to test for intended results and hidden or unintended consequences as these three perspectives are integrated in action.

Diagnostic Stages of Rapid Due Diligence

There are six progressive stages to the Rapid Due Diligence method of diagnostics for strategic decision-making. These stages include the following:

- Scope of the inquiry
- Preparatory investigation
- On-site discovery
- Analysis and observation development
- Synthesis and formulation of recommendations
- Delivery of process results

Table 2.1 shows these six stages and the respective set of players involved in each stage, the process steps, targeted outcomes, and typical timeline for the Rapid Due Diligence diagnostic method.

Chapters Three through Eight provide deeper definitions and descriptions for how to conduct each of these separate stages, supported by a variety of diagrams, constructs, models, and perspectives that aim toward the Triple Win. Within each chapter, illustrative examples of applications are drawn from several case studies of organizations operating in North America, Europe, Asia, and Australia. To protect trade secrets, the identity of the organizations remains anonymous throughout this text.

TABLE 2.1 Rapid Due Diligence Method of Diagnostics

	Stage One	*Stage Two*	*Stage Three*	*Stage Four*	*Stage Five*	*Stage Six*
	Scope of the Inquiry	*Preparatory Investigation*	*On-Site Discovery*	*Analysis & Observation Development*	*Synthesis & Formulation of Recommendations*	*Delivery of Process Results*
Players Involved	• Owner of situation • Organizational key contact • Principal researcher • Research team (if any)	• Organizational key contact • Principal researcher, • Research team (if any)	• Organizational key contact • Subject matter experts • Principal researcher • Research team (if any)	• Principal researcher • Research team (if any)	• Principal researcher • Research team (if any)	• Owner of situation • Organizational key contact • Principal researcher • Research team (if any)
Process Steps	• Secure clarity on situation, process, outcomes & timeline. • Organize to collect evidence. • Prepare draft research design.	• Gather background information. • Conduct preliminary analysis. • Pinpoint areas for inquiry.	• Conduct on-site interviews & direct observations. • Distribute any online survey & collect input.	• Organize all sources of data. • Conduct separate analyses of all sources of data.	• Conduct more complex analyses & synthesis of all sources of data. • Capture gaps.	• Prepare written report & supporting documents.

	• Confirm access to information & people. • Prepare for on-site work.	• Confirm research design & protocol. • Secure discovery schedule. • Prepare surveys.	• Gather any new background information. • Manage data. • Provide key contact with updates.	• Apply initial filters to findings. • Capture gaps. • Record observations.	• Record conclusions. • Formulate specific steps to move from current to targeted outcomes.	• Present summary of key findings. • Facilitate discussion with designated decision-makers.
Outcomes	• Mutual understanding of situation, process, and desired outcomes	• Initial findings • Research design with protocol, fields of inquiry & discovery process	• Findings from subject matter experts	• Initial analytical results & observations about findings	• Conclusions • Recommendations for action	• Deliverables completed • Organization prepared for strategic decision-making
Timeline	1 day	3–5 days	5–10 days	3–5 days	3–5 days	2 days

12 Definition of Rapid Due Diligence

Rapid Due Diligence and Applied Social Science Research

There are similarities between the Rapid Due Diligence method of strategic organizational diagnostics and case study methods used extensively in applied social science research. The case study method is a preferred approach when research questions of "how" and "why" are posed, when the focus of study is a contemporary issue in a specific context, and when the investigator or researcher has little or no control over the series of events under study.[2]

Case study methodology is particularly appropriate for organizational and management diagnosis or research in professional fields such as management science and business administration. Adaptation of this methodology allows the Rapid Due Diligence diagnostic process to retain the meaningful characteristics of real-life situations, such as organizational and managerial processes, business development relationships, organizational performance management, and strategy execution.

The case study methodology can be used for exploratory, descriptive, or explanatory purposes. It can be used to illuminate one or more decision opportunities and create a framework for discussion and decision-making. While the method requires careful attention to diagnostic design, analysis, observations about the findings, and formulation of recommendations for discussion and decision-making, it does not require the same type or depth of rigorous empirical data collection and factored analysis as formal hypothesis testing or other experimental forms of applied social science research.

The Rapid Due Diligence diagnostic method shares many of the characteristics of exploratory field studies or non-experimental inquiries focused on discovering relationships and interactions among variables in real social structures, such as organizations and institutions. Similar to field studies, the Rapid Due Diligence diagnostic method is strong in realism, the number of variables, and the opportunity for application of theory and heuristics. This approach has the capability to process a wide variety of evidence such as descriptive documents, interviews, survey results, and direct observations of participants.

The resulting greater complexity can mean that the process can encounter some weakness or lesser precision in the measurement or evaluation of variables and impact. For these reasons, the research design for a high-quality Rapid Due Diligence diagnostic method must be particularly robust and pursued with rigorous attention to detail and precision of all process steps.[3]

Drawing upon the principles of applied behavioral or social science research, the Rapid Due Diligence diagnostic method requires a research design, plan, or overall scheme with an outline of the purpose of the investigation, what the researcher will do throughout the inquiry process, and the operational implications of selecting evidence and analyses of data to arrive at findings and conclusions.

Just as in conducting case study work, the researcher deploying the Rapid Due Diligence diagnostic method needs to be vigilant in capturing and reporting all evidence in a fair, accurate, and complete way, free of potential bias. This is a particular distinction with resources that rely too heavily or exclusively on their own models, formulas, or prepackaged solutions to skew findings and recommendations to further their own advantages.

The Rapid Due Diligence diagnostic method, in emulating the case study research methodology, relies on the investigation of multiple sources of evidence, the triangulation and convergence of these sources, and the application of constructs and theoretical propositions in guiding both the data collection and various forms of analysis.

The investigation research design or plan of the Rapid Due Diligence diagnostic method draws upon logic that links the evidence to be collected with the analysis, interpretation, and formulation of the decision framework. In doing so, the Rapid Due Diligence diagnostic method relies on an underlying logical model of proof that allows the researcher to draw inferences about the causal relationships among the variables of the investigated situation.

The Rapid Due Diligence investigation research design or plan serves as a blueprint to determine or refine the scope of the inquiry, identifies relevant evidence, shapes the triangulation and convergence of any or all findings, guides the analysis, and establishes the criteria for interpretation of all data to create a set of recommendations. Where possible, the investigation should include a mix of both qualitative and quantitative evidence. Direct, detailed behavioral observations, supported by rich, thick descriptions, are desirable but not required. Such methods are used to illuminate one or more critical decisions and create a framework for decision-making. Use of these methods will ensure a responsible, professional level of investigative rigor and critical thinking throughout the application of the Rapid Due Diligence diagnostic method.

Characteristics of the Researcher

The nature of the Rapid Due Diligence diagnostic method places greater demands on the intellect, ego, and emotions of the researcher than other, less intensive forms of diagnostic investigation. In part, this is because there is continuous, rapid-fire interaction with a host of data and a number of models, concepts, issues, and disciplines. The researcher also needs to exercise initiative in responding to unexpected discoveries or in identifying and leveraging any emerging opportunities during the investigation.

The fundamental capabilities and skills required for a researcher to effectively conduct the Rapid Due Diligence diagnostic method include the following:

- An inquisitive mind that can quickly and easily formulate incisive questions and interpret responses
- Deep listening skills and intake capacity that can assimilate large amounts of new information and do so without preconception or bias
- The capability to accurately capture and assess mood, affectation, and perceptions of interviewees

14 Definition of Rapid Due Diligence

- The ability to balance the rigor of the investigative process with adaptability and flexibility to accommodate unanticipated events
- A firm grasp of strategic, governance, process, policy, and performance execution factors in motion
- A keen understanding of how, when, and why evidence may be contradictory and require further investigation
- Sufficient fluency in several dimensions, models, frameworks, heuristics, and disciplines to enable virtually autonomous sensing of important data points while maintaining the integrity of the results
- The ability to simultaneously apply multiple perspectives as filters, thus speeding up the diagnostic process and yet ensuring highly integrated analysis and synthesis, free of bias

Similar to case study methodology, the Rapid Due Diligence diagnostic method includes development and application of investigative protocol. This includes a set of procedures, rules, and any instruments for conducting interviews, direct observations, or staging surveys. This protocol increases the reliability of the Rapid Due Diligence diagnostic method and focuses attention to the central purpose and scope of study, provides for unanticipated events, reduces the introduction of potential bias, and guides the researcher during high-intensity data intake periods such as field studies or on-site discovery activities.

This depth of working knowledge about frameworks, models, disciplines, or heuristics must not, however, introduce bias toward substantiating a preconceived observation or solution. This is one of the risks inherent in relying on researchers who are connected with purveyors of prepackaged solutions or application of a single model.

To help reduce the potential for unintentional introduction of bias into the Rapid Due Diligence diagnostic method, the researcher is instructed to observe the following guidelines:[4]

- Be aware, as the researcher, of the natural tendency of the mind, temperament, and intentions related to the inquiry.
- Avoid the reliance on such interests in shaping the scope of work, selection of evidence to be pursued and captured, choice of analyses, and the final exposition of findings and process results.
- Prepare to be competent and fastidious in selecting and reporting evidence.
- Recognize or acknowledge underlying assumptions that can skew the process.
- Complete the entire Rapid Due Diligence diagnostic process in ways that exhibit scholarly virtues of accuracy, order, thoroughness, logic, honesty, self-awareness, and imagination.
- Ensure the final analysis, observations, conclusions, and recommendations are based on factual evidence, not implications based on bias.

Future chapters include more detail on reducing the potential for introducing bias into the Rapid Due Diligence diagnostic process.

Discussion Questions

- In what types of situations is the Rapid Due Diligence method a preferable diagnostic approach? Why?
- What are the benefits of adapting applied social science research to the Rapid Due Diligence diagnostic method?
- Why are the characteristics and qualifications of the researcher important?
- Why is it important to be vigilant about the introduction of bias into the process?

Notes

1 Joyce A. Thompsen, *Achieving a Triple Win: Human Capital Management of the Employee Lifecycle* (London: Routledge, 2010), 3.
2 Robert K. Yin, *Case Study Research: Design and Methods, Second Edition* (Thousand Oaks, CA: SAGE Publications, 1994), 1–5.
3 Fred N. Kerlinger, *Foundations of Behavioral Research, Third Edition* (Fort Worth, TX: Harcourt Brace, 1992), 374–375.
4 Jacques Barzun and Henry F. Graff, *The Modern Researcher, Fifth Edition* (Fort Worth, TX: Harcourt Brace Jovanovich, 1992), 186–192.

References

Barzun, Jacques, and Henry F. Graff. 1992. *The Modern Researcher, Fifth Edition*. Fort Worth, TX: Harcourt Brace Jovanovich.

Kerlinger, Fred N. 1992. *Foundations of Behavioral Research, Third Edition*. Fort Worth, TX: Harcourt Brace.

Thompsen, Joyce A. 2010. *Achieving a Triple Win: Human Capital Management of the Employee Lifecycle*. London: Routledge.

Yin, Robert K. 1994. *Case Study Research: Design and Methods, Second Edition*. Thousand Oaks, CA: SAGE Publications.

Selected Bibliography

Listed below are a number of works and sources that have been useful in writing this textbook. The list is intended as a convenience for those who wish to pursue additional study in the fields covered in this chapter.

Bailyn, Lotte, Joyce Fletcher, and Deborah Kolb. "Unexpected Connections: Considering Employees' Personal Lives Can Revitalize Your Business." *MIT Sloan Management Review*, Summer 1997.

Barney, J. "Firm Resources and Sustained Competitive Advantage." *Journal of Management* 17, 1991.

Bassi, L., and D. McMurrer. "Maximizing Your Return on People." *Harvard Business Review*, March 2007.

Bersin, Josh. "High-Impact Talent Management: State of the Market and Executive Overview." Bersin & Associates paper, May 2007.

———. "Talent Management: Is It Too Important to Delegate to HR?" Bersin & Associates paper, March 2007.

16 Definition of Rapid Due Diligence

Borton, Greg. "Managing the Productivity and Costs of the Employee Job Life Cycle." Primary Matters paper, October 2004.

Boudreau, John W., and Peter M. Ramstad. "Talentship and the Evolution of Human Resources Management: From Professional Practices to Strategic Talent Decision Science." University of Southern California Center for Effective Organizations working paper #G04–6, 2004.

Bryan, Lowell L. "The New Metrics of Corporate Performance: Profit per Employee." *The McKinsey Quarterly*, (June 2007).

Bryan, Lowell L., and Claudia I. Joyce. "Better Strategy through Organizational Design." *The McKinsey Quarterly*, no. 2 (2007).

———. *Mobilizing Minds: Creating Wealth from Talent in the 21st-Century Organization*. New York: McGraw-Hill, 2007.

Bryan, Lowell L., Claudia I. Joyce, and Leigh M. Weiss. "Making a Market in Talent." *The McKinsey Quarterly*, no. 2 (2006).

Byrne, John. "How to Lead Now." *Fast Company* magazine, August 2003.

Cauldron, Shari. "How HR Drives Profits." *Workforce* magazine, December 2001.

Center for Workforce Development. "The Teaching Firm: Where Productive Work and Learning Converge." Newton, MA: Education Development Center, 1998.

"CEO Challenge 2004." The Conference Board paper, August 2004.

"CEO Takes HR to Primetime – Between the Lines – Jim Goodnight, SAS." *Workforce* magazine, December 2002.

Center for Workforce Preparation (CWP), a not-for-profit affiliate with the U.S. Chamber of Commerce report.

Charan, R., S. Drotter, and J. Noel. *The Leadership Pipeline: How to Build the Leadership-Powered Company*. San Francisco: Jossey-Bass, 2001.

"2007 Chief Learning Officer Business Intelligence Industry Report: Executive Summary." *Chief Learning Officer* magazine, May 2007.

Courtney, H. *20/20 Foresight: Crafting Strategy in an Uncertain World*. Boston: Harvard Business School Press, 2001.

Cross, Rob, and Wayne Baker. "What Creates Energy in Organizations?" *MIT Sloan Management Review* 44, no. 4 (Summer 2003).

Davidson, Glenn, Stan Lepeak, and Elizabeth Newman. "The Impact of the Aging Workforce on Public Sector Organizations and Mission." International Public Management Association for Human Resources, February 2007.

Fitz-enz, J. *The ROI of Human Capital: Measuring the Economic Value of Employee Performance*. New York: AMACOM, 2000.

Goffee, Rob, and Gareth Jones. "Leading Clever People." *Harvard Business Review,* March 2007.

Grant, R.M. "The Resource-Based Theory of Competitive Advantage: Implications for Strategy Formulation." *California Management Review* 33 (1991).

Guthridge, Matthew, Asmus Komm, and Emily Lawson. "The People Problem in Talent Management." *The McKinsey Quarterly*, no. 2 (2006).

Hall, R. "A Framework Linking Intangible Resources and Capabilities to Sustainable Competitive Advantage." *Strategic Management Journal* 14 (1993).

"Hallmarks of Success: Strategies for Improving Leadership Quality and Executive Readiness." Corporate Executive Board and Corporate Leadership Council, 2003.

"High Impact Talent Management: Top 22 Best Practices." *What Works in Enterprise Learning and Talent Management* newsletter, May 2007.

"HR Executive Review: Implementing the New Employment Compact." The Conference Board paper, 1997.

"Introducing High Impact Talent Management Research Findings." *What Works in Talent Management* newsletter, May 2007.

"It's 2008: Do You Know Where Your Talent Is? Connecting People to What Matters." Deloitte Research paper, 2007.

Jaques, E., S. D. Clement, C. Rigby, and T.O. Jacobs. "Senior Leadership Requirements at the Executive Level." ARI Research Report Number 1420. Alexandria, VA: U.S. Army Research Institute for the Behavioral and Social Sciences, 1986.

Kamoche, K. "Strategic Human Resource Management within a Resource-Capability View of the Firm." *Journal of Management Studies* 33 (1996).

Kichak, Nancy. "Statement of the Associate Director for Strategic Human Resources Policy, U.S. Office of Personnel Management, before the Subcommittee on Federal Workforce, Postal Service, and the District of Columbia Committee on Oversight and Government Reform on Diversity in the Senior Executive Service." U.S. House of Representatives, May 10, 2007.

Kiger, Patrick J. "Explaining Executives' Dim View of HR." *Workforce Management*, June 26, 2007.

Landsman, Diane. "Talent Management at the Best Workplaces." *Talent Management* magazine, April 2007.

Leibs, Scott. "Measuring Up: Many Companies Still Struggle to Use Metrics Effectively." *CFO Magazine*, June 2007.

Lexis-Nexis Deutschland, GmbH. "Ergebrisse der Wissensmanagement Studies," March 2004.

Mahoney, J.T. "The Management of Resources and the Resource of Management." *Journal of Business Research* 33 (1995).

Mankins, M., and R. Steele. "Turning Great Strategy into Great Performance." *Harvard Business Review*, July-August 2005.

Michael, E., H. Handfield-Jones, and B. Axelrod. *The War for Talent*. Boston: Harvard Business School Press, 2001.

Parsons, George D., and Richard T. Pascale. "Crisis at the Summit." *Harvard Business Review*, March 2007.

Penrose, E. *The Theory of the Growth of the Firm*. New York: John Wiley & Sons, 1959.

"Performance and Talent Management Trend Survey 2007." Business Performance Management Forum and Success Factors report, March 2007.

Perlow, Leslie. "Finding Time: How Corporations, Individuals, and Families Can Benefit from New Work Practices." Cornell University paper, 1997.

Porter, Michael E. "Toward a Dynamic Theory of Strategy." Article in *Fundamental Issues in Strategy: A Research Agenda* by R. P. Rumelt, D. E. Schendel, and D. J. Teece, eds. Boston: Harvard Business School Press, 1994.

"Retiring Workforce, Widening Skills Gap, Exodus of 'Critical Talent' Threaten U.S. Companies: Deloitte Consulting Survey." *CFO Magazine*, February 15, 2005.

Siebert, Scott, Maria Kroimer, and Robert Lider. "A Social Capital Theory of Career Success." *Academy of Management Journal*, April, 2001.

Spender, J. C. "Making Knowledge the Basis of the Dynamic Theory of the Firm." *Strategic Management Journal* 17 (1996).

Sterman, John D. *Business Dynamics: Systems Thinking and Modeling for a Complex World*. Boston: Irwin McGraw-Hill, 2000.

Sullivan, John. "The True Value of Hiring and Retaining Top Performers." Report of the California Strategic HR Partnership. *Workforce: HR Trends and Tools for Business Results,* October 1, 2002.

Taub, Stephen. "MVPs of MVA: Measuring How Much Market Value Companies Created." *CFO* magazine, July 2003.

"The Battle for Brainpower." *The Economist* magazine, October 5, 2006.

"The Leadership Benchstrength Challenge: Building Integrated Talent Management Systems." Executive Development Associates study, 2005.

"The 'Masculine' and 'Feminine' Sides of Leadership and Culture: Perception vs. Reality." Knowledge@Wharton, October 5, 2005.

Thomas, Nancy, Scott Iaslow, and Pam Watkins. "Executive Skills: Talent at All Levels." *Talent Management* magazine, March 2007.

Thompsen, Joyce A. "A Case Study on Achieving Return on Critical Talent in Technology-Intensive Organizations." Portland International Conference on Management of Engineering and Technology proceedings, July 20, 2003.

———. "Achieving Return on Critical Knowledge." Proceedings of Portland International Conference on Management of Engineering and Technology, August 1999.

———. "Achieving Return on Critical Knowledge and Talent." Presentation to the American Society of Training and Development, Houston, TX, September 2001.

———. "Achieving Return on Critical Talent in Technology-Intensive Organizations." Proceedings from IEEE International Engineering Management Conference, St. John's College, Cambridge University, UK, August 18, 2002.

———. "Aligning Learning Content with Workforce Competencies." *Chief Learning Officer* magazine, April 2006.

———. "Current Trends in Succession Planning and Management" presentation, Washington, D.C., June 12, 2007.

———. "Gaining Greater Benefit from Lean Six Sigma and Leadership Initiatives within the Military." Proceedings of the IEEE International Engineering Management Conference, St. John's, Newfoundland, Canada, September 11, 2005.

———. "Managing the Employee Relationship Lifecycle" presentation. Houston ASTD Conference, September 25, 2007.

———. "Strategy to Results: Achieving Greater Return on Critical Talent." AchieveGlobal research paper, October 2004.

———. "The REAL Impact of People" presentation. Arizona Society for Human Resource Management Conference, September 7, 2004.

Thompsen, Joyce, and Anne E.P. Smith. "Building Leadership Bench Strength: Current Trends in Succession Planning and Management." AchieveGlobal research paper, October 2005.

Thompsen, Joyce, and John Center. "The Virtual Enterprise Framework and Tool Box: A Convergence of Communications, Computing, and Energy Technologies." Proceedings of the IEEE International Conference on Engineering and Technology Management. Vancouver, British Columbia, Canada, August 1996.

Watkins, Michael. *The First 90 Days.* Boston: Harvard Business School Press, 2003.

Watson Wyatt press release on their fourth Human Capital Index study, October 28, 2002.

"Within Reach ... But Out of Synch: The Possibilities and Challenges of Shaping Tomorrow's Government Workforces." Report by The Council for Excellence in Government and the Gallup Organization, December 5, 2006.

Zaccaro, S. *The Nature of Executive Leadership: A Conceptual and Empirical Analysis of Success.* Washington, D.C.: American Psychological Association, 2001.

3
STAGE ONE – SCOPE OF THE INQUIRY

Learning Objectives

- To understand the elements of the first stage of the Rapid Due Diligence diagnostic method.
- To acquire guidelines for preparing an effective investigative research and diagnostic plan.

In the first stage of the Rapid Due Diligence diagnostic method for strategic decision-making, the researcher focuses upon establishing the scope of the inquiry. For reference, the description of the first stage has been excised from the full six-stage table in Chapter Two and appears in Table 3.1.

The players involved in the first stage include the owner of the organizational situation, the designated organizational key contact, the principal researcher, and

TABLE 3.1 Rapid Due Diligence Method of Diagnostics: Stage One – Scope of the Inquiry

Players Involved	• Owner of situation • Organizational key contact • Principal researcher • Research team (if any)
Process Steps	• Secure clarity on situation, process, outcomes & timeline. • Organize to collect evidence. • Prepare draft research design. • Confirm access to information & people. • Prepare for on-site work.
Outcomes	• Mutual understanding of situation, process, and desired outcomes
Timeline	1 day

20 Stage One – Scope of the Inquiry

any other members of the diagnostic research team. It is important to distinguish the roles of the players.

The owner of the organizational situation is the person who bears ultimate responsibility for the success or failure of a specific strategy for the organization. This is typically a person in an executive role with profit and loss accountability in a for-profit organization. If the scope of the work is an entire enterprise, the owner is most often at the senior executive level with a title such as chief executive officer, chief operations officer, or chief sales or marketing officer. For a large business division, the owner is likely the division general manager. For a geographic location, the owner may be the country manager or regional manager with responsibility for portions of a country, more than one country, or continent. In some cases, the scope of the inquiry is confined to a specific singular location or group of production facilities, in which case the owner is often the production vice president or production manager. In other cases, the scope of the inquiry focuses upon a market category, customer group, or product development area; and the owner carries similar functional executive or managerial titles. In a governmental agency or not-for-profit organization, the owner of the situation is the individual who carries the ultimate accountability for achieving the assignment or mission. In all situations, the owner carries the ultimate responsibility for deciding on the course of strategic action and guiding the achievement of results from the execution of that strategy. The owner determines who else may be involved in the investigation process, in receiving the final recommendations from the Rapid Due Diligence diagnostic process, and how the final decision-making will occur.

In nearly all cases, the owner of the situation appoints another individual to serve as the organizational key contact for the day-to-day work of arranging and completing the Rapid Due Diligence diagnostic process details. The key contact is a trusted member of the organization who has significant knowledge about the nature of the business situation in question, the current strategy that is planned or in motion, the supporting processes, and identity of others who can effectively serve as subject matter experts in the investigation. The key contact is granted the authority to access relevant information and set schedules for all forms of on-site discovery. This person is readily available for regular contact or to respond to clarifying organizational questions from the researcher or research team. The key contact also has sufficient depth of understanding of the importance and scope of the inquiry, the viewpoints of the owner, the nuances of cultural practices and organizational norms, distinctive behavioral characteristics of the subject matter experts, market competition, or customers to serve as an able and trustworthy internal resource to the researcher or research team.

The organizational key contact also receives periodic interim reviews and may be asked to provide clarification or verification of emerging findings during the course of the Rapid Due Diligence diagnostic process. If the key contact does not personally possess sufficient information to provide such guidance, this individual knows where to secure such information or when to engage the owner of the business situation in discussion. The key contact is also the individual who previews the first draft of Rapid Due Diligence diagnostic results, including supporting evidence, conclusions, and recommendations for future decision-making.

The principal researcher is the individual who has primary responsibility for the design, conduct, and completion of the Rapid Due Diligence diagnostic process. This individual crafts the investigative research design or plan, sets the investigative protocol, determines the forms of on-site discovery, chooses the types of analysis and synthesis to be conducted, establishes the criteria for reaching conclusions and formulating recommendations, designs the delivery of all process results, takes steps to ensure high process integrity, and oversees the execution of every stage of the process.

The principal researcher is expected to have a deep understanding of the entire Rapid Due Diligence diagnostic process and a working knowledge of all types of discovery, analysis, and synthesis, plus the likely impact of proposed recommendations. The principal researcher also bears responsibility for ensuring that there is no encroachment of bias in any of the process stages. The principal researcher is the primary communications link with both the owner of the business situation and the organizational key contact.

Depending upon the scope and complexity of the business situation, the principal researcher may be supported by one or more assisting resources. These individuals may have deep expertise in a particular aspect of the on-site discovery, any of the tools or techniques used in the analysis or synthesis stages, data management, or documentation requirements. In all cases, the team members are expected to fulfill any or all of the stages of the Rapid Due Diligence diagnostic process with bias-free integrity, confidentiality, accuracy, thoroughness, and sense of urgency. Each team member is expected to maintain a complete record of communications, actions taken, results secured, and disposition of all assigned data.

Upon the identification of a business situation that warrants a Rapid Due Diligence diagnostic process, the initial step in this first stage consists of a discussion between the owner of the business situation, the designated organizational key contact, and the principal researcher or research team. This opening discussion occurs irrespective of the choice to assign an internal resource or engage an external consulting resource to conduct the diagnostic process. The purpose is to confirm the scope of the inquiry and organize for the diagnostic process.

In preparation for this opening discussion, the principal researcher conducts a preliminary review of any website information on the organization to gain familiarity with high-level fundamentals of the business, its field of competitive play, products and services, and geographic reach. This brief review enables the researcher to ask logical questions and begin to build credibility with the owner of the business situation and the organizational key contact.

22   Stage One – Scope of the Inquiry

The principal researcher then creates the agenda and facilitates the discussion to achieve at least the following:

- Secure a mutual understanding and clarity on the presenting circumstances of the business situation, the desired strategic outcomes, the stages of the Rapid Due Diligence diagnostic process, roles and responsibilities of all parties, and expected deliverables.
- Identify all the key stakeholders and subject matter experts who are expected to be involved in the process and confirm accessibility.
- Set the timeframe for the Rapid Due Diligence diagnostic process and completion of all deliverables.
- Begin to prepare for any site visits, interviews, possible surveys, or other potential forms of discovery.
- Identify and organize any relevant background information or documentation for advance review by the researcher.

It is quite common for the owner of the situation to grant the researcher access to the appropriate levels of people or privileged information while choosing to refer any decisions on the details of site-visit discovery or provision of other relevant background information to the key contact. This means that the initial step may be bifurcated into an opening discussion with the owner of the situation being actively involved, followed by a more detailed working session with only the organizational key contact.

A preliminary list of people is identified who are expected to have valuable perspectives on the business situation and who are willing and available for on-site discovery of any type. This discovery may take the form of in-person interviews, telephone calls, panel discussions, direct observations of a process or facility operations, field visits with customers, or perhaps surveys. Given the short timeframe of the Rapid Due Diligence diagnostic process, the list of people for in-person contact is typically within a smaller range of perhaps twenty to fifty persons, depending upon the nature of the situation and scope of the inquiry. Ideally, these people have a direct executive or managerial interest in the strategic outcome as well as others who represent a diagonal slice of all other roles, functions, and structural levels within the organization. Representatives of the market or customer base may also be included in the discovery stage in order to gain a full understanding of the dynamics and potential of the business situation. This array of people includes a balance of at least the following:

- Executives who likely have specific information and perspectives about the strategic implications of the business, both historically as well as aspirationally for current and future strategic plans
- Middle managers or other leaders who play key roles in directing the strategy, supporting processes, and guiding the performance of others to achieve targeted goals

Stage One – Scope of the Inquiry **23**

- Employees who are expected to perform any functions in the fulfillment of the strategy or may be involved in any current or future skill development processes to support the business situation or strategy under review
- Customers or representatives of the markets who are directly affected by the provision of products or services emanating from the business situation or strategy

The organizational key contact provides preliminary notice to all of the subject matter experts who are expected to be involved in the discovery process. As the researcher completes the draft investigation research design and plan, information about the identity of the participants and timing of the discovery process are confirmed with the key contact. The researcher assists the key contact is preparing any advance communications about the Rapid Due Diligence diagnostic process, its purpose, and expectations.

As noted earlier, during the opening discussion, the researcher and organizational key contact determine the identity of any information sources that are relevant to the business situation under review. The key contact arranges for prompt provision of any pertinent documents to the researcher for preparatory investigation. Typical documentation may include any or all of the following:

- The most current set of strategic plans, goals, priorities, and measures of success related to the business situation
- Any previous internal or external assessments, interviews, findings, or recommendations related to the situation
- Any enterprise or business group scorecards or performance dashboards that are used to track the performance of the business strategy or the situation in question
- The most recent customer or market satisfaction, loyalty, or reference surveys
- Measures of process or transaction effectiveness and efficiency
- Any comparative external association or benchmark data, such as A.M. Best, Moody's, J.D. Power, or others
- Current marketing, branding, or communications strategies to the marketplace, including the customer value proposition or other primary tools used to describe how the organization brings value to the targeted market and customers
- Any data on behavioral economics, customer choice analytics, particularly any trigger points tied to customer decision-making, plus any comparisons or commentary on current product or service performance and targets
- Information about current and future targeted customers and their potential requirements of the organization, plus any descriptions of preferred customer experiences, and any data or opinions about the type and degree of change required to meet those requirements
- Any evaluation of competitive positioning and market distinctions

24 Stage One – Scope of the Inquiry

- Information that provides clarity or insight into the business mission, vision, charter, or the value the organization brings to its customers, plus how success is or will be measured
- Details of any operating or business models and correspondent economic value-producing paths
- Relevant public information, such as any Security and Exchange Commission reports, annual or quarterly reports, such as 10-K, 8-K, or 10-Q reports, investment analyst briefing notes, press releases, management discussion and analysis segments, and any inherent risks or opportunities that have been shared with financial analysts or investors with respect to this business situation
- Identification or clarification of Critical Knowledge Areas© that may be at work within the targeted situation[1]
- Specific competencies, any descriptions of behavioral anchors, relevant reliability validations, and how those competencies or behaviors are inculcated and managed throughout the human capital system
- Curricula, training, and development evaluations of any type that relate to the business situation, including any business impact tracking
- Human capital data, such as engagement levels, pulse indices, climate surveys, turnover rates, employee value propositions, performance data, and related analytics
- Description of employee geographic dispersion, supporting infrastructure, policies, practices, and any impact on the situation
- Any assessments, calibrations, or other gauges on the current organizational effectiveness, efficiency, performance, or talent levels that may be relevant to the targeted situation
- A summary or description of key strategies, programs, initiatives, policies, or practices that guide the management and performance of employees and their roles in fulfilling the targeted strategy or situation
- Any process flow charts, roadmaps, playbooks, value stream analyses, or initial design or reengineering documents that map the current key processes required to fulfill the targeted strategy
- Descriptions of the current and intended culture, any sub-cultures, stated organizational values, planned organizational culture changes, and any descriptions about how the employees operate among themselves and with customers
- Any articulated employee value propositions, employment branding, or summary statements of why people would choose to become and remain an employee of this organization
- Any other data that directly or indirectly can reveal insights about the targeted situation or the opportunity to achieve a Triple Win for the organization, its customers, and its employees

Draft Investigative Research and Diagnostic Design

Upon completion of the initial discussion, the owner of the business situation, organizational key contact, and researcher will have reached agreement on the scope of the inquiry, the preliminary identity of subject matter experts, provision of relevant information resources, tentative work within each stage of the Rapid Due Diligence diagnostic process, and targeted date for completion.

With this preliminary information in hand, the researcher commences to build a draft investigative research and diagnostic design or plan. The researcher examines the six stages of the Rapid Due Diligence Method of Diagnostics table, shown in Chapter Two, and verifies the process steps and outcomes that match the requirements of this specific scope of inquiry. The researcher confers with any supporting team members in preparing the draft plan. The draft plan document includes at least the following:

- Statement summarizing the business situation and scope of the inquiry
- Identity of key players, roles, and responsibilities
- Identity of subject matter experts who will be contacted for data collection and for what form of discovery process
- Description of any written sources of evidence, relevant documentation, and when and how that information will be provided for review
- Identity of the on-site or other forms of discovery process and description of appropriate adaptations of case study research methodology to fulfill the discovery
- Listing of the types of analysis and synthesis that are most appropriate to the nature of the business situation and scope of the inquiry, including the unit of analysis that will be used
- Instructions for data management
- Description of all deliverables
- Timeline for each of the stages
- Instructions for the management of any contractual documents, terms, and business relationships

In preparing the draft investigative research and diagnostic design, the researcher needs to consider the typical strengths and weaknesses of various sources of evidence. A sound plan seeks as many sources as practical to corroborate or augment evidence. A description of the typical sources appears in Table 3.2.

A sample of a draft investigative research and diagnostic design appears in Box 3.1. In this situation, there was an urgent need to discover insights for improving client relationship results in an exceptionally short timeframe to accommodate an existing executive strategic decision analysis and review schedule.

26 Stage One – Scope of the Inquiry

TABLE 3.2 Sources of Rapid Due Diligence Evidence

Source	Weaknesses	Strengths
Archival Records	• Accessibility	• Coverage of broad span of time & events
Documentation	• Accessibility • Potential unknown bias	• Precise data & details
In-person Interviews	• Potential unknown bias • Recall inaccuracies	• Potential causal relationships • Behavioral incident recall
Surveys	• Difficulty with follow-up actions • Dependent on question construction	• Ease of implementation with large numbers of respondents
Direct Observations	• Costly • Time-consuming • Performance skewed by anxiety • Potential manipulation	• Contextual • Based in reality
Panel Interviews	• Group think potential • Withholding contradictory information	• Richer, comparative viewpoints • Broader, balanced input from several perspectives at one setting • Efficiency

---

BOX 3.1 DRAFT INVESTIGATIVE RESEARCH DESIGN

Summary of Situation

- A very large, publicly held, financial services organization is seeking even greater efficiencies and effectiveness in its financial advisor and client relationships.
- Results of the diagnostics are requested within ten working days due to a pre-planned executive-level strategy review.

Identity of Key Players

- Owner of situation: chief executive officer
- Organizational key contact: director of employee development
- Principal researcher and support team

Subject Matter Experts

- Executives and directors of each functional area
- Client service managers
- Agents

Stage One – Scope of the Inquiry **27**

Archives and Documentation

- Current strategic vision
- Service delivery goals
- Organization charts
- Recent service ratings by outside benchmarking organizations
- Description of current performance management process
- Current and planned development for leaders and service agents
- Online research on SEC reporting documents

On-Site Discovery

- Protocol and questions to focus on the current client-focused strategy and measures
- In-person interviews with subject matter experts
  - o All executives and directors
  - o Panel interviews: twenty-five service agents and five supervisors

Types of Analysis and Synthesis

- Uncover points of alignment and degree of strength among strategic dimensions.
- Analyze trigger points for client preferences and loyalty, behavioral drivers, and any trace of economic value-producing stream and metrics.
- Detect any contradictory initiatives or messaging and resulting competition for resources.
- Conduct any causal flow diagramming to test for unintended consequences.
- Test adherence to performance management system and best-in-class policies and practices.

Data Management

- Record all sources of data.
- Hold all sources as anonymous.

Timeline and Deliverables

- Complete preparatory investigation and on-site discovery in four days.
- Complete analysis, synthesis, conclusions, and recommendations by day seven.
- Complete written report by day eight.
- Preview findings and recommendations with organizational key contact, then owner of situation on day nine.
- On day ten, prepare any implementation planning documentation in format to support executive strategy review session.

28 Stage One – Scope of the Inquiry

In another situation, the Rapid Due Diligence diagnostic method was used to conduct a baseline assessment as an initial step for developing a comprehensive human resources strategy in the aftermath of several acquisitions. The intent was to secure a clear understanding of activity already in place across a score of independent sites and to identify opportunities to build on that foundation. Key executives were anxious to secure the results within less than fifteen business days. The scope of inquiry appears in the partial investigative research design in Box 3.2.

BOX 3.2 EXAMPLE OF SCOPE OF INQUIRY

In a post-merger situation, the Rapid Due Diligence diagnostic process is being applied to secure a baseline assessment as an initial step toward developing a broader human resource strategy.

In this scope of inquiry, the researcher will engage approximately seventy contacts representing as many as twenty independent properties. The purpose is to accomplish the following steps:

- Take careful stock of what is known or already in place.
- Gauge how well those elements are working and producing any positive impact.
- Understand the future business context and performance targets.
- Identify critical competencies (skills, knowledge, abilities, and motivations) required for the business success the organization is seeking.
- Compare all findings with best practices, research, and experiences of best-in-class organizations.
- Pinpoint specific opportunities for building on what is already in place and creating a more cohesive, integrated approach to talent management, while at the same time accommodating the unique cultural aspects at the various properties and business units across the entire enterprise.

To prepare for highly focused interviews with at least seventy subject matter experts from as many as twenty independent sites within a five-day timeframe, the researcher will conduct preparatory investigation of a specified list of relevant documents. Focus groups and individual interviews will be compactly scheduled at a mutually convenient central location. The interview guide and protocol will be confirmed with the organizational key contact in advance.

The results from all discovery, analysis, synthesis, observations, conclusions, and recommendations will be previewed with the organizational key contact no later than twelve days after the start of the Rapid Due Diligence diagnostic process. The final written report and supporting evidence will be delivered by the fifteenth day.

With the completion of the scope of the inquiry stage, the researcher is ready to begin the next stage of preparatory investigation. This draft investigative research and diagnostic design or plan is distributed to all members of any research team for the purposes of any further input and to prepare for the next stage of the diagnostic process. The draft document is refined as needed in the second stage of preparatory investigation.

Discussion Questions

- How does the researcher set boundaries for the scope of the inquiry?
- Why is it useful for the researcher to seek on-site discovery with a diagonal slice of participants representing the organization's structure?
- When should customers be included in any form of discovery?
- How does a shorter or more urgent timeframe affect the diagnostic process and results?
- Why does the researcher create a draft investigative research and diagnostic plan?

Note

1 Joyce A. Thompsen, *A Case Study of Identifying and Measuring Critical Knowledge Areas as Key Resource-Capabilities of an Enterprise* (Ann Arbor, MI: UMI Dissertation Services, 2000).

Reference

Thompsen, Joyce A. 2000. *A Case Study of Identifying and Measuring Critical Knowledge Areas as Key Resource-Capabilities of an Enterprise.* Ann Arbor, MI: UMI Dissertation Services.

4
STAGE TWO – PREPARATORY INVESTIGATION

Learning Objectives

*   To understand the elements of the second stage of the Rapid Due Diligence diagnostic method.
*   To acquire guidelines for designing the investigation in on-site discovery.

In the second stage of the Rapid Due Diligence diagnostic process, the researcher and any supporting team engage in preparatory investigation and refinement of the final investigative research and diagnostic design or plan. For reference, the description of the second stage has been excised from the full six-stage table in Chapter Two and appears in Table 4.1.

TABLE 4.1 Rapid Due Diligence Method of Diagnostics: Stage Two – Preparatory Investigation

Players Involved	• Organizational key contact • Principal researcher • Research team (if any)
Process Steps	• Gather background information. • Conduct preliminary analysis. • Pinpoint areas for inquiry. • Confirm research design & protocol. • Secure discovery schedule. • Prepare surveys.
Outcomes	• Initial findings • Research design with protocol, fields of inquiry & discovery process
Timeline	3–5 days

Preparatory Investigation of Documentation

Using the draft investigative research and diagnostic design or plan, the researcher organizes all of the acquired documentation into broad categories, physical stacks, or folders for detailed examination. These categories include the following:

- Business information such as strategic dimensions, plans, goals, priorities, business models, and critical ratios
- Market and customer information
- Human capital information

In this preparatory investigation stage, the researcher is seeking to gather facts and descriptions of all the strategic dimensions of the organization that can have an influence on the business situation under review. These dimensions are labeled and briefly described in Table 4.2.

TABLE 4.2 Strategic Dimensions of an Organization

Strategic Dimension Label	Description
Mission	Purpose or fundamental focus of an organization
Vision	Ideal future state upon realization of the mission
Values	Desirable set of principles, standards, or qualities
Business Model	Scheme or description for how an organization creates, delivers, and captures value
Critical Success Factors	Essential, measurable ingredients and focal points for organizational attention
Primary Strategies and Goals	Plans of action or maneuvers to achieve specified targets
Customer Value Proposition	A statement summarizing the rationale for customers in choosing products and services from an organization as compared to competitive options
Employee Value Proposition	A statement summarizing the employment experience that individuals have while a member of an organization and rationale for choosing to belong to one organization as compared to other options
Shareholder or Owner Value Proposition	A statement summarizing the rationale for shareholders or owners to choose to invest in an organization
Key Processes	Primary systems of operations or series of actions and functions to produce targeted results
Key Metrics and Critical Ratios	Essential measures and evaluative comparisons that determine the success of a strategy or organizational viability
Critical Knowledge Areas©	Unique bodies of specific key resource-capabilities which lie at the core of the value proposition of an organization
Competitive Distinction	Point of differentiation between an organization and its rivals

32 Stage Two – Preparatory Investigation

The researcher commences the detailed review of all website material and physical documentation to capture information that describes each of the strategic dimensions, as well as key supporting information that addresses the central business issue under review. This can be done in either handwritten or electronic notes, according to the preference and ease of the researcher.

The notes are intended for multiple uses throughout the Rapid Due Diligence diagnostic process and need to be constructed with care. The original documents are numbered and marked with the review date and name of the researcher. The precise label, document title, source, and origin of each document are recorded at the top of each notes page. The left-hand column is available for the researcher to identify categories of evidence, record questions for further investigation, or make other organizing notations for future reference. All notations include the description of the finding, source, and any identifying page number from the original document. Quotations are captured with appropriate attribution and contextual notes. A sample of the document review notes page is shown in Box 4.1.

A summary list of all documents, key references to strategic dimensions, and questions for further investigation is a useful tool. All of these tasks are performed for purposes of thorough data management. A sample of this summary page appears in Box 4.2.

The preparatory investigation of documentation sequence begins with the business information sources, proceeds with any market and customer information, and concludes with human capital information. When all website and

---

BOX 4.1 DOCUMENT REVIEW NOTES

Project Title _____

Reviewer _____

Date _____

Document Title _____

Source _____

Reviewer Notations	Page Reference	Document Findings

Stage Two – Preparatory Investigation   33

BOX 4.2 DOCUMENT REVIEW SUMMARY

Project _____

Reviewer _____

Date _____

Document Title	Key Findings	Questions for Further Inquiry	Follow-up Actions	Comments

---

relevant documents have been reviewed, the original documents are placed in order of review and set aside for future reference.

An experienced researcher will begin to identify items of meaning from the beginning of the Rapid Due Diligence diagnostic process. These items may include recognition of potential regularities or irregularities, specific recurring patterns, causal flows and relationships, explanations, and alignments or misalignments of resources. Such items may emerge as early as the opening discussion with the owner of the business situation and organizational key contact and are likely to be recognized or amplified through the preparatory investigation of website and documented materials. In all cases, a competent researcher makes notes of such items while maintaining an open mind to new findings as the investigation progresses.

The next step in the discovery process is to fashion appropriate research techniques to affirm, augment, or refute the earlier findings from the preparatory investigation and identify missing information. The researcher examines and compares the elements of strategic dimensions of an organization with findings in the document review or document review summary. Any open or new fields of inquiry are highlighted. Fields of inquiry are set to uncover, define, expand, clarify, or refine earlier findings from the documentation and website review. If earlier findings have been ambiguous, unclear, or contradictory, the additional research technique needs to be designed to seek clarity or verification of the accurate details. The researcher also needs to identify the roles and responsibilities of subject matter experts who are most likely to possess the highest degree of clarity and

34 Stage Two – Preparatory Investigation

veracity about the targeted strategic dimensions and fields of inquiry. In all cases, the fields of inquiry need to include investigation about all three broad categories related to the business, its customers, and its employees in order to effectively move toward a Triple Win.

The early findings from this preparatory investigation of documentation and website material are used to refine the investigative research and diagnostic design or plan. These initial findings form the basis for the development and application of investigative protocol and critical questions for further inquiry. The researcher matches the questions for further inquiry with the most reliable or likely source of illumination, as well as the best method of discovery.

Investigative Protocol for Discovery

The investigative protocol includes a set of procedures and rules. The protocol gives shape to any instruments for conducting interviews, direct observations, or staging surveys. The protocol is designed to increase the reliability and integrity of the Rapid Due Diligence diagnostic process and its subsequent findings, observations, conclusions, and recommendations. It further provides guidance for dealing effectively with unanticipated events, reduces the potential for introducing bias, and guides the researcher and any team members during high-intensity data-intake periods during on-site discovery or field activities.

The core of the investigative protocol is the specific set of questions that are posed by the researcher to interviewees. When an online survey is used, the protocol includes the precise questions and instructions accompanying the survey. For direct observations, the protocol includes introductory comments and instructions for how the observations will be conducted. The purpose of the inquiry, identity of sponsoring personnel, and how the findings will be used, with or without anonymity, are disclosed to each participant. In all cases, the discovery techniques and process steps follow ethical rules for conducting applied social science research and remaining free of intrusive bias.

The Rapid Due Diligence diagnostic method can draw upon any of the following classic survey methods:

- In-person interviews
- Mail or online survey questionnaires
- Panel interviews
- Telephone interviews

Of these methods, the strongest and principal approach is the in-person or personal interview. This method requires the careful construction of a schedule of relevant questions. For the Rapid Due Diligence diagnostic method, the questions focus heavily on the respondent's knowledge, or subject matter expertise, about the situation under inquiry. The researcher also needs to gather any beliefs, attitudes, opinions, or points of view about cognitive objects of interest within the scope of study[1].

Telephone surveys can be used for purposes of time and cost efficiencies; however, the findings can be limited by the respondent's reluctance to answer questions fully or the researcher's inability to capture nonverbal cues and corollary inflections that may reveal important attitudes about the subject matter. There can be situations where the researcher needs to take extra steps to draw out valuable information.

Mail or online survey questionnaires can present significant drawbacks unless combined with other discovery techniques. Those drawbacks include the potential failure to respond and little to no provision for response verification or deeper investigation.

Online questionnaires or surveys, rather than paper surveys by mail, are a better choice for the Rapid Due Diligence method of diagnostics. The timeline is reduced substantially; and there is no requirement for scanning or hand-entry of data, thereby eliminating opportunities for error in the transfer or recording of responses.

The scope of the inquiry and research design will be used to set or confirm the description and number of participants who will be surveyed by any method. It is desirable for the interview method to be used with all executive and managerial level individuals who will serve as subject matter experts. Where possible, the interview method is also preferred for a strong sample of other contributors, including front-line personnel or representatives of related functions within the value stream under investigation. In situations where travel costs and time are limited, the interviews can be conducted by telephone. When there is a need for large numbers of respondents and they are widely dispersed, online surveys provide more efficient means for gathering responses. An example of deploying multiple discovery methods appears in Box 4.3.

Questions in all discovery methods must be carefully constructed. In interviews, open-end questions are preferred in order to elicit broader explanations and provide cues for further research. Open-end questions supply a frame of reference with a minimum of restraint or qualification on the respondent's answers. A series of open-end questions can serve as an effective funnel for securing important information on a specific topic. The funnel can also reveal more detail on practices, processes, results, and attitudes. When possible, the inclusion of more open-end questions provides richer data even though the physical management of those responses is more complicated.

Online or mail surveys can be constructed to capture "yes" or "no" answers with closed-end or poll questions. The difficulty with such questions is the inability to probe for further explanation or information.

A Likert-type scale of responses can be presented to gather degree of agreement or disagreement with questions or statements. Results from scale questions can be more reliably checked against responses to open-end questions.

36 Stage Two – Preparatory Investigation

BOX 4.3 SAMPLE OF MULTIPLE DISCOVERY METHODS

A large military command deployed the Rapid Due Diligence diagnostic process to define the equivalent of an employee value proposition for a critical role and, further, to identify practical ways to measure progress in the application of that proposition.

Based upon the approved scope of inquiry and preparatory investigation of considerable volumes of relevant documentation, it was mutually agreed upon by the command and the research team to expand the discovery stage. The nature of the issue warranted broad participation from hundreds of subject matter experts in providing reflective input and critical incident data.

A set of open-end survey questions was developed. These questions did not limit responses or seek opinions about any preconceived answers. A set of criteria was established to define a reliable representative sample of soldiers who were expected to be in the best situation to answer the questions. A criteria matrix was used to identify individuals from six groupings, representing a breadth of experience, demographics, geographic locations, and range of performance.

Specific instruments, tools, and protocol were created for three methods of survey: in-person interviews, online surveys, and a virtual broadcast with live interaction with voluntary callers. In combination, several hundred individuals were able to respond to the same set of open-end questions and provide a rich array of responses from their personal experiences.

There are a number of criteria that need to be considered in the creation of questions of any type for the discovery methods. Questions should have the following characteristics:

- Related to the scope of inquiry of the Rapid Due Diligence diagnostic process
- Appropriate type to secure full information and rationale for the interviewee's chosen behavior
- Clear and unambiguous language
- Short in length to avoid confusion
- Contain a single idea
- Focus on securing information the respondent is likely to possess
- Non-judgmental
- Non-leading, not suggesting certain answers
- Able to elicit rich, thick descriptions

The researcher compiles an interview guide with the complete set of opening commentary, embedded protocol, procedures, a series of questions which focus upon the fields of inquiry, potential follow-up questions, and closing comments.

Stage Two – Preparatory Investigation **37**

This document is used with all subject matter experts. Space is allotted within the interview guide for making handwritten notations at the time of the interview. Additional space is desirable for analytical notations in future stages. If the researcher prefers, electronic records can be used.

A sample interview guide is shown in Box 4.4. It incorporates the opening and closing comments required by the Rapid Due Diligence diagnostic method protocol. In this example, the researcher is interviewing a subject matter expert who is expected to be able to provide significant information to help the organization create a more effective, efficient, and sustainable business development process. The primary areas of inquiry are supported by a series of additional questions to gain further depth and insights. The questions probe for information that can also support a Triple Win for the organization, its customers, and its employees. For purposes of a usable interview guide, the spacing in this sample would be expanded for notes.

BOX 4.4 SAMPLE INTERVIEW GUIDE

Rapid Due Diligence Diagnostic Process
Interview Guide and Protocol
Project Title _____
Interviewee Name _____
Role _____
Contact Info _____
Interviewer _____
Date/Time _____

Opening Comments

- Introduce yourself.
- Confirm interviewee's availability for an interview of up to (sixty) minutes.
- Verify interviewee's data.
- Announce that you are conducting data collection and interviews with key people in a number of roles in conjunction with a significant project for the organization.
- Propose the following agenda and process for the interview:
  o The purpose of this interview and other data collection is to gain a clear, complete, and mutual understanding of important background information to help create an effective, efficient, and sustainable sales process and high performing organization.
  o During the interview, you will ask for the interviewee's personal perspective on a series of important factors and issues that help pinpoint

(Continued)

38 Stage Two – Preparatory Investigation

developmental needs and the results your business is seeking. The topics will include:
- o The business and its customer relationships as they exist today and as envisioned for the future
- o Sales performance metrics and how you use them
- o The skills and practices of high performers
- o Current training systems and recommended changes
- o Any challenges or other factors that can either propel or impede the attainment of your sales organization's strategy
- o Other insights you should know for planning purposes
- o Announce that the interviewee's answers will be shared with the core project team. Anonymity will be preserved on specific comments if requested.
- o The interviewee's input will be combined with other data and used to shape the developmental curriculum and implementation process for this initiative.
- o The benefit to the interviewee and assigned functional area is the provision of specific content to meet key needs.
- Check for acceptance.

Interview Questions

- How would you describe the current state of the business?
  - o How well are you achieving your current targeted results?
  - o What is the status of key metrics, such as:
    - o Revenue growth (percent)
    - o New business penetration
    - o Closing ratio
    - o Customer service, satisfaction or loyalty data
- What changes or challenges do you expect in your business in the next twelve to twenty-four months? For example:
  - o New, more aggressive revenue or new business targets?
  - o Any strategic shifts?
  - o Changes to your customer value proposition?
  - o The condition of the market?
  - o Any changes in customer choice analytics? Specifics?
  - o How is the business demonstrating responsibility for them and delivering the brand in ways that customers notice?
  - o Any major new product introductions?
  - o Any organizational structure or system changes?
  - o What are customers telling you – ease of doing business with you, their changing needs, cues that indicate their preferences?

Stage Two – Preparatory Investigation **39**

- What metrics do you use regularly to gauge the performance of your salespeople?
  - o What threshold or criteria do they need to meet expectations?
  - o To be calibrated as a high performer?
  - o What percent of your sales team qualifies as high performing?
- What skills, knowledge, and practices have you observed that are distinctive to your high performers?
- What do you personally do to specifically assist high performers?
- How do you distribute your time among high, moderate, and low performers?
- How well does the current curriculum prepare you for your role?
- In what knowledge or skill areas do you need more development? Why?
- How do you focus your time to fulfill your role? How does that compare with the average – or recommended – activity profile for managers?
  - o Supervision, goal setting, and management (forty-four percent) – including observing field work (thirteen percent), discussing or analyzing weekly sales activity with representatives (five percent), role playing exercises (two percent)
  - o Administration (twenty-one percent)
  - o Teaching, training, coaching (ten percent)
  - o Recruitment, selection, and assimilation of new sales representatives (eight percent)
  - o Following the guideline of sixty percent in field activity
- What challenges do you anticipate with the pursuit of this initiative?
  - o What recommendations do you have to address these challenges?
- What other advice or information should we have as we shape the content and implementation for this initiative?

Closing and Next Steps

- Affirm the access and/or delivery of any additional planning documents, survey results, or other data that are important to review.
- This interview information will be combined with other input and data.
- Verify whether there are any sensitive data for which the interviewee's identity needs to be protected.
- The core project team will scope and plot the preliminary plan for content and implementation.
- Any questions?
- Here is how the interviewee may contact you or the project team if there is other information to share.
- May you contact the interviewee again if there new questions or a need to clarify information?
- Thank the interviewee for valuable input.

40 Stage Two – Preparatory Investigation

Refined Investigative Research Design

The principal researcher confers with any other team members to affirm the refined investigative research and diagnostic design or plan. The identities of subject matter experts, types of on-site or field discovery, research instruments, further documentation needs, adjustments to the intended analysis and synthesis process, and any changes to the stages within the agreed-upon timeline for deliverables are incorporated in the draft plan. The final version of the investigative research and diagnostic design document is distributed to all team members.

The principal researcher engages the organizational key contact to review portions of the plan. The explicit identity of all subject matter experts and types of discovery processes are reviewed and scheduled. The interview schedule typically allows up to ninety minutes for in-person interviews at the executive level and up to sixty minutes for people in non-executive roles. Ninety minutes to two hours are allowed for panel discussions. Depending upon the nature of the direct observations, these are typically thirty to sixty minutes in length. For the purposes of maintaining the Rapid Due Diligence diagnostic timeline, it is desirable to complete all of the interviews, panel discussions, and direct observations within a concise period, preferably within a few days on-site. This compact schedule also allows the researcher to more easily engage in any appropriate follow-up questions with any subject matter experts, as well as move quickly into the analysis and synthesis processes.

The researcher conducts a preview of the investigative questions with the organizational key contact and makes edits as required for clarification. The key contact is requested to provide any important cultural or behavioral background that may have an influence on the discovery process with any individual subject matter experts, groups, or site visits. This information provides an early alert to the researcher or team members of the potential for known tendencies of contrarian views, hostility, any patterns of avoidance behaviors, masking key information, embellishments, duplicity, or other forms of disruption or bias that can interfere with the diagnostic process or accuracy of findings and conclusions.

Clear communications are prepared and delivered to all subject matter experts and discovery sites with sufficient time for mutual preparation and travel, as required. Field activities such as direct observations of production facilities and processes are scheduled. All communications need to include the business purpose of the inquiry, introduce the researcher, acknowledge how any responses will be used, whether or how anonymity will be preserved, the schedule, and allotted timeframe.

All of the steps within the second stage of preparatory investigation typically take place within a quite intensive three to five days. The next stage of on-site discovery commences as quickly as possible, usually as soon as travel arrangements can be confirmed.

Discussion Questions

- Why are all of the strategic dimensions of an organization important to the Rapid Due Diligence diagnostic method?
- What is the value of organizing document review notes?
- How does the researcher determine the techniques for discovery?
- Why is the preparation of questions and interview protocol important to the diagnostic process?

Note

1 Fred N. Kerlinger, *Foundations of Behavioral Research, Third Edition* (Fort Worth, TX: Harcourt Brace, 1992), 378–380.

Reference

Kerlinger, Fred N. 1992. *Foundations of Behavioral Research, Third Edition.* Fort Worth, TX: Harcourt Brace.

5
STAGE THREE – ON-SITE DISCOVERY

Learning Objectives

- To understand how to conduct various types of on-site discovery activities.
- To learn how to prepare, organize, and manage evidence.

In the third stage of the Rapid Due Diligence diagnostic process, the researcher and any supporting team members prepare and conduct on-site discovery and other information-gathering techniques. For reference, the description of the third stage has been excised from the full six-stage table in Chapter Two and appears in Table 5.1.

TABLE 5.1 Rapid Due Diligence Method of Diagnostics: Stage Three – On-Site Discovery

Players Involved	• Organizational key contact
	• Subject matter experts
	• Principal researcher
	• Research team (if any)
Process Steps	• Conduct on-site interviews & direct observations.
	• Distribute any online survey & collect input.
	• Gather any new background information.
	• Manage data.
	• Provide key contact with updates.
Outcomes	• Findings from subject matter experts
Timeline	5–10 days

Interviews

To prepare for the actual on-site discovery, the researcher and any supporting team members who will engage in these activities complete a thorough review of all findings acquired to date and all open fields of inquiry. The researcher is steadily achieving a command or reliable recall of the content uncovered in the preparatory investigation and can engage subject matter experts with a level of confidence in understanding the scope of the inquiry and strategic dimensions at work. The researcher also prepares to deliver opening commentary from the interview guide protocol in a way that engenders a positive atmosphere.

Every subject matter expert deserves to be treated with respect and neutrality. Even though the organizational key contact may have provided the researcher with a profile of contentiousness or irascibility for any particular subject matter expert, the researcher must portray an even-handed, respectful demeanor. Such individuals can often possess important information, insightful perspectives, or unexpected evidence that can cast a different point of view, reveal new or additional truths, substantiate other assumptions, or raise essential new fields of inquiry for further investigation.

At no time during an interview does the researcher reveal the identity of any other subject matter experts who have presented a different or contradictory point of view. While a current interviewee may surmise a differing view from another person and may so state this to the researcher, no confirmation is given. It is acceptable for the researcher to probe for the interviewee's rationale for this conclusion. It is important to make note of any such statements.

In keeping with the protocol of case study research methodology and applied social sciences research, it is essential that each researcher set forth the same primary set of questions or fields of inquiry, using the same initial language. In contrast, however, with the Rapid Due Diligence diagnostic method, the researcher is welcome to conduct follow-up, probing questions to gain further insight into the response to any given question. Further, if the initial response reveals the potential for greater insight into any of the fields of inquiry or a particularly important strategic dimension, then the researcher is invited to continue the line of questioning to pursue a more precise perspective of the subject matter expert. The researcher is expected to note any additional questions and responses.

In some cases, a subject matter expert may choose to remain parsimonious and exceptionally brief in responding to one or more questions. In these situations, the researcher is recommended to respectfully repeat or rephrase a question to secure a more complete response. If this technique does not work, the researcher may choose to directly ask for more information or seek the rationale for the earlier response. The intent is to set the subject matter expert at ease as quickly as

44 Stage Three – On-Site Discovery

possible by a consistent show of respect and neutrality. If necessary, the researcher may choose to assure the subject matter expert of the anonymity of all responses and the importance to the business issue to gather a complete view even with differing or contradictory information.

In those situations where hostility is evident, the researcher is expected to maintain a neutral and bias-free stance. The subject matter expert may refuse to actively engage or passively avoid responding to questions. In other cases, the subject matter expert may respond with sharp commentary, expletives, or high degrees of animation which behaviorally display discontent with the business situation, specific individuals, or the expectation to participate in any interview. At all times, the researcher needs to maintain a calm demeanor. When such instances occur, it is helpful for the researcher to take a pause in the conversation, allowing the subject matter expert to momentarily regain composure and reflect upon the situation. If the hostility continues, the researcher may directly ask the subject matter expert why specific behaviors are being displayed. One or more follow-up questions may be necessary to uncover the rationale. In response, the researcher is cautioned not to show bias toward or against the perspective of this or any other resources. This is an acute time for the researcher to maintain eye contact with the subject matter expert and remain calm, confident, respectful, and neutral. The role of the researcher during this discovery process is to gather information, not make evaluations or judgments about the character of subject matter experts. After the interview and separation from the subject matter expert, the researcher needs to make detailed notes of such instances.

There may be situations when a subject matter expert challenges the credentials, credibility, or integrity of the researcher in conducting the Rapid Due Diligence diagnostic research. At this point, it is essential for the researcher to not become defensive. A good approach is to take a momentary pause, quickly consider exactly what question is being raised, and restart the conversation with a simple question of why the subject matter expert has presented this view. Again, in a calm manner, the researcher is seeking to understand the underlying meaning or intent of the subject matter expert in raising such issues. When the subject matter expert has revealed any further information, the researcher is in a more sound position to accurately address the underlying question or concern. As the researcher is able, a response may include reference to similar Rapid Due Diligence diagnostic projects without attribution or directly naming an organization.

Another technique is to refer to the care in crafting the investigative research design, inclusion of important protocol for the on-site discovery process, and verification of all steps with the organizational key contact, or perhaps even with the owner of the business situation. Typically, any or all of these approaches will settle the subject matter expert's concern; and the interview process can proceed more smoothly. The intent is to begin to build a sufficiently trustworthy interpersonal relationship for this brief period of interaction in order to secure accurate and complete information of importance to the scope of the inquiry and resolution of the business issue.

At the end of each interview, the researcher follows the protocol for closing commentary. This includes a clear description of how the information received from the subject matter expert will be treated during the remainder of the Rapid Due Diligence diagnostic process. The researcher is advised to position the potential for raising additional or clarifying questions with the subject matter expert at a later time. The researcher gives assurance of anonymity, as noted in the interview guide. If the subject matter expert is expected to participate in the receipt of the results of the Rapid Due Diligence diagnostic process, it is appropriate for the researcher to set expectations and provide a brief description of the timeline and format for presenting the results.

Following the completion of each day of on-site discovery, the researcher and any participating team members gather to briefly review the activity of the day. At this point, it is unnecessary to delve into excessive detail or engage in premature analytical activities. A brief assessment is made of the progress of the on-site discovery work in that timeframe in gathering responses which yield usable information about the open fields of inquiry. Any significant areas of inquiry which are as yet unanswered are pinpointed. If additional probing questions or interview techniques are required to address the open fields, this is the time to create those questions. If contradictory information has been provided, a tactic for securing clarity and suitable verification is devised by the researcher and any team members. The researcher may choose to counsel with the organizational key contact in such situations.

After the researcher and any team members have engaged in this review of the day, it is a useful step to have a brief conversation with the organizational key contact. The purpose is to provide an abbreviated description of the progress that was achieved during the interviews of the day. The primary researcher is expected to enumerate one or more top-of-mind findings or observations, as well as identify any need for other source data or avenues of inquiry. Interviews with additional subject matter experts may be required, or there may be a need to examine newly identified documentation. If there had been any instances of intentional withholding of information, subject matter expert hostility, or other troublesome or confounding circumstances, this daily briefing provides an opportunity to explore causation with great care with the organizational key contact. To the degree possible, it is preferable not to reveal too many specifics of any given situation. Doing so places an unwelcome burden on the key contact, who may feel duty-bound to report such circumstances to the owner of the business situation or others. Depending on the nature of the circumstances, the results of the Rapid Due Diligence diagnostic process could become tainted. This daily briefing practice is designed to provide assurances to the organizational key contact and may also ameliorate unwelcome backlash to the delivery of potentially significant surprises at some point in the future.

46 Stage Three – On-Site Discovery

There may be several instances in which subject matter experts can only be contacted by telephone interviews, due to scheduling conflicts or significant geographic dispersion. Telephone interviews are established to begin at a very specific time and conclude within the allotted time period. Most subject matter experts express gratitude if an interview is completed in less than the expected timeframe.

The researcher is expected to follow the investigative protocol and established questions in the interview guide. In order to capture the complete response of subject matter experts, the researcher is advised to routinely inquire if there is more to add to any responses. The researcher needs to carefully capture and clarify any instances of inflection cues throughout the interview. These subtleties can sometimes be barely perceptible, and the researcher is expected to be particularly skillful in identifying any expressions or even nonverbal cues that beg for further investigation. All such cues may signal important revelations about the fields of inquiry or the broader scope of inquiry. The results of telephone interviews are included in the daily review and briefings with the organizational key contact.

An example of a situation where several types of discovery techniques were required appears in Box 5.1.

BOX 5.1 CONDUCTING A VARIETY OF DISCOVERY TECHNIQUES

As a central strategy to become a more formidable international competitor, a scientific organization determined to improve the productivity and effectiveness of its sales force. The Rapid Due Diligence diagnostic method was deployed to identify ways to engage this strategy.

A variety of discovery techniques was used. Upon creation of an interview guide and protocol, telephone interviews were arranged with sales managers and sales professionals from seven countries in Europe, plus Australia and India. These interviews were followed by another set of in-person interviews on-site with sales managers and sales professionals representing the United Kingdom, Germany, and Northern and Central Europe.

The researcher then completed direct observations of sales professionals in a variety of business development visits with a number of customers in the United Kingdom and Germany.

Following all of these discovery activities, a panel of eight subject matter experts from the European countries was engaged in a three-day working session to gather more detailed data. The researcher facilitated discussions to refine a new sales process matched with customer buying profiles. Best practices and opportunities for improvement were identified across all global operations.

Direct Observations

In contrast to interviews with subject matter experts, direct observations are typically intended to gather in-stream evidence of the fulfillment of a specific task or process which is particularly important to the scope of the inquiry or the business situation under review. Following are examples of typical instances of direct observations:

- Watching and/or listening to the exchange between a customer and an organization's customer service representative
- Listening to a business development conversation between an account representative and a potential new customer
- Observing the conduct of a team meeting about a production process
- Following the execution of designated steps within a production process
- Visiting field facilities to interview and observe site leaders and employees contributing to key processes or providing essential services to customers
- Gathering information about the virtual conduct of designated business processes
- Observing unique cultural distinctions across boundaries with respect to business processes, practices, or relationships

These direct observations provide another layer of depth to the discovery process. Similar to the investigative protocol used with an interview guide, the researcher and any team members are expected to make opening statements about the purpose of the Rapid Due Diligence diagnostic process, identify what process is being observed, why it is important to the overall scope of the inquiry, position questions that do not interrupt the flow of the subject matter expert's responsibilities, seek clarity when needed, and provide closing commentary.

It is helpful for the researcher to have access to any process description, flowchart, roadmap, or design document in advance of the direct observation. The researcher is expected to have sufficient familiarity with the process prior to the direct observation in order to identify the fields of inquiry and craft appropriate questions. In demonstrating at least some degree of familiarity, the researcher is more likely to set the subject matter expert at ease. The subject matter expert is also less likely to perform the designated task or process in an uncomfortable or halting manner. When possible, the researcher should seek opportunities to observe the subject matter expert perform the targeted task more than once.

In the example in Box 5.2, there were several discovery techniques including direct observations in a large production operation.

Similarly to the interview process, the researcher is expected to make detailed notes of the performance of the task or process, plus responses to planned or follow-up probing questions. If there have been direct observations of several subject matter experts performing similar tasks, the researcher is expected not to reveal any type of evaluative commentary about previous observances. If a distinctive difference in the completion or performance of the task becomes evident,

BOX 5.2 DISCOVERY TECHNIQUES IN PRODUCTION OPERATIONS

A military organization was seeking ways to provide the highest quality equipment at the right time and most cost-efficient manner to soldiers in combat. A combination of Lean 6s and Six Sigma process improvement initiatives were already underway at several production sites, but the results to date were mixed. The Rapid Due Diligence diagnostic method was deployed to determine how to consistently improve and sustain results.

In preparation for the on-site discovery, the research team created a structured direct observation process, protocol, communications plan, and observation grid worksheets to capture behavioral evidence of leadership, teamwork, and process management behaviors in the natural flow of multiple rapid improvement events in production operations. The research team conferred in advance to ensure a consistent approach to gathering observation data and assessing its effectiveness. The intent was to secure accurate, rich depth of valid data that could be used to pinpoint specific opportunities.

To aid in these direct observations, the research team used the following list of core competencies required for effective Lean 6s and Six Sigma process improvement:

- Recognizing opportunities
- Taking initiative beyond requirements
- Thinking and acting strategically
- Dealing effectively with ambiguity
- Focusing on the critical-to-quality needs of customers
- Identifying unspoken needs
- Communicating effectively
- Involving others
- Practicing group effectiveness
- Planning and organizing complex projects
- Managing projects for results
- Applying technical or statistical problem solving proficiency
- Gathering relevant data
- Paying attention to detail
- Defining work flow
- Analyzing and interpreting data for meaning
- Applying creativity and innovation
- Discerning distinguishing differences
- Formulating criteria for decision-making
- Applying judgment
- Making decisions

Stage Three – On-Site Discovery **49**

- Setting performance standards of Six Sigma excellence
- Sharing information
- Demonstrating accountability for results
- Embracing change
- Monitoring and measuring performance
- Evaluating performance
- Providing feedback to others
- Coaching others
- Maintaining and promoting Six Sigma quality
- Driving for results

The direct observations were conducted in all key operations and work shifts at the site over a five-day period. Together, the research team observed the day-to-day production work, process improvement team meetings, brief-out presentations to operational group leaders, and portions of their value stream analysis sessions. There were numerous other opportunities to observe project team activities.

All relevant behavioral data were captured in detailed notes, then labeled and classified for further analysis. Specific attention was given to the occurrence of positive, negative, or missed opportunities for application of the Lean 6s and Six Sigma core competencies listed above.

the researcher is expected to ask appropriate follow-up questions to secure the underlying rationale. The guidelines related to passive, nonresponsive, or hostile behaviors encountered in interviews also apply to direct observations.

The practice of daily reviews and briefings with the organizational key contact are followed with direct observations. Because observations may be occurring at a number of separate locations, sometimes across multiple time zones, with members of the research team or distant from the organizational key contact, the timing and length of daily reviews may need to be adjusted to accommodate these circumstances.

Panel interviews are deployed in situations where several people hold the same role and responsibilities and can gather without inconvenience to the subject matter experts or significant interference with the fulfillment of any daily duties. The panel is also an effective choice when there is an urgent need to include a large number of people in the on-site discovery process. The proclivity for any degree of agreement in their respective responses to any questions is immaterial to the inquiry process. As with the other techniques, the organizational key contact is instrumental in identifying the subject matter experts who will participate, establishing the schedule, and conducting the preparatory communications. Similarly, the researcher is expected to follow the investigative research protocol of an interview guide designed to secure responses to the designated fields of inquiry.

In the opening steps of a panel interview, the researcher makes a brief self-introduction and, as needed, invites all members to identify themselves to the group. The researcher may ask participants to complete name tents. The researcher makes the required commentary about the purpose and importance of this gathering and how any information will be used throughout the Rapid Due Diligence diagnostic process. The researcher announces how members of the panel will be invited to respond to all questions, ensuring that all members have an equal opportunity to express points of view. In instances where there are members who tend to say much more than others, the researcher is required to respectfully ask for the responses of all others in the panel. As any differing responses emerge, the researcher is expected to calmly move forward in taking extra steps to ensure that all members respond. Appropriate follow-up or probing questions are positioned to secure more depth or uncover rationale for the differences.

If it is apparent that there is agreement by all panel members, the researcher may choose to summarize the responses and ask directly for an indication of agreement or disagreement. If a consensus arises, the researcher makes that notation with the explicit details of any dissenting responses. The researcher makes notes on all the perspectives, including the identity of the contributors. The researcher makes the closing remarks. Following the departure of all participants, the researcher is advised to make any additional notes to capture further details and identify any surprising information. The experience and results of any panel interviews are included in the daily briefings.

The example in Box 5.3 describes the discovery process with customer visits in multiple locations.

BOX 5.3 CUSTOMER SITE VISITS

An international pharmaceutical organization was seeking to refine its strategy to relationship-centered business development. The Rapid Due Diligence diagnostic method was used to gauge the current reality and identify opportunities for improvement.

The investigative research plan required a series of visits to operations in multiple geographic locations. Individual interviews, panel interviews, and direct observations were completed with employees at multiple sites.

The researcher also accompanied business development managers and account representatives as they made routine visits to several customer offices and field operations. The customer took the researcher on a brief tour of the offices and operations to provide additional background information.

The researcher observed the business meetings between customers and the organization's representatives, followed by private interviews with the customers to gain further insights into their perspectives of the business development process and relationship. Closing sessions were then completed with all parties present.

Online Surveys

With the Rapid Due Diligence diagnostic method, there is a preference to rely on in-person, telephone, or panel interviews and accompanying direct observations or field visits. If it is desirable to capture the input of a significantly greater number of subject matter experts and those people are greatly dispersed in time or geography, an online or mail questionnaire or survey may be simultaneously deployed. As noted earlier, the timeline of the Rapid Due Diligence diagnostic process is better suited to the use of online surveys than paper surveys handled in both directions by postal delivery. The tendency is to craft surveys with primarily closed-end questions or Likert-type scalable inquiries that produce more easily and quickly recorded responses.

If a survey is used to bolster other forms of discovery, the researcher and organizational key contact take great care to specifically identify the participants for the survey and craft the accompanying communications. In alignment with the investigative research protocol shaping interviews and direct observations, the announcements need to include the purpose of the survey, clear instructions on the process for completing and submitting responses, precise time deadlines, and any ways in which subject matter experts can offer additional commentary beyond what is invited in the survey.

Ideally, the survey responses are electronically submitted directly to the researcher or team member designated with responsibility for capturing all results. It is customary for the survey responses to be required within a relatively brief period of time, typically no more than a five-day window, to more quickly secure responses while accommodating people who are traveling or unavailable for any reason. The monitoring researcher checks the number of responses and samples results at the close of each day.

In situations where there is an abnormally low response rate early in the submittal window, the organizational key contact is notified immediately. Additional communications may be launched as respectful reminders to stimulate a higher rate of responders within the allotted window.

As the monitoring researcher is technically able, any responses arriving within two days after the close of the announced window can be captured and identified as beyond the time boundary. Therefore, if the collective responses during the allotted time window have been low, have been disrupted by unexpected circumstances, or do not provide a reasonably acceptable ratio of responses from all invited subject matter experts, the monitoring researcher or the research team may choose to include and so note the late arrival responses.

As with all other forms of discovery, daily reviews and briefings about online survey results are conducted.

Data Management

Data management is an important operation within the Rapid Due Diligence method of diagnostics. The investigative research and diagnostic design

52 Stage Three – On-Site Discovery

includes instructions for preparing, organizing, and managing evidence. This includes techniques for classifying, labeling, coding, categorizing, notating, tracking, cross-referencing, and networking sources and content of evidence in preparation for effective diagnostic analysis. Whether dealing with quantitative or qualitative data, the researcher needs to plan in advance to perform the following:[1]

- Make complete notes, identifying the name of the researcher, date, name and role of people involved, location, content, and protocol.
- Edit or revise notes immediately to ensure accuracy and completeness.
- Make memo notes to the researcher for future, deeper consideration or analysis.
- Capture potential insights.
- Identify items for immediate follow-up.
- Note any surprising data.
- Code notes with key words or label tags to permit easy retrieval and future reference.
- Store notes in an organized, accessible format, whether handwritten or in a computer database, to enable ease in search, retrieval, and inspection.
- Mark notes for relevant cross-referral to assist in forming categories, clusters, or networks of information.
- Count frequencies of similar content and identify patterns.
- Triangulate data among multiple sources to avoid over-reliance on a single datum.
- Condense data and prepare for any appropriate display for further inspection or analysis.
- Use network diagrams, causal networks, or other graphic displays to draw observations and conclusions about the data.
- Make clear notes about the decision rules or constructs that are applied with each step of analysis and making observations or conclusions.
- Prepare graphic display or mapping of the findings and recommendations.
- Write any interim, final, and executive summary reports with references to the database.

The research design flow plan should also include instructions for coding and tabulating responses from all of the deployed survey methods. Coding is the translation of responses to specific categories for use in analysis. Content analysis will also be used. Tabulation is the recording process of the numbers of types of responses in the various categories. All of these steps are used to organize and prepare all findings as complete, accurate, and bias-free information for the next steps.

Discussion Questions

- How does the researcher determine which types of on-site discovery techniques to use?
- Why is the investigative protocol important?
- Why are direct observations helpful in collecting evidence?
- Why is a data management plan important to the Rapid Due Diligence diagnostic method?

Note

1 Matthew B. Miles and A. Michael Huberman, *Qualitative Data Analysis, Second Edition* (Thousand Oaks, CA: SAGE Publications, 1994), 44–46.

Reference

Miles, Matthew B., and A. Michael Huberman. 1994. *Qualitative Data Analysis, Second Edition*. Thousand Oaks, CA: SAGE Publications.

6

STAGE FOUR – ANALYSIS AND OBSERVATION DEVELOPMENT

Learning Objectives

- To understand a series of data management moves to prepare for analysis.
- To acquire an understanding of several analytical techniques used in the Rapid Due Diligence diagnostic method.

In the fourth stage of the Rapid Due Diligence diagnostic process, the researcher and any team members commence the analysis of all findings secured during the preparatory investigation and on-site discovery stages. For reference, the description of the fourth stage has been excised from the full six-stage table in Chapter Two and appears in Table 6.1.

The investigative research and diagnostic design or plan specifies a series and sequence of analytical techniques and applications of models or constructs to address the central issue in a direct, effective, and efficient manner. Depending upon the results of the preparatory investigation and on-site discovery, this original set and sequence may also be augmented by additional techniques to further

TABLE 6.1 Rapid Due Diligence Method of Diagnostics: Stage Four – Analysis and Observation Development

Players Involved	• Principal researcher
	• Research team (if any)
Process Steps	• Organize all sources of data.
	• Conduct separate analyses of all sources of data.
	• Apply initial filters to findings.
	• Capture gaps.
	• Record observations.
Outcomes	• Initial analytical results & observations about findings
Timeline	3–5 days

Stage Four – Analysis and Observation Development **55**

identify and trace causal relationships and gain new or deeper insights. Previously unanticipated or contradictory information may emerge that requires a fresh look at findings to date and perhaps additional discovery. Furthermore, the nature of the unanticipated information may require the consideration of additional techniques or different forms of analysis. These discoveries may occur during the data management work to prepare for the analytical applications.

Data Management to Prepare for Analysis

In correlation with the data management steps discussed in the previous chapter, a classic series of analytic moves can be deployed with the sets of responses to any of the discovery methods and field observations to prepare for separate analysis. These moves include the following:

- Code the notes.
- Make reflective notes or comments.
- Sift or sort data to identify similar phrases, codes, relationships, themes, causal flows, patterns, common sequences, or specific contrasts.
- Isolate specific processes, patterns, or distinctions for further analysis.
- Compare these findings with a variety of appropriate constructs, models, or theories.
- Formulate observations about the findings to express degree of contrast.
- Reduce data to sharpen, focus, condense, organize, or perhaps set aside data to enable observations.
- Compress data into an organized, easily understood display that permits drawing conclusions.

The following series of sample data management tables (Tables 6.2 through 6.5) illuminates a number of these analytical moves. These examples demonstrate the adaptation of case study research methodology in preparing data for analysis, synthesis, and drawing conclusions.

TABLE 6.2 Code List for Analysis Operations

	Readying Data for Analysis
CAT	Categorizing
DASH	Referencing dashboard measurement system
DELIB	Revealing evidence of deliberation
DEC-CRIT	Expressing decision criteria for answer
DIFF	Expressing difficulty in forming an answer
FUNC	Expressing functional or professional perspective
NO ANSR	Expressing no answer
PO-CKA	Identifying potential Critical Knowledge Area©
PO-MEAS	Identifying potential measure for Critical Knowledge Area©
SUMM	Summarizing language

(Continued)

Drawing Conclusions	
AGREE	Agreeing fully on response
ALT	Expressing alternative response for the record
BIAS	Controlling for researcher bias
CONS	Achieving consensus on response
CONT	Contrasting idea
DIS	Identifying source of disagreement
EXPL	Building explanation
NEG	Presenting negative evidence
PATT	Seeing a pattern or common theme
SUPP	Supporting theoretical framework for Critical Knowledge Areas© as key resource-capabilities
UNDC	Undecided; not ready to declare choice
Confirming Conclusions	
FDBK	Corroboration from participant feedback
GEN	Analytic generalization from study to the theory
TRI-DATA	Triangulation from data

TABLE 6.3 On-Site Discovery: Interview Content and Analysis Notations

Participant Name _____

Interview Date _____

Researcher _____

Analysis Notations	Interview Content	Clarification Requirements
	Researcher: What is the value proposition that X Organization brings to its customers?	
1002 PO-COMP	Participant A: Our value proposition is different than what another organization can bring. We are truly looking at providing the most cost effective pharmaceutical care	
2001 PATT	benefit. So we adjust our priorities and align all of our products and services so that they look the best. An example of that would be the disease state management programs that are fully integrated. We support and secure the accreditations.	
	Researcher: What is your focus right now?	
1003 FUNC	Participant A: Cost management is number one on our list so we have all of our resources aimed toward managing down the costs and not doing a lot of other fluffy programs that were important, say, two years ago.	

TABLE 6.4 On-Site Discovery: Panel Interview Content and Analysis Notations

Group Identity _____

Panel Interview Date _____

Researcher _____

Analysis Notations	Panel Interview Content	Clarification Requirements
1207–1210 PO-CKA	Participant C: I would categorize the broad categories as four: managing a retail channel delivery system for our client, managing a mail channel, adding clinical value and quality to the process, and fourth, the prescription with cost and utilization management.	2126–2128 PATT
1211 PO-CKA

1212 DELIB

2129 CONT | Participant A: Another essential body of knowledge beyond the pharmacy piece is knowing the health care environment. Knowing what our customers face in the marketplace and knowing their organization. Knowing how we can deliver those four areas of knowledge that Participant C described. How to make that actually happen in the customer's environment. Knowing the weak links of the sales force so that we can supplement their work and the customer can get the maximum value from the pharmacy benefit. There are lots of different bodies of knowledge within understanding the customer. | Note: expanded definition or list of what Participant A meant by "health care environment." |
| 1213 PO-CKA

2130 PATT | Participant D: The pharmacy knowledge – with the health care knowledge – and the financial knowledge – and how all of those things interact. | |

TABLE 6.5 Analysis Operation: Readying Data for Analysis

Project Identity _____

Researcher _____

Data Source	Code	Source Tag	Data	Comment
Individual Interviews	DASH	1001	Participant A: I was the one who brought in the dashboard. We used it at the beginning to turn around the company. Now we are pretty stabilized so it does help us monitor the business. These are always top of mind. I have to get involved with the day-to-day business transactions. It goes to the very core of our business.	

(Continued)

58   Stage Four – Analysis and Observation Development

Data Source	Code	Source Tag	Data	Comment
"	PO-COMP	1002	Participant A: Our value proposition is different than what another organization could bring. We are truly looking at providing the most cost effective pharmaceutical care benefit to the customer.	
"	DIFF	1003	Participant A: I'm not sure if that is what you are looking for.	
"	PO-CKA	1004	Participant A: The terminology that would be used, customer intimacy, would be our focus. For us, it is always looking at the total health care costs. So we make our pharmacy recommendations based on total health care costs, not just the piece that we manage.	

As time permits, the researcher may choose to combine findings from the sources, fill in the codes, and attach a numerical sequence of source tags for more explicit data management in the future stages of the Rapid Due Diligence diagnostic process. Similarly, the data may be sorted to accommodate the analytical moves for drawing conclusions, as shown in Table 6.6.

TABLE 6.6 Analysis Operation: Coding for Drawing Conclusions

Project Identity _____

Researcher _____

Data Source	Code	Source Tag	Data	Comment
Individual Interviews	PATT	2001	Participant A: We are truly looking at providing the most cost effective pharmaceutical care benefit.	Focus on cost, efficiency, or prescription management calculation
"	PATT	2002	Participant A: So – customer intimacy would be our focus.	Focus on customer intimacy
"	PATT	2003	Participant A: For us, it is always looking for the total health care costs. So we make our pharmacy recommendation based on total health care costs, not just the piece that we manage.	Focus on cost, efficiency, or prescription management calculation

Stage Four – Analysis and Observation Development 59

Data Source	Code	Source Tag	Data	Comment
"	PATT	2004	Participant A: The knowledge area would be the architecture of those strategies within prescription management, analyzing that data and determining the way or the strategies to achieve the needs of our business. This includes all of the strategies in the cost and utilization components. Cost x utility = the ultimate cost. Can be affected by the mix, the use of generics, the rates negotiated in retail and mail order rebate contracts. All of those build into the architecture. The Drug Utilization Review models are another part of the architecture. These may increase or decrease the drug utilization to offset more expensive treatments or greater pain and anxiety. The balance with the customer timeframe of members is also used to determine the payback.	Focus on cost, efficiency, or prescription management calculation

Categories of Analysis

The analytical stage in the Rapid Due Diligence diagnostic method is designed to search for four initial, broad categories of potential strategic vulnerability, inconstancy, deficiency, instability, lapse, or opportunity for innovation or advancement. These four initial categories include the following:

- Degree of alignment or fit among strategic dimensions of an organization
- Execution of strategies to achieve targeted results
- Capabilities and capacity to perform and achieve targets
- Tracing the economic value-producing path from the strategy platform to results

The findings from each of these broad areas of analysis are also compared with value propositions for the organization's owners or shareholders, customers, and employees to determine the potential for achieving a Triple Win.

60 Stage Four – Analysis and Observation Development

The analysis of these four categories includes at least the following techniques:

- Determine the degree of fit among the strategic dimensions captured for this organization, referring to Table 6.7 below.
- Apply the elements and questions of the Integrated Strategic Human Capital Alignment Framework, to be shown in this chapter.
- Identify how the organization engages its distinctive Critical Knowledge Areas© and critical talent.
- Trace the economic value-producing path from the strategy platform to results.
- Examine market and customer choice analytics.
- Seek degrees of agreement among multiple value propositions and operations.
- Uncover flaws in strategy execution.
- Identify sources of dissonance among the business model, strategy, execution, or perceptions of the organization, customers, and employees.

Degree of Alignment or Fit among Strategic Dimensions

This category of analysis begins with a host of critical questions applied to the complete set of findings from all sources, including the document review and all forms of on-site discovery. For reference, the questions are applied to the list of thirteen strategic dimensions revealed in Chapter Four and shown again in Table 6.7.

TABLE 6.7 Strategic Dimensions of an Organization

Strategic Dimension Label	Description
Mission	Purpose or fundamental focus of an organization
Vision	Ideal future state upon realization of the mission
Values	Desirable set of principles, standards, or qualities
Business Model	Scheme or description for how an organization creates, delivers, and captures value
Critical Success Factors	Essential, measurable ingredients and focal points for organizational attention
Primary Strategies and Goals	Plans of action or maneuvers to achieve specified targets
Customer Value Proposition	A statement summarizing the rationale for customers in choosing products and services from an organization as compared to competitive options
Employee Value Proposition	A statement summarizing the employment experience that individuals have while a member of an organization and rationale for choosing to belong to one organization as compared to other options
Shareholder or Owner Value Proposition	A statement summarizing the rationale for shareholders or owners to choose to invest in an organization
Key Processes	Primary systems of operations or series of actions and functions to produce targeted results

Stage Four – Analysis and Observation Development **61**

Strategic Dimension Label	Description
Key Metrics and Critical Ratios	Essential measures and evaluative comparisons that determine the success of a strategy or organizational viability
Critical Knowledge Areas©	Unique bodies of specific key resource-capabilities which lie at the core of the value proposition of an organization
Competitive Distinction	Point of differentiation between an organization and its rivals

The researcher makes appropriate notations of the responses to all of the critical questions for use in all further analysis, synthesis, and formulation of conclusions and recommendations. The critical questions include at least the following:

- Does the organization have all of the thirteen strategic dimensions in place?
- If not, which strategic dimensions are missing, inadequately described, unused, or too dated to be reliable?
- Which strategic dimensions have been affirmed with any depth of strategic review in the most recent six- to twelve-month period?
- How are the strategic dimensions supported and on what basis?
  - o Explicit statements of assumption?
  - o Current, direct market research and analysis by the organization of customer needs and preferences?
  - o Reliance on accuracy of any recent sector analyses completed by others, such as industry associations, economic or scientific studies of universities or independent institutes, government agencies, or related non-profit organizations?
  - o Any evidence of intentional conformation or symmetrical arrangement that can be projected from one strategy to another, or in the cascade of strategic dimension factors throughout the organization?
  - o Past practices or traditions of the organization?
  - o Intuitive guesses or estimates without explicit supporting evidence?
- How are the strategies dimensions applied or integrated with the following:
  - o Strategic planning process?
  - o Development of the specific strategy currently under review?
  - o Execution of the strategy?
  - o Performance management process?
  - o Evaluation of results and impact on the condition of the strategic dimensions?
- Where do the strategic dimensions reside on a continuum of influence or degree of fit? Refer to Figure 6.1.

62 Stage Four – Analysis and Observation Development

Absent, Non-existent, No Degree of Fit	Incomplete, Crude Connection	Moderate, Directional Alignment	Fully Consistent, Correspondent, Logical Inference of Similarity

FIGURE 6.1 Continuum of Strategic Fit.

- What is the origin or source of each of the strategic dimensions?
  - o Specific research conducted by or for the organization?
  - o Agreement or consensus among the owners or leaders of the organization, based upon their individual information on the subject?
  - o Definition or description adapted from an outside source, for example, a published book or article?
  - o Provision by an outside consulting resource?
  - o Considered as an incunabulum, i.e., an artifact from an earlier period in the existence of the organization?
- How are the strategic dimensions evident in the operations and culture of the organization?
  - o Explicitly inculcated in the routinely evaluated measures of strategic performance?
  - o Culturally distinctive in a unique set of observable behaviors?
  - o Visible or traceable indicators of the active presence or quality of a strategic dimension?
  - o Concrete, line-of-sight alignment throughout the performance management process at all levels?
  - o Clearly established as a sentinel of organizational viability?
  - o Descriptions or conditions that give rise to organizational sententiousness, i.e., readily emoting aphorisms, principles, or observations about the organization that can stimulate increased levels of engagement?
- How are the strategic dimensions communicated?
  - o To what levels and locations throughout the organization?
  - o To customers and targeted markets?
  - o To the investing public or community?
  - o In what level of descriptive detail?
  - o With what frequency?
  - o From which author or originator?
  - o With what evidentiary statements or descriptions?
- How and why are any of the strategic dimensions considered proprietary in nature and thus protected? Are any of the following present?
  - o Critical Knowledge Areas© such as patents, copyrights, secret formulas, or processes?
  - o Primary strategies or supporting tactics that depend upon constant or temporary subterfuge?

Stage Four – Analysis and Observation Development **63**

- o A business model that embodies unique or competitively disruptive practices?
- o A competitive distinction that is under development and not yet sufficiently mature for dehiscence, exposure, or revelation?
- What is the relationship of any of the strategic dimensions to customers?
  - o Of primary significance or a driver of customer choice analysis?
  - o Centric to the brand?
  - o Well publicized and recognizable throughout the targeted market?
  - o Of little, unknown, or untracked value to the customer?
- What is the relationship of any of the strategic dimensions to employees of the organization?
  - o Principal source of identification or sense of belonging?
  - o Primary driver of employee roles and responsibilities?
  - o Explicitly pinpointed function of individual and/or group performance and contribution to targeted results?
  - o Inherent factor for stimulating positive engagement?
  - o Central description giving intentional shape to the culture?
  - o A qualifier for selection, development, and employment retention?
  - o Irrelevant, unknown, or untested in relationship to employees?
  - o Source of mildly differing perspectives, disagreement, hostility, agitation, discontent, apathy, or indifference?
- In what ways do the current definitions, descriptions, conditions, stature, or application of any of the strategic dimensions reveal any symptom of the following:
  - o Missed opportunity?
  - o Fresh or newly discovered opportunity?
  - o Leverageable distinction from competitive offerings or sources?
  - o Opportunity for disruptive competitive challenge?
  - o Insight into previously untapped aspect of customer, investment community, or employee relationships?
  - o Misalignment that impedes the full realization of targeted results?
  - o Previously unknown toxicity to the culture?
  - o Inhibitor to the effective engagement and productive achievement of results?
- To what degree are the strategic dimensions intentionally crafted as a coherent, fully aligned set? Which strategic dimensions are out of alignment or inadequately executed?
- How do any of the strategic dimensions serve as an effective stimulant or incubator for innovation? What supportive practices are in place or missing?
  - o Does the organization regard innovation as critical to future growth?
  - o Have risk-balanced portfolios of potential innovative initiatives been defined?

64 Stage Four – Analysis and Observation Development

- o Have the prospects of digitization been incorporated to displace or augment more conventional approaches?
- o Are investments routinely made in innovative initiatives?
- o Are sufficient resources provided to produce positive results?
- o Have new business models been created to leverage innovations and to generate scalable profitability?
- o Does the organization have a reputation for developing and launching innovations quickly and effectively?
- o Are employees organized, motivated, and rewarded for innovation?
- o Are there penalties for failure?
- Are there any interstitial areas which may unknowingly impede or accelerate execution of the strategy or business issue under review?

There are a number of ways in which the researcher can proceed. Each of the questions may be the point of singular analysis of all of the sets of findings. A more experienced researcher may combine certain critical questions into bundles for review of all findings. A particularly facile researcher may simultaneously filter all of the documentation or on-site discovery sources for potential evidence in response to a majority of the critical questions.

Other techniques or tools can be useful in plotting the degree of alignment and fit among the strategic dimensions. A chart may be created to visually juxtapose all key strategic initiatives that are currently underway with the strategic dimensions to analyze potential degree of impact. An example appears in the table below.

This chart presents a visual array of initiatives that are currently in motion and the relative importance to the advancement of the respective strategic dimensions. It is useful in initially identifying initiatives that consume resources without sufficient return to the effectiveness or long-term viability of the organization. The findings can assist in isolating areas for further inquiry or analysis. This tool can also be used for facilitating a working session of panel interview participants or a group of decision-makers. The discussion can provide a rich source of discovery.

A generic strategic thinking set of questions can be assembled for application to the business issue under review. This technique can be used by only the researcher or with a research team to collaboratively compare separate segments of initial findings. The responses to the strategic thinking questions can assist in setting the direction for deeper analysis. A sample worksheet appears in Table 6.8.

A flow network diagram can be assembled to visually capture all or most of the strategic dimensions. As the analytical review of the findings yields the identity of the various strategic dimensions, the remaining fields open for eventual discovery are highlighted. Relationships among the strategic dimensions and degree of conformability can also be traced in this compact tool. This diagram can also serve as a

TABLE 6.8 Integrated Strategic Focus and Potential for Impact

Current Initiatives	Mission	Vision	Values	Business Model	Critical Success Factors	Primary Strategies and Goals	Customer Value Proposition	Employee Value Proposition	Owner Value Proposition	Key Metrics and Critical Ratios	Key Processes	Critical Knowledge Areas©	Competitive Distinction	Impact Total	Action Steps
New product development															
Implement strategic enrollment management															
Implement new learning delivery system															
Create new organizational culture															
Facilities usage assessment															
Redefine faculty workload system															
Define new governance policy															
Diversify college workforce															
Complete accreditation self-study															

Ranking of Impact: 5=Very High 4=High 3=Moderate 2=Low 1=Nominal 0=Not Applicable

66 Stage Four – Analysis and Observation Development

TABLE 6.9 Situation Worksheet with Strategic Thinking Questions

Questions	Notes
What is the situation? What is the real opportunity or problem?	
What are the desired results?	
What is the gap?	
Who needs to be involved? Why?	
What additional information do we need?	
What behaviors or best practices apply?	
What alternatives need to be considered?	
What are the estimated risks and resources for each alternative?	
What criteria should guide and align the decision?	
What is the best course of action?	
What follow-through is required for success?	
How will we measure and recognize progress?	

helpful deliverable with the final recommendations. It can generate useful discussion and stimulate fresh insights among decision-makers. A sample flow network diagram appears in Figure 6.2.

The strategic dimension of key metrics and critical ratios, described as essential measures and evaluative comparisons that determine the success of a strategy or organizational viability, is frequently the primary target for management attention. This dimension, therefore, becomes a special area for preparatory investigation, on-site discovery, and analysis within the Rapid Due Diligence diagnostic process.

During the preparatory investigation, the researcher will have gathered considerable information from investor information sources, such as Securities and Exchange Commission reports, presentations to financial analysts, news releases, and other reports of operating results, competitive comparisons, and customer loyalty tracking. The researcher needs to especially examine the management discussion and analysis of the organization's financial condition and results of operations, appearing within the annual 10-K report. This section includes important financial highlights, the consolidated and segmented results of operations, identity and status of critical ratios, year-over-year comparisons, and sources of significant financial gains or losses. This section also contains background information on any claims, litigation, catastrophic modeling, delineation of uncertainties within the business and reserves to mitigate impact, future outlooks and expectations of key drivers for results of operations and the organization's capital position,

Strategic Targets and Descriptors	Mission Statement: To improve the health of the people we serve				Value Proposition: (not available)
	Strategic Objective Statement: We will be among the best and biggest in our industry by delivering the best product value with the best people.	**Strategic Objectives:** • Achieve the targeted performance characteristics of our best competitors in each region. • Increase our scale and market share in targeted regions. • Create competitive edge through product value. • Become the employer of choice in the health management industry and in targeted regions.			**Operating Imperatives:** • Grow profitable enrollment. • Reduce administrative cost. • Reduce cost of care. • Improve the health of our members. • Improve the level of service. • Develop our associates.
	Core Values: Customer Focus, Commitment to Excellence, Continuous Improvement and Innovation, Results with Integrity, Teamwork	**Four "Fs":** Fast, Fun, Flexible, Focused			**Six "Cs":** Capability, Commitment, Contribution, Continuity, Collaboration, Conscience
Potential Critical Knowledge Areas©	Knowledge of the economics of our health care insurance business and systemic influences among members (employers), provider network, clinical/medical care management.	Knowledge of actuarial and underwriting practices in determining rates that meet the needs of our customers.	Collective knowledge about our targeted markets, competition, and our customer relationships.	Knowledge about how to translate customer needs into profitable business (risk assessment and management).	**CKA© Needed:** Knowledge about how to effectively do our business through e-commerce.
Potential Critical Talent Descriptions	**Experience:** • Health care industry insurance experience • Health care system experience of any type (brokerage, medical care management, insurance, etc.) • Work experience within multiple functions in health care	**Education and/or Professional Credentials:** • Actuarial credentials • Medical/clinical credentials • Appropriate licensure with state departments of insurance	**Behavioral Profile:** • Strategic, systemic thinking with short/long term view • Critical thinking and creative problem solving • Disciplined analysis, judgment, and decisiveness • Willingness to take initiative • Personal and professional credibility • Ability to communicate complex situations with clarity • Collaboration	**Behavioral Profile:** • Accountability and drive for results • Willingness to share information • Ability to identify meaningful patterns and opportunities • Flexibility and openness to change • High standards of excellence • Sense of urgency • Change leader • Customer service orientation (internal and external) • Ability to influence others to action	
Potential Measures of Influence or Return on Critical Talent	Efficiency and effectiveness of the combination of Critical Knowledge Areas© and Critical Talent may produce the following potential changes: • Reduction in internal and external transaction cost factors • Increase in effect of deep knowledge about the triangle and systemic effects • Increase in return factors such as revenue, operating margins, and sales • Increase in customer loyalty and market share				

FIGURE 6.2 Flow Network Diagram.

68 Stage Four – Analysis and Observation Development

critical accounting estimates, identity of potential risk factors, and market risks with quantitative and qualitative disclosures.

The researcher examines all of these sources for the identity and condition of key metrics or critical ratios that can have a bearing on the business issue under review. If the central business issue includes a heightened concern about the financial viability of the organization, the researcher is encouraged to seek additional professional resources such as research reports and opinions issued by outside, objective financial analyst firms to gain evaluative data. Such third-party research perspectives can be useful to the researcher in understanding the potential confidence or anxiety of the market and a possible underlying source of concern to the owner of the business issue. A listing of commonly used ratios appears in Table 6.10.

In conversation with the owner of the business issue and the organizational key contact, the researcher identifies the key metric or critical ratio of particular concern. The researcher isolates the factors at work within the key metric or critical ratio and pursues deeper detail and causal relationships. There can be primary, secondary, or tertiary relationships within the organization, market or customer base, or employee productivity.

The researcher can use an analytical technique for mapping strategic drivers through the organization's economic value-producing path to specific key metrics or ratios. This technique permits the researcher to trace factors of influence or productivity and pinpoint specific performance areas for correction, development, or other types of attention. An example of this mapping technique appears in Box 6.1.

An important underlying perspective that supports the principle of seeking a Triple Win for the organization, its customers, and its employees relates to the measurement of the impact of learning and development strategies as a valuable form of business intelligence. In the course of conducting the Rapid Due Diligence diagnostic method, this means the researcher creates a visible line of sight from the business strategy under review to the learning strategy, its intended outcomes, the application of newly acquired knowledge and skills, and eventually to targeted results. This measurement process illuminates a tracer between the strategy and results.

The precision of the overarching learning strategy and its direct connection to the economic value-producing path for the business will often determine the degree of impact on both the short and long-term position of the organization. Such information is ideally built upon the unique economics of the organization and presents a useful guide to strategic decision- making and competitive advantage.

This position is highly compatible with management's growing reliance upon facts and evidence as the foundation for strategic decision-making, managing resources, and leading people. It is fundamental to the development of deep wisdom about the success factors for the business, the customers' choices, plus the relationship between human capabilities and the performance of the organization.

TABLE 6.10 List of Commonly Used Ratios

Label or Description	Acronym	Ratio Calculation
Gross margin, gross profit margin, or gross profit rate	GM or GPR	$\dfrac{Gross\ Profit}{Net\ Sales}$
Operating margin or return on sales	OM or ROS	$\dfrac{Operating\ Income}{Net\ Sales}$
Profit margin or net margin	PM or NPM	$\dfrac{Net\ Profit}{Net\ Sales}$
Return on equity	ROE	$\dfrac{Net\ Income}{Average\ Shareholders\ Equity}$
Return on assets	ROA	$\dfrac{Net\ Income}{Average\ Total\ Assets}$
Return on net assets	RONA	$\dfrac{Net\ Income}{Fixed\ Assets + Working\ Capital}$
Return on capital	ROC	$\dfrac{EBIT\ (1 - Tax\ Rate)}{Invested\ Capital}$
Return adjusted return on capital	RAROC	$\dfrac{Expected\ Return}{Economic\ Capital}$
Return on capital employed	ROCE	$\dfrac{EBIT}{Capital\ Employed}$
Cash flow return on investment	CFROI	$\dfrac{Cash\ Flow}{Market\ Recapitalization}$
Current ratio, working capital ratio, or liquidity ratio	WCR	$\dfrac{Current\ Assets}{Current\ liabilities}$
Operating cash flow ratio	OCFR	$\dfrac{Operating\ Cash\ Flow}{Total\ Debts}$
Asset turnover	AT	$\dfrac{Net\ Sales}{Total\ Assets}$
Debt ratio	DR	$\dfrac{Total\ Liabilities}{Total\ Assets}$
Earnings per share	EPS	$\dfrac{Net\ Earnings}{Number\ of\ Shares}$
Price to book value ratio	P/B or PBV	$\dfrac{Market\ Price\ per\ Share}{Balance\ Sheet\ Price\ per\ Share}$

Stage Four – Analysis and Observation Development

> ## BOX 6.1 MAPPING STRATEGIC DRIVERS TO SALES PERFORMANCE METRICS
>
> The economic value-producing path demonstrates the linkage between:
>
> - The business strategy platform with identification of key drivers of economic value,
> - A series of cascading performance scorecards, and
> - The performance targets and responsibilities delineated within those scorecards to achieve targeted strategic sales results.
>
> Primary business strategies typically include knowledge and data-supported assumptions about at least the following significant categories or key strategic drivers of economic value:
>
> - Market space and customer choice analytics on their unique needs and triggering decision points that produce predictably favorable results
> - Leveraging economic fulcra or balance points for the business, targeted markets and channels, products, and services
> - The organization's value proposition with its customers and comparisons with current competitive intelligence
> - Impact on targeted shareholder value, such as assets under management (AUM) or return on invested capital
>
> The key drivers of economic value frequently fall into four components of measurable targets and are visually displayed for simple communication and tracking purposes on an enterprise scorecard. Examples of these components and potential target areas are listed below:
>
> - Create shareholder value, e.g., growth of AUM year-over-year, a specific target $AUM by a certain date, or specific AUM by channel.
> - Customer focus, e.g., Return on Customer such an increased transaction and advisory fees, or growth in targeted investment products and services. (To gain more precision and predictability in driving greater Return on Customer, it is helpful to note that customer choice analytics may often produce valuable data that can be used to more effectively inform the application of resources and techniques in sales and service to produce favorable results. For some customer populations, such as those with smaller transactional size, the calculations may be considered too complex, unpredictable, or unknowable to determine useful, reliable ways to capture trigger points and decisions related to individual customer investment choices. However, there may be sufficient information to discern patterns that identify probable trigger points and the causal relationship with sales or service actions that can produce desirable customer choice results.)

Stage Four – Analysis and Observation Development **71**

- Operational excellence, e.g., efficiency and yield of the sales process or impact of applied skills within a sales process to reduce sales cycle times or produce greater yield per territory or channel
- People development, e.g., demonstrated mastery of skills via assessments, impact of applied skills to business results, or convincing, observed anecdotal evidence

The sales performance scorecard reflects the assigned performance expectations that will contribute directly to the enterprise scorecard. Typically, a similar quadrant is created with brief descriptions or labels of the respective sales targets for each of the four components (shareholder value; customer focus; operational excellence; people development).

- In composite, the aggregate sales performance scorecards for all business units, divisions, or channels are expected to deliver the total value of assigned enterprise targets. Not all categories or targets may apply equally to each contributing sales group.
- The sales performance scorecards often are cascaded through one or more sales management level, then converted ultimately into personal scorecards for assigned territories.
- Sales management level sales performance scorecards correlate with coaching issues diagrams for regularly scheduled, integrated coaching and feedback discussions of skills, knowledge, and performance to date on assigned metrics.
- Scorecard content also is correlated with territory action plans, all performance review documentation, any adaptation of the four-box sales opportunity model, and sales management performance reviews.

Personal scorecards capture the specific performance expectations for personal achievement within the business cycle.

- These are also directly matched to the content of territory action plans and simultaneously appear in any performance management process tools.
- Ideally, the personal scorecards are used as self-tracking tools to ensure focus and attention to performance metrics that matter most to the enterprise.
- Personal scorecards may also include explicit personal development expectations.

The intent is to create clear, simple, meaningful connections between the strategic drivers to key enterprise metrics to the contribution of the sales organization and individual performance objectives of sales executives.

Listed below are sample sales performance metrics that an organization might consider for insertion within sales performance scorecards and

(Continued)

72 Stage Four – Analysis and Observation Development

personal scorecards. These can be used in routine sales management reviews and coaching discussions at multiple levels plus self-tracking. There is an emphasis upon process focal points and skills effectiveness to ultimately produce lower cost of sales, plus greater yield on selling time and effort. These metrics are often called key performance indicators and typically represent a combination of leading and lagging indicators.

- Progress toward achieving targeted AUM annual dollar targets required for performance leader status (measures ongoing, cumulative yield throughout the year)
- Number of prospects identified and qualified (measures focus and sufficiency of prospecting activity to eventually reach AUM targets, ideally also expressed as a percent of sufficiency, based on known sales analytics)
- Dollars of opportunity within an active pipeline, minimum of dollars and percentage of annual AUM target (measures sufficiency of the entire pipeline; compares with sales analytics on the each stage plus close rates required to achieve AUM target)
- Conversion ratio of at least X percent over the most recent Y days (measures efficiency or cycle time of the sales process and applied skills, in converting prospects to advanced stages or higher probability closing stage)
- Closing ratio of at least X percent within Y days (measures complete sales process efficiency and proficiency of process and applied selling skills; again compares with known sales analytics on the average or targeted close rate to achieve the AUM targets)

Other sales performance metrics may be added to emphasize performance in specific channels, products, or services. Examples include:

- Specific progress measures on growth in targeted investment management products and services, or growth in specific types of advisory and transaction fees (bases, transaction, and performance)
- Specific market or channel penetration, typically year-over-year percentage growth
- Measurable increase in the amount of selling time

High-quality measurement and evaluation methods produce information that is designed to provide reliable links between insights and actions. It is free of assumptive bias and designed to deliver facts that are used to:

- Illuminate factors that have previously been gray areas of uncertainty or the unknowable.
- Convert insights on such situations into well-organized, reliable evidence that can be used to accurately guide and frame critical thinking and decision-making.

Stage Four – Analysis and Observation Development

- Pinpoint areas that require management attention.
- Uncover unexpected insights.
- Shape the ongoing execution of a specific strategy.
- Isolate areas that require further coaching and reinforcement.
- Gauge progress toward a targeted goal.
- Trace the economic value-producing path from the business strategy platform to key drivers of value to work group and individual actions.

Often, the best measurement and evaluation methods start with a close examination of the organization's business model, operating model, the core roadmap, or playbook of how it does business with its customers. Within this model are trails of behavioral activity that flow from the business mission, key strategies, platform drivers within functional areas such as product development, marketing and customer relationship processes, and data management systems and tools.

Whether applied in sequence or in non-linear paths, these value driver trails are filled with critical knowledge, decision points and rules, and behaviors, all of which can be directly sharpened or influenced by precise learning strategies and can be monitored, measured, and evaluated to determine the impact of those learning strategies.

Many organizations have successfully harnessed these linkages within an enterprise scorecard or dashboard. At least the following areas are routinely captured and examined in combination:

- Market space and customer choice analytics on their unique needs and triggering decision points that produce predictably favorite business results
- Leverageable economic balance points for the business, its targeted markets and channels, and mix of products and services to meet current needs
- The organization's value proposition with its customers and comparisons with current competitive intelligence
- Impact on targeted shareholder value, return on invested capital, or similar financial viability metric

These key drivers fall into typically four components of measurable targets. They are often visually displayed for simple, regular communication and tracking purposes, as shown in Table 6.11.

Frequently, an enterprise scorecard, dashboard, or similar visual tool is translated for business units, functional areas, or work groups with equivalent quadrants

TABLE 6.11 Components of Measurable Targets

Create Shareholder Value	Operational Excellence
Customer Focus	People Development

74 Stage Four – Analysis and Observation Development

and targets for which those areas carry prime accountability. These tools are further delineated into personal versions to capture the specific performance expectations for individual achievement within a given business cycle.

The intent is to create clear, simple, meaningful connections from the strategic drivers to key enterprise metrics, to the contribution of the business unit or functional segments, and ultimately to individual performance objectives. This set of connections can be described as creating line of sight from the strategy platform to all levels of employees, as shown in Figure 6.3. It can also be described as comparable to the phenomenon of syzygy, or the configuration of the sun, moon, and earth lying in a straight line.

Wherever possible, it is preferable to apply measurement and evaluation methods that trace these value drivers to align directly within the natural business and performance management processes. In this way, the measurement of the learning strategy is embedded within the business and uses the organization's own language and familiar metrics. It is not a detached, mysterious activity. As a result, the analytical findings and recommendations of the Rapid Due Diligence diagnostic process are more readily accepted and applied.

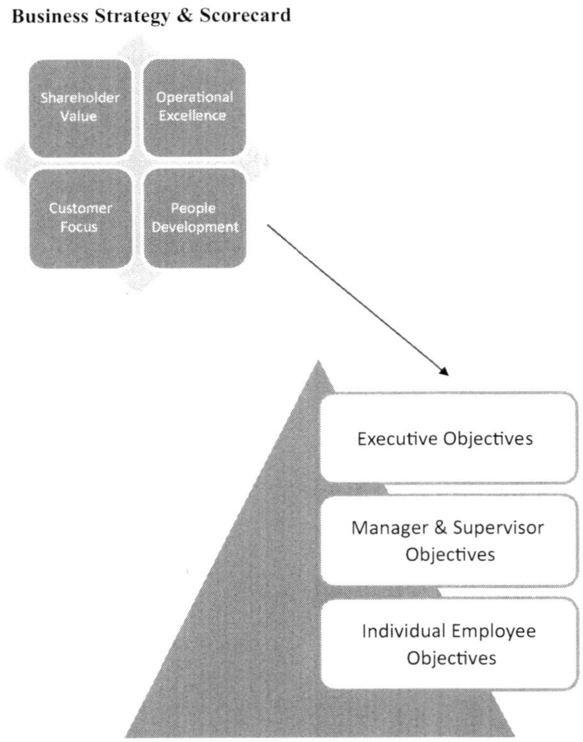

FIGURE 6.3 Achieving Syzygy within Organizational Performance.

The typical steps the researcher can use for tracking the impact of a learning strategy on the business include the following:

- Identify the strategic goal of the enterprise, business unit, or function for which the learning strategy was designed.
- Isolate the key drivers and enablers necessary to meet the strategic goal.
- Identify the required observable behaviors (knowledge, skills, abilities, and motivations) necessary to activate the drivers or enablers.
- Determine the precise components of the learning strategy or training experience that build capability in those behaviors.
- Clarify the ways in which those components and the application of behaviors will be measured and evaluated.
- Match the behaviors with the strategic measures.
- Narrow the data to minimize other variable influences.
- Track, evaluate, and convert data as appropriate to economic terms that are useful and understandable to the organization.
- Frame the results for fact-based or evidence-based decision-making.

An example of a specific approach to measuring the effectiveness and impact of a learning strategy appears in Box 6.2.

BOX 6.2 MEASURING THE EFFECTIVENESS AND IMPACT OF A LEARNING STRATEGY

Purpose

- To regularly track and report trustworthy, organizationally credible data that gauges the effectiveness and impact of the training system.
- To set specific, practical measures that simply and effectively capture critical information that ties the training to any updated strategy on customer service and operational efficiency and effectiveness.
  - o Watch especially those trigger points that matter most to customers.
  - o Examine the current metrics, surveys, and feedback mechanisms from customers and employees.
  - o Trace the economic value-producing path within the operating model.
  - o Adapt all forms of dashboards, scorecards, performance monitoring processes, and reports to include these practical, critical-to-quality metrics from customers.
- To collect, interpret, and disseminate data in practical, actionable formats that are readily usable by senior leaders, branch and area managers, and front-line sales and service representatives.

(Continued)

76 Stage Four – Analysis and Observation Development

Process Alternatives

Performance Gates for New Sales Representatives On-Boarding Process

- Prepare and conduct mastery tests for technical and product knowledge and skills.
  - o Create tests to match the new streamlined product lines.
  - o Complete mastery tests on selling skills.
  - o Conduct these tests at the end of the week in which the correlating training segment is completed.
  - o Participants need to have a minimum of seventy percent score on technical and product knowledge tests on the first try. Any re-testing scores must be at least eighty-five percent.
  - o Participants need to have a minimum of eighty-five percent score on the selling skills mastery test. Plus, applications in exercises or skill practices must demonstrate at least an acceptable grasp of skills.
  - o Management and the human resources function will collaborate in confirming the consequences for failure to pass. The range of action can include provisional status with precise developmental activity for the remainder of the on-boarding process or termination.
- The comprehensive simulation and assessment center conducted in the eleventh week will be designed to include specific assessment guidelines and decision rules on what constitutes an acceptable level of performance, provisional status, or failure. A participant must demonstrate at least an acceptable level of performance in order to qualify for graduation and certification as a new sales representative eligible to go on plan. In all cases, participants will be provided with individualized feedback and future developmental recommendations.
- The aggregate set of participant scores from weeks two, three, four, seven, and eleven will be further evaluated for deeper insights into curriculum adjustments, future developmental recommendations, and baseline data for gauging future performance and business impact.

Application of Classic Levels of Learning Evaluation

- Level one (class survey or program module evaluations to gauge the participant's learning experience)
  - o Complete surveys at the close of each session.
  - o Take immediate action on feedback where warranted to improve the learning experience.
  - o Conduct an after action review process to gain further understanding of unusual results.

Stage Four – Analysis and Observation Development **77**

- o Conduct an analysis of data at least once each quarter to draw comparisons and promote continuous improvement in the learning experience.
- Level two (knowledge test to discern proficiency and understanding of key concepts)
  - o These are the mastery tests that are strongly recommended as performance gates in the new sales representative on-boarding process.
  - o Results are often further compared with level one participant reactions to determine where there may be any causal relationships in the level two scoring results.
- Level three (application of learning or 360 degree feedback and observations by others)
  - o This evaluation can be conducted via an assessment instrument or discerned from tailored performance review data.
  - o Investigate electronic level three assessment tools for its sales performance training content.
    - o If the organization chooses this option, it is suggested that the assessment be conducted between ninety and 180 days after the training experience.
    - o It is further recommended that any assessment data be used for developmental purposes only.
    - o Organizational trends can be used to identify opportunities for continuous improvement, further emphasis in coaching and reinforcement, and heightened communications strategies.
  - o For a tailored performance review approach, key training behaviors/skills need to be explicitly incorporated in performance expectations for the training participants.
    - o For best results, the respective managers will engage in routine observation, coaching, and feedback to reinforce the application of the skills.
    - o Learners and managers may use the following variation of the critical incident method of data collection for anecdotal evidence.
      - o Situation
      - o Action taken
      - o Results achieved for the business
      - o Impact on the people involved
    - o Both mid-year and year-end evaluations are recommended to focus on the ratings of these specific behaviors.
    - o Comparative ratings can be gathered from performance review data and used for organizational trending and further individual development.
- Level four (impact on the business with anecdotal, qualitative, or quantitative measures)

(Continued)

78 Stage Four – Analysis and Observation Development

- o Track changes to sales productivity via new policy production, per capita, quotations, yield, and close rates.
- o Consider creating precise standards of competency and performance.
  - o Using current financial and business analytical data, establish predictive financial performance modeling with threshold performance expectations for the phases.
    - o Sample sales process or pipeline metrics are listed below for reference:
      - o Qualify a specified number of prospects of X size over Y period of time (measuring focus and sufficiency of prospecting)
      - o Active current year pipeline of X size coverage, totaling at least Y dollars (measuring sufficiency of pipeline to achieve revenue targets)
      - o Transition ratios of at least X percent over Y period of time (measuring conversion of prospects to later stages of sales process or pipeline)
      - o Quotes of at least X number per Y period of time (measuring effectiveness with any intermediary)
      - o Closing ratio of at least X percent within Y period of time (measuring complete sales process and proficiency)
    - o Communicate these expectations within the training process, in before-during-after communications, within coaching and reinforcement techniques, as well as in the performance management process.
    - o Evaluate performance against these standards on at least an annual basis.
- o Test whether any sales productivity results are correlated with any production integration (cross-sell/up-sell) targets per household.
- o Trace any impact of the business development process and training content on customers' experiences and results reported in any related scorecards.
  - o Trace high value trigger (or decision migration) points within the customer analytics of the value driver trees, paths of greatest opportunity, or similar reports.
  - o Match those findings to the granular detail within the steps of the business development process, performance standards and goals, and learning outcomes of the training system.
  - o Isolate the most direct points of influence on performance and contribution to customer satisfaction ratings.
  - o Refer to any form of impact scale, color-coded indices, or performance scores by component.
  - o Follow the flow of any platform drivers to both sub and key drivers, then to the overall outcomes for business units.

Stage Four – Analysis and Observation Development **79**

- o Watch especially for movement within ninety to 120 days of the training experience.
- o Trace the performance data on customer satisfaction to the enterprise scorecard. Watch especially for performance changes in customer service, retention rates, operational efficiency and effectiveness, and financial growth.
- o Evaluate any influence of the training system on any forms of employee engagement index or pulse survey data.
  - o Compare the survey question sets and results for the most recent survey period with any results after the training system implementation.
  - o Isolate any questions that relate to the sales process, operating model, and direct influencers of sales performance.
  - o Evaluate pre and post-training results for those zones, areas, or locations that completed the training system.
  - o Test the ratings and results in the following path:
    - o Employee engagement data
    - o To individual skill development
    - o To individual performance expectations, performance review data, and zone, branch, or area scorecard data
    - o To sales performance (production or per capita)
    - o To enterprise scorecard data
    - o To current gauges of Return on Customer (customer satisfaction indices + revenue production + retention data)
  - o If available, conduct a further test of the degree of zone, branch, or area involvement in formal coaching, reinforcement, or mentoring process activities in direct support of the training system.

Further Considerations

As time and resources permit, additional analytical actions can be undertaken to secure more precise and perhaps metadata in gauging the business impact of the training system.

- Examine and evaluate the detailed implementation plans. Construct the following data into a comparative organizational action timeline with performance tracking:
  - o Who participated by zone, branch, area, or other functional area?
  - o Who were the sales leaders at the time of the learning experiences and key changes in sales or market leadership?
  - o What structural or assignment changes occurred over the timeline?
  - o What strategy or operating model shifts or significant organizational changes occurred?
  - o Plot sales productivity by zone, branch, or area.

(Continued)

80 Stage Four – Analysis and Observation Development

> - o Plot any sales model pipeline changes.
> - o Identify degree of application of the mentoring process.
> - o Confirm actions deployed by field developmental specialists or internal performance consultants in conjunction with zone, branch, or area managers.
> - o Assess the application of the coaching and reinforcement process.
>   - o When and where deployed with regularity
>   - o Tracing any variations in performance tied to coaching
>   - o Comparisons with coaching practice heuristics
> - o Verify the application of detailed communications strategy.
>   - o Key messaging before-during-after the training experience
>   - o Comparisons
> - In the coming year, test for sales productivity changes that may correlate to both the training system plus the organizational restructuring and any change in span of control.
> - Compare any results from this implementation and execution analysis with the earlier noted levels one through four results.
> - Draw further causal relationships and patterns from the historical data.
> - Compare results with sales performance training system heuristics available from other sources.

In those situations where the behavioral change can be observed and may not be easily quantifiable, other analysis, measurement, and evaluation methods can be applied. These include variations of the long-accepted critical incident methodology from social science research, such as the Situation-Action-Result-Impact (SARI) technique. Anecdotal evidence can be collected to isolate:

- The stimulating circumstances or situation (S)
- The action (A) that was taken in response to that situation
- The result (R) for the business
- The impact (I) on the people that were involved

This is an analytical technique that is incorporated in the approach to the on-site discovery stage and then coded in the analysis stage. Behavioral assessment of such SARI examples can produce either negative or positive evidence. A collection of similar data can provide stronger predictive evidence of likely impact. These examples can be further validated and used as behavioral anchors or performance guideposts.

Another form of measuring the learning strategy has been connected to comparative benchmarking. While such activity can produce information of some level of interest to management, most organizations gain greater insight from seeking more direct, robust competitive intelligence. This more direct information serves as a point of departure in more accurately defining and fulfilling the customer value proposition that matters most in the marketplace. The learning strategy is then designed to be tightly connected to providing the skills, knowledge, and full capabilities required to precisely deliver on the customer value proposition.

As the researcher pursues this analysis, an alternative point of view deserves consideration, especially if there are time or budgetary constraints. If there is sufficient reliable evidence available, this alternative perspective or recommendation is to avoid the investment of limited staff time, energy, and budgetary resources on additional measurement and evaluation.

From the perspective of the Rapid Due Diligence diagnostic method, the researcher needs to address whether it is practical or necessary to prove the causal relationship or the degree of impact if the organization already has sufficient evidence for sound decision-making and action-taking. As the Rapid Due Diligence diagnostic method proceeds through its sequential stages, the researcher may choose instead to focus on other recommendations, such as clarifying the strategy, engaging in flawless execution, coaching and reinforcing the newly acquired skills and knowledge, and managing leading and lagging indicators through existing or more precise performance management or scorecard mechanisms.

Execution of Strategies to Achieve Targeted Results

This category of analysis delves more deeply into operations, practices, and organizational behavior to identify potential deleterious effects on the execution of strategies that are planned or already in motion.

Longitudinal research investigating strategy execution has revealed important insights into the effectiveness of strategy execution. Beginning with the identification and ranking of non-financial factors that are most highly valued among the investment community, the following five factors are shown below in rank order:[1]

- Strategy execution
- Management credibility
- Quality of strategy
- Innovativeness
- Ability to attract talented people

Throughout the stages of the Rapid Due Diligence diagnostic method, all five of these factors are included in the investigative process. Critical questions pursuing the factor of innovativeness were introduced in the previous category seeking degree of alignment or fit among strategic dimensions. This section will focus upon strategy execution.

Another finding of the longitudinal research, noted above, revealed significant loss of potential value during the typical execution of a strategic plan. The data show that, on average, an organization achieves only sixty-three percent of the

82 Stage Four – Analysis and Observation Development

realizable potential value of a given strategy. The remaining thirty-seven percent of potential value is primarily lost to the following three barriers.

- Inadequacy of performance management systems in fully aligning with the strategy
- Failure to commit sufficient and timely resources to the strategy
- Organizational failure to engage in necessary changes

These three areas of possible value erosion (Figure 6.4) are the targets of specific analytical review during this stage of the Rapid Due Diligence diagnostic process. Nearly one-half of the lost value is attributable to inadequacy of performance management systems in fully aligning with the targeted strategy.

Performance management presents a rich target area of opportunity during the Rapid Due Diligence diagnostic process; therefore, more background information is provided in this segment for analytical review. Effective performance management frameworks include the following ten elements:

- Understanding the organization's mission, vision, values, strategies, and goals
- Linking individual and team goals, expected contributions, and behaviors
- Setting verifiable targets and priorities for results and development
- Coaching for optimal performance
- Tracking progress

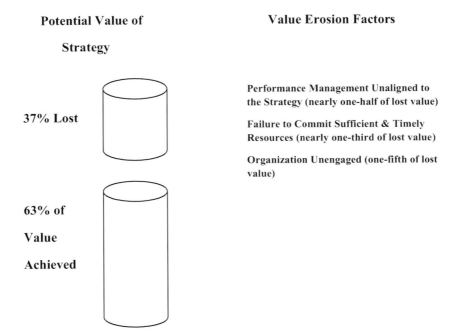

FIGURE 6.4 Barriers to Effective Strategy Execution.

Stage Four – Analysis and Observation Development **83**

- Giving periodic feedback on performance results and behaviors
- Communicating any changes in course
- Measuring verifiable or observable results and impact
- Recognizing performance contributions and developmental growth
- Determining compensatory and other rewards

While the inadequacy or absence of any one of these elements can substantially weaken the organization's capability to deliver the desired performance, the most frequent barriers are listed below:

- Failure to clearly connect performance to organizational strategies and goals
- Absence of setting performance expectations
- Little or no provision of feedback on performance
- Difficulty receiving feedback for improvement
- Lack of coaching
- Failure to provide meaningful recognition for performance results
- Poor conduct of any performance discussions
- Weak or nonexistent calibration of performance with any compensatory or other rewards

During the analytic process, the researcher needs to identify the existence of any one of these eight frequent barriers to effective performance management as prime opportunities for strategy execution improvement. The evidence of these barriers is most likely to be revealed in the on-site discovery stage. In practice, these weaknesses or barriers are not revealed until the latter portion of the interviews when the researcher probes for insights into the individual connections and sense of responsibility for specific strategic results.

Effective performance management flows as a continuous process, not the typically observed annual event. Effective performance management focuses on driving high performance and flawless execution of the organization's business strategy and flows in a dynamic set of three interactive phases as also shown in Figure 6.5:

- Planning
- Tracking and providing feedback
- Appraising

For purposes of the planning phase of the performance management cycle, there are several steps that need to be observed. The researcher needs to verify that all steps are routinely followed.

- Seek, clarify, and share business direction, goals, and priorities.
- Balance the focus upon results and competencies required for achieving those results.

84 Stage Four – Analysis and Observation Development

FIGURE 6.5 Performance Management Cycle.

- Establish individual performance objectives that directly link to the business strategy and the matching metrics.
- Identify key competencies (knowledge, skills, abilities, and motivations) that drive the desired performance, produce flawless execution, and demonstrate the organization's values.
- Create a fully aligned employee development plan to bolster those competencies.

In preparing the individual performance objectives, the respective managers and individuals have sufficient dialogue to build a full understanding of the organization's strategy, goals, priorities, and expected contributions. The individual performance objectives fall directly into line-of-sight alignment with other levels within a business unit, division, or corporate hierarchy, similar to Figure 6.3 (Achieving Syzygy within Organizational Performance).

For organizations which practice any version of a balanced scorecard approach to measuring strategic progress, the individual performance objectives are directly connected to one or more of the quadrants, depending upon the role and responsibilities of the employee. An example of individual performance objectives that demonstrate alignment to scorecard quadrants appears in Figure 6.6.

The researcher may find that the organization's managers are required to establish individual performance objectives that are tightly linked to the strategy yet may not be supported by full accretion or commitment. From either an individual or collective perspective, this phenomenon also directly relates to the execution barrier of organizational failure to adopt necessary changes. Within the findings, the researcher needs to seek evidence of difficulty or even absence of managerial preparation and actions to secure individual commitment to goals or objectives in which the individuals have little or no input. Specific techniques can be practiced to gain commitment by reluctant individuals. If these techniques are not routinely practiced, the missing behaviors can be identified as part of the recommendations to the organization. These include the following actions by the manager:

Stage Four – Analysis and Observation Development **85**

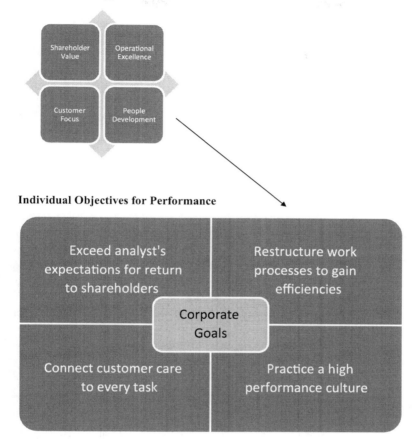

FIGURE 6.6 Establishing Objectives Aligned to the Business.

- Clarifying the specific goals and expected contributions
- Resolving any self-concerns and anticipating the likely objections of individuals
- Presenting the goals and expectations in direct linkage with the business strategy
- Encouraging the individual to voice any concerns
- Asking for ideas on how to achieve the goals and charting an agreed-upon path
- Offering assistance and support to the individual in pursuit of the goals

Individual performance objectives typically are weighted to aggregately account for seventy percent of the performance management plan. The remaining thirty percent is reserved for observable practice and potential development of specified

86 Stage Four – Analysis and Observation Development

competencies. For purposes of the Rapid Due Diligence diagnostic process, competencies are defined as the specific set of knowledge, skills, abilities, and motivations that produce the desired performance and contributions to the organization's strategy and goals. An example of primary competencies by job family in a sample organization is shown in Table 6.12.

In actual practice, the researcher can identify the inclusion of competencies in the performance management system by seeking documentation such as shown in Figure 6.7.

The researcher also seeks evidence of individual development plans as part of the performance management system. It is a typical practice for individual development plans to focus on no more than two specific competencies within a performance management cycle timeframe. This pace permits sufficient concentration for successful acquisition and practice of a competency in order to trace effective application on the job.

Moving to the second phase of the continuous process of performance management, the researcher seeks to uncover evidence of successful tracking or monitoring of progress, provision of timely feedback and coaching, adaptation to any changes in course, and periodic assessment of progress. Providing feedback is one of the more difficult managerial behaviors and is, therefore, frequently avoided. The researcher needs to determine how well this behavior is performed and with what degree of frequency. Weakness in this behavior is a very common finding in organizations that are struggling to achieve strategic results. Specific techniques for the effective provision of feedback include the following actions.

- Open the conversation with an expression of positive intent.
- Describe the behavior or action that has been specifically observed and connects to the goal or results in question.
- Convey the impact of the behavior or action on the results.

TABLE 6.12 Sample Competencies by Job Family

Management	*Sales/Marketing*
Change Management	Striving for Excellence
Performance Management & Development	Managing Resources
Teamwork & Diversity	Consultative Selling Skills
Supervisor	*Customer Service*
Change Management	Adaptability
Managing Resources	Personal Responsibility
Teamwork & Diversity	Customer Focus
Professional Contributor	*Field Operations*
Striving for Excellence	Adaptability
Managing Resources	Personal Responsibility
Problem Solving	Safety Orientation

Stage Four – Analysis and Observation Development **87**

Change Management		Weight 10 x Score ____ = Total of ____			
Unsatisfactory Performance	Needs Improvement	Fully Satisfactory	Exceeds Expectations	Performance Leader	
Resists making changes. Complains about changes. Challenges supervisor demands. Loses control of emotions. Unwilling to take on new tasks. Holds attitude of maintaining the status quo.		Implements best practices to accommodate changes. Embraces and supports change. Helps others adapt to change. Views obstacles as opportunities. Challenges the status quo.		Implements practices that have significant positive effects. Champions the need for change. Models effective behaviors.	
Example:		Example:			

Teamwork & Diversity		Weight 20 x Score ____ = Total of ____			
Unsatisfactory Performance	Needs Improvement	Fully Satisfactory	Exceeds Expectations	Performance Leader	
Resists helping others. Shows indifference. Looks out only for self. Places blame on others. Refuses to accept responsibility. Responds defensively to feedback.		Establishes trust and respect among peers. Encourages others to help one another. Values and respects the ideas of others. Views feedback as a learning process.		A model for establishing high levels of trust and respect. Seeks feedback for personal growth. Helps others understand the value of diverse points of view.	
Example:		Example:			

FIGURE 6.7 Examples of Performance Management Competencies.

- Invite the individual's response.
- Collaborate to craft a remedial action plan to achieve the desired change.
- Provide support without weakening or removing the individual's responsibility for performance.

As noted above, the lack of coaching within a performance management system can weaken the organization's capability to achieve targeted results. The researcher needs to seek specific evidence that coaching is routinely practiced and performed well by those with managerial or supervisory responsibility. Specific techniques for effective coaching with the objective of flawless strategy execution include the following actions:

- Identify a specific opportunity to assist an individual in acquiring or expanding skills, abilities, or knowledge.
- Ask questions to determine the individual's readiness for any coaching activity.

88 Stage Four – Analysis and Observation Development

- Clarify the specific situation and potential benefits to both the individual and the organization.
- Collaborate to identify the best actions and likely consequences.
- Offer support to the individual without removing responsibility.

The researcher then turns attention to discovery in the third phase of appraisal in the performance management cycle. In this phase, it is preferable for managers and individuals to prepare for a collaborative evaluation or performance review. An example of a commonly used employee performance and development evaluation form is shown in Figure 6.8.

The researcher may uncover weaknesses in the appraisal phase that can contribute to varying levels of employee disengagement, dissatisfaction, resentment,

Coaching Record – Mid-Year Review	
Comments	Dates
Overall Performance Comments	
Manager	Employee
Performance Ratings: Performance Leader: Significantly exceeds all expectations for the position. Exceeds Expectations: Exceeds all expectations for the position. Fully Satisfactory: Meets all expectations for the position. Needs Improvement: Meets some but not all expectations for the position Unsatisfactory: Fails to meet expectations. A performance plan must be completed. **Overall Rating and Comments:**	

Signatures:

_____
Employee's Name and Date

_____
Manager's Name and Date

_____
Next Level Manager's Name and Date

FIGURE 6.8 Employee Evaluation Form.

Stage Four – Analysis and Observation Development **89**

or conscious withholding of energy or productivity. In the on-site discovery, such weaknesses may be described as the absence of any collaboration in the evaluation activity, disregard for plausible circumstances which have affected productivity or results, failure to adequately explain the connections between performance and organizational achievement of results, incomplete description of the rationale for making any compensatory changes, vague references or lack of specificity in describing actions and behaviors, lack of acknowledgment for any attributing factors to management or supervisory responsibilities for providing no interim feedback or coaching, or discouraging the individual's appeal of evaluation judgments. Any of these behavioral findings can ultimately lead to erosion of realizable strategic value and are subject to remedy in the recommendations of the Rapid Due Diligence diagnostic process.

A particularly sensitive area of concern to employees can be the incomplete description of the rationale for making any compensatory changes and the resulting perception of inequity. For these reasons, it is useful for the researcher to learn how managers and supervisors seek to establish precise alignment and adherence with a host of compensatory elements, as noted below:

- Organizational compensation policies
- Budgetary guidelines or constraints
- Balance of the variable and non-variable portions of compensatory considerations
- Fixed incentive pools
- Impact on pay banding
- Correlation with any explicit retention strategy
- Application of practices such as top-grading, A-B-C ranking or banding, forced ranking, or intentional internal talent competition
- Employee value proposition and any explicit or implied compensatory promises
- Geographic, sector, or competitive influences
- Intent for high potential or fast track employees
- Awareness of procedural justice issues or the potential of perception of unfairness or inequity among employees

The researcher needs to be aware of any practices or policies which have become a distinctive source of employee discontent, disillusionment, and disengagement. Such findings are often hidden and only reluctantly revealed by employees who fear retribution. For this reason, the researcher needs to exercise special care in the preservation of anonymity of sources while addressing the organizational practices or policies.

Another area for the researcher to uncover in the analysis is any evidence of the organization's failure to commit sufficient and timely resources to the strategy. While the on-site discovery individual interviews, panel interviews, or any online

90 Stage Four – Analysis and Observation Development

surveys may reveal the potential pattern for resource deficiency, this finding is often more difficult to discern. This phenomenon may be revealed as a burden of excessive numbers of strategic initiatives expected to be pursued by a segment of the organization within a constrained period of time.

The researcher may also uncover a talent mismatch or misalignment of the bundle of skills, abilities, knowledge, and motivations required to accomplish the objectives. In such cases, the allotment of time and talent may be insufficient for any of the strategic initiatives to contribute expected results; and specific priorities, gating, stacking, talent realignment, or go/no-go decision techniques may be required to relieve the situation.

As noted above, approximately twenty percent of the value erosion in strategy execution is attributable to organizational failure to engage all of its capabilities and capacities in necessary changes. This finding overlaps with the third broad category for analysis and is included in the next section.

Capabilities and Capacity to Perform and Achieve Targets

This category of analysis warrants the introduction and clarification of specific elements which are underlying keys to uncovering an organization's capabilities and capacity for performance.

Critical talent is centered on Critical Knowledge Areas© that serve as the organization's principal sources of competitive advantage. An organization achieves its greatest level of return when it activates and competitively leverages what it knows best (Critical Knowledge Areas©). These are specific bodies of knowledge that produce value at the core of the business mission. These Critical Knowledge Areas© are the principal source at work within the value proposition an organization brings to its customers. This knowledge and how it is activated clearly and distinctively set an organization apart from its competition.

The concept of Critical Knowledge Areas© and their value as a competitive advantage to an organization are drawn from earlier research conducted by the principal researcher and author of this text.[2] The conceptual foundation is derived from a combination of the Penrosean resource-based theory of the firm and competitive advantage models. A number of the resources contributing to the formulation of this concept are included in the section for further reading at the end of this chapter.

Critical talent is the superior capability to apply a specific Critical Knowledge Area©. Effective activation of a Critical Knowledge Area© draws upon a combination of experience, education, perhaps professional credentials, and culturally effective behavioral profile, in order to achieve results and produce value for the business and its customers.

As shown in the formula below, talent is the product of an individual's capabilities (knowledge, skills, and behaviors) multiplied by the number and quality of opportunities presented for development and practical experience.

Talent = (Knowledge, Skills, and Behaviors) × (Opportunities and Experience)

These findings reflect and simplify related research by Jaques, Clement, Rigby, and Jacobs.[3] An individual's level of work capability has been defined as follows:

$$LoC = (PE \times CP \times O)$$

The ingredients in this definition include:

- LoC is the level of work capability.
- PE is the psychological equipment, including skills, knowledge, values, and the personal temperament required for work completion.
- CP is the cognitive power, i.e., the maximum level of capability of any given individual.
- O is the combination of developmental experiences and opportunities that blend to forge an acquisition of skills and knowledge.

Combining the LoC and CKA findings produces:

$$Critical\ Talent\ (CT) = (PE \times CP \times O)(CKA)$$
$$Critical\ Talent\ (CT) = (LoC)(CKA)$$

An organization that engages in focused management attention to talent gains a clear understanding of the specific combination of distinctive knowledge, skills, and behaviors that most directly contribute value to its mission and the expectations of its customers. Employees with that combination are given multiple opportunities for focused development and gaining experience. As a result, the value of the employees' talent increases in depth, breadth, and wisdom of application. The value realized by both the organization and its customers rises accordingly.

If the researcher discovers significant opportunity with the application of Critical Knowledge Areas©, there are a number of related concepts to track and evaluate. For example, in knowledge management valuation, the focus is on the additional value that will be created with the investment to leverage a given Critical Knowledge Area©. This valuation contrasts with the typical financial valuation of intangible assets that rely on cost, market, or revenue approaches.

Value driver visualization and value trees are occasionally used to trace the discrete and measurable aspects of workflow, operation, and creation of economic value of Critical Knowledge Areas©. These techniques can be applied, supported, and tested with sensitivity analyses to determine which Critical Knowledge Area© serves as the key value driver. With this Critical Knowledge Area© in motion within a declared customer value proposition, it is the most highly leverageable source of Return on Critical Talent. This discovery becomes a particularly

92 Stage Four – Analysis and Observation Development

significant finding in business issues such as mergers, acquisitions, major growth strategies, and improvement of human performance.

If further economic value calculations are warranted, the researcher may choose to apply the Real Options Value (ROV) formula as a modification of the classic Black-Scholes model.[4] The Real Options Value formula can be used to gauge the investment in knowledge assets and quantify an estimated value of learning.

Attentive management of transactional costs can create substantial economic value, for example, in governance, leadership focus, organizational structure, and transaction details in internal coordination, cooperation, and communications networks. These costs or opportunities within knowledge architecture can be amplified in virtual, cross-functional matrix, or newly synthesized structures.

The researcher can also trace the identity and application of Critical Knowledge Areas© in organizational networks, extended geographic or dispersed enterprises, or value constellations of suppliers, business partners, customers, and the organization which can co-produce greater economic return within a value creation system. The researcher can trace the value signature of the Critical Knowledge Areas© throughout the key metrics and critical ratios of the strategic dimensions.

For the purposes of Rapid Due Diligence diagnostic methodology, it is important to acknowledge that most organizations have vast reservoirs of talent of many types. A wide range of talent is required in supporting processes and systems. The critical talent that effectively activates Critical Knowledge Areas© ensures the most powerful contribution to business results, i.e., delivering on the value proposition or keeping the organization's promise to its customers.

While a growing number of organizations have been influenced by published literature and trends toward more attention to managing talent, significant opportunities for improved strategic impact remain with the identification and intentional application of the inherent capabilities and capacity of Critical Knowledge Areas© and critical talent. In those cases where the analysis reveals either a vacancy or insufficiency of this strategic dimension, the researcher has uncovered a valuable source of future opportunity and strategic leverage.

Shown below are two tables constructed during a Rapid Due Diligence diagnostic process in which the researcher was seeking first to identify potential Critical Knowledge Areas© and then to convert those findings into a potential critical talent profile for use in performance management and achievement of more reliable strategic results in multiple locations of one organization. The findings from the on-site discovery stage were secured from the three states in which the organization had operations (A, B, and C as noted in Tables 6.13 and 6.14). Individual interviews were followed by panel interviews. The researcher then facilitated a ranking and voting process with the panel participants to gauge priorities.

Stage Four – Analysis and Observation Development 93

TABLE 6.13 Potential Critical Knowledge Areas©

Item	Description	A	B	C
1	Depth of targeted market knowledge (local and regional) applied in customer relationships (customer needs, product preferences, criteria and fit, regulatory influence and impact, product performance with member groups) (24)	★	★	★
2	How we translate customer needs into specific products and services that meet our profitability requirements (12)	★	★	★
3	Understanding the implications of short and long-term rate changes on both the organization and customers (spotting and interpreting trends faster than our competition, actuarial analysis to assess risk) (11)	★	★	★
4	Technical discipline in determining rates that provide acceptable levels of financial security to the organization and rate stability for our customers (10)	★	★	★
5	Actuarial data base, guidelines and decision rules, and analytical process to configure risk tolerance, determine pricing, and meet profitability thresholds (10)	★	★	★
6	Knowledge of how all systems converge to provide value to customers (combination of product knowledge, customer needs, and medical care management) (10)	★	★	★
7	Understanding the balance of the economics of the business and choices of each part of the triangle (members+employers/provider network/organization; what drives costs, behaviors, and patterns of use and choices as the basis for pricing (9)		★	★
8	Depth and breadth of fundamental knowledge of our insurance industry (the big picture and systemic influences) (6)	★	★	★
9	Clear, in-depth understanding of the full health care delivery system (players, economics of the business, distribution channels, cause and effect relationships) (5)	★	★	
10	Understanding the financial implications of clinical health management (4)	★	★	★

TABLE 6.14 Potential Critical Talent Profile To Effectively Activate Critical Knowledge Areas©

Item	Description	A	B	C
1	Willingness to take initiative (13)	★	★	★
2	Strategic thinking based on the long-term, big picture, and matching micro with macro view (11)	★	★	★
3	Actuarial plus business experience combined with creative, critical thinking and problem solving (11)	★	★	★

(Continued)

94 Stage Four – Analysis and Observation Development

Item	Description	A	B	C
4	Credibility that earns trust within an ongoing business relationship (10)	★	★	★
5	Strong communications skills, particularly the ability to translate complex issues into clear, simple, and practical messages (10)	★	★	★
6	Critical thinking, judgment, and decisiveness (10)	★	★	★
7	Actuarial credentials and analytical skills (9)	★		
8	Ability to understand the economics of our business (9)	★	★	★
9	Collaboration (8)	★	★	★
10	Accountability for results and commitment to follow through (8)	★	★	★
11	Sharing information (8)	★	★	★
12	Problem solving, disciplined analysis, and decision-making based on astute attention and translation of emerging patterns (8)	★	★	
13	Helping others see and understand connections to the business (8)	★	★	
14	Flexibility and openness to different perspectives (7)	★	★	★
15	Vigilant attention to trends, emerging patterns, and likely implications (6)	★	★	★
16	Experience in the health care business and markets (6)	★	★	
17	High standards of excellence (accuracy, completeness, methodical analysis) (6)	★	★	★
18	Capability to discern usable, actionable data for sound decision making (what retrospective and predictive data applies reliably to our customer needs) (6)	★	★	
19	Systems thinking across boundaries (6)		★	★
20	Demonstrating energy and a sense of urgency (5)	★	★	★
21	Adopting an integrated strategic focus on the whole business (5)		★	★

Employee Value Proposition

The strategic dimension labeled the employee value proposition is described as a statement summarizing the actual employment experience that an individual has while a member of an organization and the rationale for choosing to belong to one organization as compared to other options. This description contrasts with the description of an employment brand, wherein the brand refers to how the work experience is perceived and portrayed to current or prospective employees. While the employee value proposition and employment brand can co-exist within an organization, it is important to define and develop the employee value proposition prior to the employment brand. For such a brand to be effective and avoid the risk of losing employees who become disillusioned, the reality of the work experience needs to confirm the expectation or value proposition described in the employment brand.

The employee value proposition strategic dimension is a product of growing research into talent management and broader recognition of the importance of employee contributions to the strategic success of organizations. Such research suggests that organizations which create and apply employee value propositions tend to outperform those which at best take a more casual approach. As a summary of the actual benefits derived from the work experience while employees demonstrate commitment, effort, and contributions to an organization, the relationship de facto becomes at least an informal psychological contract or expression of implicit agreement between an organization and its employees.

In conducting the analysis stage of the Rapid Due Diligence diagnostic method, the researcher seeks the existence of an explicit statement which meets the employee value proposition description, whether or not it is titled as such. The researcher also verifies the degree to which all of the following categories of value are represented within the description:

- Attributes of the organization, such as corporate appeal, working conditions, culture, demonstrated work/life balance practices, or social responsibility
- Work design
- Opportunities for career development and advancement
- Compensatory benefits

These four categories are typically comprised of a compilation of a longer list of likely elements shown in Table 6.15.

TABLE 6.15 Elements Contributing to an Employee Value Proposition

Great Company	Great Job	Compensation and Lifestyle
Values and culture	Freedom and autonomy	Differentiated compensation by merit
Managed well	Exciting challenges	Attractive geographic location
Exciting challenges	Career advancement	Respect for personal lifestyle
Strong performance and financial viability	Personal growth potential	High total compensation potential
Industry and market leader	Personal fit with others	Acceptable pace of work
Many talented people		Acceptable stress level
Inspiring mission and vision		
Pays attention to development		
Promotes fun in the workplace		
Offers job security		

96 Stage Four – Analysis and Observation Development

The researcher is also advised to compare the findings from on-site discovery interviews, panel interviews, or online surveys with any employee value proposition statements in order to again confirm the reality of the work experience. In the example appearing in Box 6.3, the Rapid Due Diligence diagnostic method was used to describe the actual work experience and ultimately define an employee value proposition that would attract people seeking career assignments. The definition and comparison with the desired work experience revealed significant opportunities for improvement and contributed to a recruitment business issue.

BOX 6.3 DEVELOPMENT OF AN EMPLOYEE VALUE PROPOSITION

A military organization identified a strategic need to increase the percentage of individuals who would voluntarily seek a particular assignment. The primary task was to determine the rationale for why members of the military organization would make such a choice. The Rapid Due Diligence diagnostic method was engaged to discover the current reality and to shape a future description of an employee value proposition for this assignment.

Upon completion of a variety of discovery methods, including in-depth preparatory investigation of a host of relevant documents and reports, in-person interviews, a voluntary online survey, and broadcast invitation, the research team gathered findings from hundreds of individuals who were considered subject matter experts in the targeted field of inquiry. The complete set of findings from all sources were analyzed and synthesized to arrive at a set of observations about the data, conclusions, and two descriptions.

The first description constituted the current reality of the military command and the set of rationale for why an individual had been selecting the targeted assignment. The volume of findings was condensed into five simpler elements listed below.

Current Reality of Our Employee Value Proposition

- Today, military professionals seek to join this command for the opportunity to:
  - o Build the all-volunteer force
  - o Change lives with this military experience
  - o Live at home
  - o Develop valuable skills
  - o Advance in a military career

As requested by the command, the research team was also able to distinguish a set of rationale that was expected to fit the cultural and organizational transformation that was already in its early stages of implementation. This description was proposed as an employee value proposition that would deliver on the intended future state of the command. The findings produced a longer set of elements as shown in the list below.

Future Reality of Our Employee Value Proposition

- Upon realization of the organizational transformation, military professionals will seek to join this command for the opportunity to enjoy:
  o A positive command climate where together we simultaneously make mission and take care of the soldiers, their families, and civilian employees
  o A stimulating, respectful, and supportive culture based on building skills, coaching, and mentoring for mutual success
  o A preferred assignment that demonstrates the desired image to the public
  o A period of stability and relief from deployment
  o Assignment to a desirable location
  o Capability to be home every night
  o Opportunity for meaningful career advancement
  o Gratification in building the all-volunteer force and helping people choose a career, grow, and change their lives
  o Personal growth with the acquisition of valuable, transferrable leadership, interpersonal, and marketing skills
  o A degree of day-to-day autonomy in achieving mission
  o Special duty incentives

For the purpose of producing a shorter version for practical application, the research team condensed these findings about the future reality into the following shorter employee value proposition description.

  o Contribute in a positive command climate
  o Secure valuable skills and support for life success
  o Have a life at home
  o Show the military image with pride
  o Build the all-volunteer force
  o Change lives with the military experience
  o Advance in a military career

Integrated Strategic Human Capital Alignment Framework

Another analytical technique that is essential to the Rapid Due Diligence diagnostic process is the application of the Integrated Strategic Human Capital Alignment Framework. This framework is an in-depth tool that is used to examine

98 Stage Four – Analysis and Observation Development

how well the organization engages all of its human capital in the strategic pursuit of its business. The researcher uses this tool to examine the full cycle of human capital management to identify potential opportunities for improvement in the organization's practices.

The Integrated Strategic Human Capital Alignment Framework, shown in Table 6.16, specifies six stages that encompass the human capital management cycle:

- Emergence of new organizational need, strategy, or direction
- Definition of human capital plan
- Recruitment and selection
- Employee orientation or on-boarding
- Development of ongoing capabilities or career growth
- Employee departure

Each stage of this framework is illuminated with a set of key tasks to be completed, the preferred set of outcomes, consequences of unsuccessful effort, and a series of issues or questions that need to be addressed. The longitudinal research into strategy execution, mentioned earlier this chapter, identified several specific areas of weakness or misalignment that contribute to disappointing realized results. These areas are incorporated into this framework and appear especially in the issues and questions that need to be addressed with each stage. The strategic dimensions of the employee value proposition, as well as Critical Knowledge Areas© and critical talent, are also incorporated into this framework.

The researcher is advised to pay particular attention to the complete sets of sequential key tasks within each stage of the human capital management cycle. If any of those tasks are not undertaken, an opportunity has been revealed. The outcomes and consequences entries provide important supporting rationale for paying close and full attention to each of the key tasks.

The researcher uses the issues or questions accompanying each stage of the human capital management cycle to more deeply probe the specific ways in which the organization conducts a number of important actions. Depending upon the initial description provided by the owner of the business situation and the scope of the inquiry, questions included within each stage of this framework can also be used in the preparatory investigation or on-site discovery stages of the Rapid Due Diligence diagnostic process.

The researcher uses all of the content as a strategic map or diagnostic checklist in directly comparing the findings from all sources. A comparison of the entries in this framework with the full set of evidence may reveal significant gaps, missteps, or incomplete attention to any aspect of the human capital cycle. Any of these deficiencies represent opportunities for improvement in identifying, developing, and retaining core capabilities and capacity to perform and achieve strategic targets.

TABLE 6.16 Integrated Strategic Human Capital Alignment Framework

Stage	Key Tasks	Outcomes of Stage	Consequences If Unsuccessful	Issues or Questions to Address
Emergence of New Organizational Need, Strategy, or Direction	• Affirm nature of new organizational need (examples: launch of new initiative; change of direction; preparation or response to new internal or external situation) • Secure facts and create compelling case for specific action and outcomes • Set overarching strategy with plan for execution • Establish process for implementation • Define human capital resources required • Specify critical knowledge and talent required for success • Align with employee value proposition • Define outcomes and measures of progress • Set communications strategy • Establish feedback loops to monitor situation	• Clarity of need and desired outcomes • Clarity of overarching strategy to achieve outcomes • Comprehensive, integrated, systemic approach to strategy execution • Thorough plan with accountabilities for results • Accurate description of required human capital, especially critical knowledge and talent • Organizational commitment to follow through • Determination of how to secure periodic evidence of progress and effectiveness of strategy and programs	• Lower probability of achieving outcomes • Untimely results • Ambiguous description of need • Outcomes may not fit situation • Wasted resources • Insufficiency and low readiness of the people to perform (do not have right people, right skills, right place, right time) • Unlikely improvement in reputation of the agency • Not viewed as attractive place to work and contribute to the public good	• How will we effectively sort competing priorities, points of view, sense of urgency, and limited resources to secure prompt clarity and direction in complex situations? • How will we build shared ownership of an important, realizable strategy? • What strategic options do we need to explore? What criteria will we use? • What risks might we encounter, and how will we mitigate them? • How will we test the strategy to avoid unintended, unfavorable consequences? • How will we determine what human capital resources are truly necessary? • Where do we have strategic vulnerability with critical knowledge and talent? • How will we communicate effectively to build broad commitment to the strategy, changes required, and responsibility for results?

(Continued)

Stage	Key Tasks	Outcomes of Stage	Consequences If Unsuccessful	Issues or Questions to Address
				• How well do our current processes, systems, policies, practices, and culture align with the proposed strategy? • How will we measure success? • How will we recognize people and celebrate success? • How will we set and monitor feedback loops?
Definition of Human Capital Plan	• Define the overarching Human Capital plan to support the new strategy • Define the competencies required for superior performance in the new strategy • Conduct a census or inventory of employee capabilities • Assess or calibrate the current set of competencies and resources • Identify specific gaps in competencies required for success	• Clarity on the precise Human Capital needs to support fulfillment of the new strategy • Accurate assessment of current capabilities • Thorough and fair plan to identify Human Capital • Reconciliation of existing talent management, bench strength, and succession planning processes	• Unclear and inaccurate identity of Human Capital needs • Unlikely to have perception of fairness • Not likely to have right people with right skills are ready at the right time and in the right place • Human resources functional support will miss the mark	• How will we accurately define the skills, knowledge, abilities, and motivations required for superior performance in fulfilling this strategy? • How will we organize and conduct a census that captures employee capabilities? • How do the targeted competencies compare with our current capabilities? • How will we pinpoint gaps for developing internally – or for hiring from outside our organization? • How will our job profiles need to change?

	• Set a comprehensive, fair, and equitable process to align the current resources – or secure additional human capital • Verify the alignment of processes, systems, policies, practices and culture • Ensure the Human Capital plan reflects the employee value proposition • Set communications strategy • Determine feedback and evaluation process	• Clear communications of the situation, intentions, and plan • Double-loop feedback stream in place		• How will we be sure our processes, systems, policies, and practices fit the Human Capital plan? • How will we ensure fair and equitable consideration for current and outside candidates? • How will we set performance expectations for all leaders to find, fully engage, develop, and retain the right people who fit the Human Capital plan? • How will we identify mission critical roles and individuals that require special retention strategies? • How will we test rewards, recognition, and compensation practices to attract the right talent? • How will we continually secure double-loop feedback and deploy new findings? • How will we set an evaluation plan to gauge impact?
Recruitment and Selection	• Clarify recruitment strategy and specific targets • Align all actions with the employee value proposition • Activate talent market that can pull through prime candidates	• Fair, efficient, and effective recruitment and selection process • Employee value proposition and branding attracts people who fit	• Not very cost-effective process • Risk securing the right people • Delay in organizational readiness to fulfill strategy or programs	• How will we ensure we're as effective, efficient, and fair as possible in our recruitment and selection process? • How will we be confident we're selecting the right people – with skills, knowledge, abilities, and motivations that best fit our needs?

(Continued)

Stage	Key Tasks	Outcomes of Stage	Consequences If Unsuccessful	Issues or Questions to Address
	• Build in any cultural transformation ingredients • Prepare details of recruitment and selection plan • Verify process, systems, policies, and practice alignment to ensure fair and equitable opportunities and efficient pipeline of qualified candidates • Prepare all interviewers and decision makers for consistent, fair, cost-effective, high quality process • Document all key steps and findings in a candidate tracking process • Secure double-loop feedback to adjust as needed	• Prompt identification of the right people with the right skills, especially critical knowledge and talent • Low-cost placement	• Overlook talent in unlikely places • Legal challenges	• How will we communicate our employee value proposition in as appealing and compelling way as possible? • How will we more effectively position our organization's opportunities as compared to others in the external talent market? • How will we activate an efficient, inclusive, pull-through process in an internal talent market? • How will we continually gather and deploy feedback? • How will we ensure we meet human capital deadlines without compromise?
Employee Orientation or On-Boarding	• Link roles to strategic outcomes and any scorecards or dashboards • Establish specific expectations for roles, responsibilities, and standards of performance • Demonstrate the employee value proposition	• Effective, efficient, and thorough initiation into the assigned roles and the organization's mission • Clarity on performance expectations, especially	• Not likely to experience accelerated learning and preparation • Delays in contributions and realizable value to the strategy and mission	• How will we accelerate commitment, learning, and contributions of new employees to the strategy of the organization? • How will we design and deliver a clear sequence of learning that produces understanding, comfort, and confidence in a new

- Develop a clear, mutual understanding and expectations for fulfilling the organization's mission, vision, values, cultural practices, and measures for performance
- Clarify the expectations for every stage of the cycle
- Equip new employees with essential, actionable knowledge about the organization, its customers, partners
- Institute mentoring and networking connections to accelerate learning
- Position on-boarding as part of an orderly developmental process over time

- The application of critical knowledge and talent to drive results
- Heightened employee engagement and validation of employer choice
- Clear understanding of the lifecycle process

- New employees experience confusion and disillusionment

organization or role – without confusion or inundation with too much detail?
- How will we communicate clear line of sight connections to the strategy and measures of success?
- How will we develop a working knowledge of the organization's mission, vision, and values?
- How will we effectively communicate essential organizational and customer knowledge?
- How will we set up mentors or a social networking system for supporting new employees?
- How will we establish systemic attention to an integrating culture?
- How will we ensure every step fits the employee value proposition?
- How will we verify the degree of employee engagement and support in this early period of employment?
- How will we position the on-boarding within the broader development process throughout the lifecycle?
- How will we secure feedback on the orientation process – and quickly learn what additional help is needed?

(Continued)

Stage	Key Tasks	Outcomes of Stage	Consequences If Unsuccessful	Issues or Questions to Address
Development of Ongoing Capabilities or Career Growth	• Identify a development process to deepen knowledge and refine skills required for defined career paths and fulfillment of strategies • Ensure enduring fulfillment of the employee value proposition • Conduct periodic assessment of capabilities and growth – compare with changing organizational needs • Provide coaching, feedback, reinforcement, and recognition of growth • Conduct formal and informal performance management • Create a talent market to accelerate growth • Reconcile actions within talent management and succession planning • Identify readiness for new opportunities for advancement	• Continual preparation and readiness of Human Capital, especially critical knowledge and talent • Continual growth and development of current and new skills • Human Capital capabilities on target with strategic needs • New career growth opportunities are identified efficiently and fairly • Employees exercise initiative to grow and contribute • Employees experience the employee value proposition as intended – and provide positive referrals	• Lower probability of organizational strategies and results being met • Human Capital needs may not be fully met – uncertainty about having the right people, right skills, right place, right time • Reduced employee satisfaction and engagement • Higher voluntary turnover • Best talent leaves first	• How will we build a comprehensive employee development plan – in timely phases – that meets the needs of the organizational and individual career growth plans? • How will we engage in formal and informal performance management discussions, coaching, feedback, reinforcement, and recognition to produce superior performance? • How will we periodically assess and gauge growth? • How will we continually verify employee engagement, satisfaction, and commitment? • How will we build in a retention strategy that's meaningful to the employees and saves organizational resources? • How will we stay apprised of unique generational or professional shifts and requirements? • How will we continually deliver the employee value proposition experience?

	• Communicate developmental opportunities and process for participation			• How will we establish a pull-through strategy in a talent market? • How will we track system dynamics over time to ensure this stage stays on track? • How will we ensure our critical talent stays and contributes? • How will we avoid redundancies, overlap, and outdating in resources?
Employee Departure	• Engage in periodic review of capabilities and early identification of possible departures for any reason • Assess impact of potential departures on the organization and customers • Identify mission critical knowledge and talent that may be at risk – and require broader or transferred coverage • Track employee engagement and other cues of potential departure – take action • Plan for effective transfer or shared knowledge with other designated employees	• Sustainment of organizational knowledge and talent, plus benefits to customers • Orderly, respectful, and dignified closure to employee career • Clarity on rationale for all departures • Promotion of a positive reputation for the organization • Follow-through on employee value proposition • Deeper understanding	• Organization loses critical knowledge and talent and suffers business shortfall and failure to perform for customers • Experience does not promote a positive reputation for the organization • Failure to keep the employee value proposition promise • Feedback and opportunities may be missed as sources of continual improvement ideas to the Human Capital strategy	• How will we identify or anticipate possible departures of all types? • How will we effectively plan for the transfer of working knowledge from current employees to others? • What are our mission critical skills and knowledge that we need to preserve? How will we easily and effectively create broader coverage? • How will we effectively and efficiently gather useful exit data and use that data in future planning? • How will we prepare people to effectively and respectfully assume the roles of departing employees, irrespective of the reasons? • How will we evaluate how well we are fulfilling our employee value proposition?

(Continued)

Stage	Key Tasks	Outcomes of Stage	Consequences If Unsuccessful	Issues or Questions to Address
	• Recognize contributions of departing employee to mission and vision • Analyze rationale for all turnover – use to improve Human Capital planning at all stages • Seek appropriate, ongoing good will • Communications planning • Seek continual system feedback	of employee's employment decision analytics	• Other employees choose to leave	• How will we reduce voluntary turnover to an acceptable level? • What will we do to promote a positive reputation for the organization? • What kinds of ongoing good will or service relationships can we establish with departing employees? • How will we tap into system feedback to gain early alerts to potential unwanted departures?

Capability and Capacity for Change

As noted earlier in this chapter, thirty-seven percent of the potential realizable value of a strategy is, on average, lost to three barriers. The third barrier is organizational failure to engage in necessary changes and accounts for approximately twenty percent of the value erosion. This statistic makes the investigation for change capability and capacity another important analytical pursuit by the researcher.

Change capability can be defined as the ability of individuals to accept, embrace, or perhaps even drive change required for the ultimate success of an organization. For the purposes of the Rapid Due Diligence diagnostic method, this definition is expanded to include the Triple Win with the accrual of benefits to the organization, its customers, and its employees.

Business literature is filled with numerous approaches to assess and calibrate organizational and individual change capability and capacity. As the researcher chooses, a specific assessment technique may be added to the on-site discovery process to gauge organizational change capability and secure qualitative descriptions or quantitative metrics of distinctive behaviors or practices.

To assist in this discovery and analysis, it is useful for the researcher to recognize the typical set of factors that tend to inhibit or interfere with the success of either international- or North American-based organizations in pursuing planned initiatives to induce change. One level of analysis needs to seek evidence of any of these factors inherent within the scope of the business issue under review. These factors appear in Table 6.17.

Another specific area for the researcher to analyze is how well the leaders of the organization demonstrate their own capability for changes and their conscious fulfillment of actions that engage others. The researcher needs to sift through the findings especially from the on-site discovery process to identify specific

TABLE 6.17 Factors Interfering with Change Initiatives

Domestic Organizations	International Organizations
Lack of communication	Lack of communication
Complacency	Complacency
Conflict	Resistance from managers
Resistance from employees	Distrust
Lack of individual buy-in	Conflict
Resistance from managers	Shifting focus
Shifting focus	Inadequate resources
Distrust	Lack of individual buy-in
Inadequate resources	Resistance from employees
Inadequate sponsorship	Inadequate sponsorship

108 Stage Four – Analysis and Observation Development

processes or actions that are routinely deployed by successful leaders of change. These actions include at least the following:

- Recognize the need for a specific change.
- Clarify the specific nature and behavioral description of the warranted change.
- Lead by example.
- Acknowledge the differing ways in which people engage change.
- Communicate the required change in complete and understandable ways, designed to engage all participants in the change process.
- Address questions and any emerging reluctance.
- Provide the resources necessary to achieve the change.
- Make appropriate adjustments to existing processes, policies, or practices to enable the change.
- Establish key indicators for success.
- Monitor and communicate progress.

The researcher needs to seek evidence that executives, managers, and supervisors are fluent in the cultural ways in which the organization tends to adopt change. This means these leaders can readily identify the behaviors of people who tend to demonstrate eagerness for change, those who seek an active role, others who crave more evidence and understanding of the need for change, those who raise challenges, and others who may exhibit hostility or champion an unchanging environment. The researcher needs to assess how well the leaders engage or respond in these varying situations.

In Box 6.4, there is an example of an organization that had already invested in building the capability and capacity of its people for strategic changes in its business model. The owner of this business issue sought deeper insights to produce accelerated and elevated results with application of the Rapid Due Diligence diagnostic method. This example describes the approach that was eventually deployed in accelerating the organization's change integration strategy.

BOX 6.4 BUILDING ORGANIZATIONAL CAPACITY FOR CHANGE INTEGRATION

Background Information

The executive team of an organization determined that its success in executing on significant business strategies and related initiatives and projects was highly correlated to the people's capacity and capability to accept, engage, and activate changes as required by those strategies. For approximately one year, the organization had been conducting a variety of projects with accelerated change ingredients and profiling the perceptions of progress and effectiveness.

With the business stakes continually growing, plus an awareness of the need for increased change capacity across the enterprise, a specialized change integration function was formed. A multi-phase approach to achieving greater enterprise-wide capacity for change integration was under development and preparing for launch in the coming year. The owner of the business situation sought a Rapid Due Diligence diagnostic process to guide the further development of its change model, levels of competency, and approach to building the organization's capacity for change. The work was designed to be completed in two steps: an initial discovery followed by recommendations for more in-depth work.

Upon completion of the initial on-site discovery of various forms, the research team recommended crafting and implementing a comprehensive, systemic, realistic, and results-focused approach to building and institutionalizing a greater capacity for change integration and implementation across the entire enterprise. The focus for this effort was positioned to drive targeted business results by activating each of the following elements:

$$\textit{Strategy} \times \textit{Engagement} \times \textit{Execution} = \textit{Results}$$

Strategy refers to the clarity and quality of the business strategy, key initiatives, and related projects, as well as targeted results to gauge success.

Engagement refers to not only the acceptance of change by the people, but also a deeper connection to the meaning of such change for themselves, the members, and the enterprise, and a willingness to activate or perform accordingly.

Execution refers to the timely, flawless, and thorough follow-through in the performance of tasks and responsibilities, especially where changes have been designed in order to fulfill the strategy, initiative, or project.

Results refers to the verifiable progress or achievement of the intended outcomes from the strategy, key initiative, or project.

The relational equation was also expressed as follows:

$$S \times E \times E = R$$

Multi-Phase Approach

The organization was already considering a series of phases to achieve its broad objectives. The desire was to gain early traction across a large population, then prepare refined models and tools for introduction in the coming

(Continued)

Stage Four – Analysis and Observation Development

year. As a result of the initial findings from the Rapid Due Diligence diagnostic process, the research team recommended the following multi-phase approach for further action on building a comprehensive, integrated capacity for change implementation.

Phase One
Awareness Building

The first phase will include focus upon awareness building across multiple levels. The internal staff will prepare and deliver awareness building sessions, using a select number of existing tools.

Development or Refinement of the Organization's Strategy, Change Model, and Competencies

This first phase can also mark the beginning of another flight or plan of action. Further discovery work is warranted with broader numbers of subject matter experts and preparation of draft deliverables for vetting within the organization.

This extension of another round of a Rapid Due Diligence diagnostic process will be completed in less than thirty days and focus as follows:

- Prepare, organize, and complete thorough data collection and discovery with designated subject matter experts who have current and recent relevant information related to the organization's change readiness, effectiveness, and needs. Actions include:
  - o Gathering relevant data from documentation such as recent change profile assessments, other related cultural or engagement assessments and surveys, plus project management plans where significant change has been introduced
  - o Conducting individual interviews or focus groups; no new surveys are planned at this time in order to save time and resources
  - o Gaining a deep understanding of primary business strategies, key initiatives, major projects, and related scorecards, metrics, and communications devices, where change is a significant ingredient
  - o Clarifying the roles among levels and functions and the specific competencies (skills, abilities, knowledge, and motivations) required to achieve superior performance in change integration and implementation
  - o Comparing the activity to date or planned with the overarching organizational human capital strategy

Stage Four – Analysis and Observation Development **111**

- o Comparing all findings with existing models inside the organization, as well as outside expert resources, best practices, or benchmarked activities
- Organize, classify, and prepare data for analysis, discovery, and extraction of key findings.
- Prepare drafts of a change integration model (refined or new) and supporting competencies for relevant levels of the enterprise.
- Assist in facilitating an internal vetting process to clarify, refine, and confirm the final content.
- Deliverables:
  - o A new change integration model
  - o Role clarity
  - o Competencies for relevant levels and roles (Determine whether these competencies need to be expanded into behavioral anchors for integration with the organization's performance management system.)
  - o Integration map, visually displaying how the plan connects with primary business strategies, key initiatives, and major projects plus related scorecards and metrics

Phase Two

A second phase can encompass two simultaneous flights or paths of action. This phase will use the findings and deliverables from the completed first phase.

Creation of Change Assessment and Measurement Tools and Processes

With the conversion of the new change model and supporting competencies into appropriate assessment and measurement instruments, these tools will be available for electronic completion and data analyses. All such assessment instruments will be designed to identify the current capacity of change and pinpoint specific developmental areas. Evaluation tools will show links and leverage points to strategic initiatives and targeted business metrics. Sample tools may include:

- Readiness assessments for individual change leaders or sponsors
- Group assessment tools for business units, functional areas, or project teams
- Change effectiveness gauges for gathering baseline and periodic progress evaluation, ideally for behavioral competencies, stages of change, and business metrics impact
- Benchmark comparisons with designated organizations or competitors

(Continued)

Creation of a New Change Curriculum

The findings and deliverables from the first phase can also be used to create the change model curriculum, reinforcement tool kits, and playbook. Where possible, existing models, tools, and curriculum will be re-purposed to meet the current and future needs of people in a variety of roles, levels, and functions across the enterprise. Specific design principles will be used to guide the design, development, and delivery of an effective curriculum for people at multiple levels and responsibilities.

- Clear language and stated intent
- Simple and straightforward approach; no clever psychobabble or excessive academic rhetoric
- Easy to understand and activate
- Direct ties to targeted business results
- Relevant, logical fit with the participants' business and cultural context; connections between the change model, tools, and real situations
- Engaging to each audience; answering the "What's in it for me" question
- Highly interactive, participant involvement with discovery and action learning
- Compelling call to action
- Practical tools that can be readily applied to real situations; following a simple outline to answer: what, why, when, how, and what to do next
- Support materials to stimulate multiple learning preferences and styles, including slide copies, wall charts, handouts, worksheets, job aids, electronic copies for future reference, reinforcement tools
- Designated people to assist with future questions and applications
- Establish a peer coaching and collaborative environment

Phase Three

The third phase will build upon the first two phases and can also include two simultaneous flights or paths of action.

Creation of the Execution Plan and Launch of the New Change Model and Curriculum

The organization will prepare a comprehensive, systemic, fully integrated, and aligned implementation plan, designed for flawless execution and thorough follow-through. The plan will also incorporate findings from the Rapid Due Diligence diagnostic and discovery activities, such as organizational or cultural issues, practices, policies, and processes that will naturally propel or impede progress. Communications planning, coaching and feedback loops, measurement methods, and key roles will be designated.

Deliverables can include:

- A project map for visually portraying the execution plan and the change model connections from the integration map
- Granular detail of action plans in a project management plan
- Longer-term plan for institutionalizing a greater capacity for change within the organization

Cultural Fit within Mergers or Acquisitions

If the business issue requiring the deployment of the Rapid Due Diligence diagnostic method is the effectiveness of a pending or recently engaged merger or acquisition, the researcher needs to apply great attention to cultural fit. Typically, there is significant attention by the proponents of the merger or acquisition to the financial or market presence benefits and little or insufficient attention to their respective organizational impact. The primary or valid business reason (VBR) for the merger is most often expressed in financial returns to the owners or shareholders. The full Return on Merger (RoM) occurs when there is also careful attention to the issue of cultural fit among the uniting organizations.

For the purpose of providing supporting rationale to the researcher, there are a number of key facts to keep in mind as the Rapid Due Diligence diagnostic process seeks to support either a merger or acquisition. First, a very high majority of mergers and acquisitions continue to fail to deliver the financial promises to shareholders. Some resources gauge this failure rate at ninety percent or more. The highest contributor to this failure is the clash or insufficient fit of the respective cultures. The evidence appears as very high employee turnover, low employee engagement, as well as low customer retention. Failure to conduct any due diligence audit on the respective cultures can quickly undermine the arrangement.

The primary reason for failure is the inability to forge a new culture that productively drives the results that were promised to the shareholders. Further, the culture has not been intentionally shaped to become a unified, driving force that is directly connected and purposefully delivering the promise of the new value propositions to either customers or employees.

The researcher needs to look for the following key actions as part of the cultural fit process:

- Determine the culture that best fits the newly defined business and the business model.
- Test the degree of fit between the existing cultures.
- Investigate the respective organizations' readiness to join forces.
- Analyze the findings to determine the required effort to unify the cultures.
- Craft the strategy to achieve the culture that can best achieve the targeted Return on Merger.

114 Stage Four – Analysis and Observation Development

Ideally, the assessment for potential cultural fit is completed very early in the merging decision process. If that opportunity has passed, the researcher should look for evidence that the assessment is underway upon consummation of the arrangement. To test the degree of fit between the merging cultures, the organizations need to seek clear and accurate answers for at least the following questions:

- How does each organization achieve success?
- How does each organization make decisions?
- Who has the most power and influence? Why?
- What causes worry?
- What is the prevalent management style?
- What matters most to the organizations?
- What is the employees' source of passion?
- What is the tolerance for taking risk, making mistakes, or speaking the truth to more powerful individuals or groups?
- What gets controlled? Why?
- Who gets promoted?
- How is the compensation managed?
- How does each organization manage relationships with customers and suppliers?
- How are the organizations' respective business models manifest in operational processes?
- How does each organization intentionally manage change?

The researcher also needs to seek evidence that the organizations are investigating the readiness of the combining populations. These steps include testing the degree of acceptance and support for each of the following actions.

- Accept the business rationale or valid business reason (VBR) for the merger.
- Support the mission, vision, business model, and value propositions of the new organization.
- Move at the required pace to achieve the targeted results.
- Apply their respective Critical Knowledge Areas© and critical talent during and after the transition.
- Relinquish their respective treasured cultural legacies in favor of a new culture.

Amidst the findings, the researcher needs to discover evidence of discernment of the type of core cultures that currently exist within the merging organizations. Cultures typically exhibit one of four sets of predominant qualifying factors:

- Excellence, capability, and competence
- Teamwork, collaboration, and emphasis on relationships

- Domination and control
- Fulfillment and growth

The researcher needs to find or recommend tests to determine the degree of coherence, cohesiveness, alignment, or focus among these types of core cultures. Using the findings from all of these earlier cultural fit analyses, a determination is made about the degree and type of effort needed to unify the organization behind the culture that best fits the newly merged business.

Typically, the most satisfying and best strategy is to move to a new culture that represents a combination of the existing cultures, celebrates compatible elements, and requires some degree of change or growth for each organization. The overriding valid business reason for the merger or acquisition becomes the primary and compelling case for making any changes to the respective cultures. The urgency for change needs to match the slope and pace necessary to achieve the targeted business results of the merger or acquisition. This change process can range from a long, slow march to a single bold stroke of decisive action.

The researcher in the Rapid Due Diligence diagnostic process needs to seek the evidence of a complete plan to achieve the required cultural fit. If such a plan is not already complete or in motion, then the researcher's analysis has revealed another significant opportunity to more fully develop the capability and capacity of the organization.

Tracing the Economic Value-Producing Path

This category of analysis takes a closer look at the business model strategic dimension, the strategy driver platform, and how well value is delivered. The researcher seeks to understand what is in place, what is intended, the current reality, and opportunities for improvement.

The business model strategic dimension is the scheme or description for how an organization creates, delivers, and captures value. The business model serves as a blueprint of the logic of the economic value-producing path in operation throughout the organization's strategy platform, structure, key processes, systems, policies, and practices. The intent is to create value for the organization, its customers, and employees, or fulfill a defining principle of the Rapid Due Diligence diagnostic method in achieving a Triple Win.

There are multiple approaches to creating a business model. Some of the more conventional options are listed below:

- Choosing a primary emphasis on one of three paths:
  o Establishing a cohesive relationship with customers
  o Engaging in innovative product development
  o Focusing on effective and efficient operations

116 Stage Four – Analysis and Observation Development

- Democratizing and digitizing the market space and delivery approach, such as is often deployed in social media models
- Activating multi-sided market platforms that simultaneously attract, serve, and network groups of customers
- Providing services to some customers without charge and assigning the costs to other customer segments
- Collaborating with resources beyond the organization to leverage under-utilized assets, such as licensure, establishing gateways, and crafting spin-off businesses

It is essential for the researcher to identify and understand an organization's business model as an organizing principle of typically nine elements as follows:[5]

- Markets and customers
- Customer value proposition
- Customer relationships
- Distribution channels
- Asset utilization
- Revenue and value streams
- Key processes and systems
- Outsourced relationships
- Cost structure

The researcher uses this understanding of the architecture, design, hierarchy, and distinctive points of competitive differentiation in crafting the scope of the inquiry, more explicitly focusing on critical fields of inquiry, selecting analytical techniques, and preparing recommendations that optimize decision-making to drive the effectiveness and efficiency of all elements in motion.

If, for example, the nature of the business issue under Rapid Due Diligence diagnostic review is seeking innovation that leads to a new or evolving business model, the scope of inquiry encompasses broader fields such as the macroeconomic and microeconomic forces, market and competitive analyses, and environmental trends. In this case, the Rapid Due Diligence diagnostic findings are typically used to shape a strategic thinking and decision-making process at the executive levels. This situation often requires significantly expanded quantitative and qualitative data and much more extensive analyses than can be accomplished within the thirty-day boundary.

During the preparatory investigation in stage two of the Rapid Due Diligence diagnostic process, the researcher will have conducted a preliminary review of a host of market segment and customer analytics. In this analysis stage, the researcher commences a deeper examination to more explicitly trace the economic value-producing path and identify new insights. The researcher returns to the Document Review Notes, Document Review Summary, and the following original documents as available:

Stage Four – Analysis and Observation Development **117**

- Current marketing, branding, or communications strategies to the marketplace, including the customer value proposition or other primary tools used to describe how the organization brings value to the targeted market and customers
- Any data on behavioral economics, customer choice analytics, particularly any trigger points tied to customer decision-making, plus any comparisons or commentary on current service performance and targets
- Information about current and future targeted customers and their potential requirements of the organization, any descriptions of preferred customer experiences, plus any data or opinions about the type and degree of change required to meet those requirements
- Any evaluation of competitive positioning and market distinctions

The researcher seeks out sources that reveal any previous in-depth review or analysis of customer intelligence, valuation of buying power, or customer sensing capability. The researcher is looking for the identification of explicit trigger points within the customer base analytics which are known to stimulate a preference for the organization's products and services and ultimately prompt loyal and referential adherence.

The researcher needs to conduct a detailed examination of the value drivers, such as the products and services offered, pricing, and service, as well as the supporting process activities, transaction quality, and behavioral characteristics evident in the provision of service. Where available, in-depth customer intelligence ideally will already include explicit descriptions and a rating scale of importance of the key trigger points for customer decision-making. In addition, the organization may have a quantitative or qualitative performance history at those trigger points. There should be separate and comparative data to capture differences in customers' shopping behaviors among all distribution channels, including in-person market contacts, digitized avenues, and any geographic and cultural commercial distinctions. Ratings and rankings ideally will include differentiation among first-time customers, price shoppers, periodic or episodic shoppers, and loyal customers who willingly advocate for the organization's products and services. In all situations, the researcher seeks to isolate high value characteristics and preferences that can be fulfilled more effectively in the organization's strategy and execution processes.

The combination of these assessments will help the researcher pinpoint specific transactions and intersections throughout the experiences of the customer buying process and relationship that can yield the highest return on performance. The researcher uses these transactions and intersections to further investigate the capability and capacity of designated processes and performers.

Specific opportunities for improvement can emerge that can raise the factors related to the quality of the customers' experiences and relationships. In those circumstances where an organization has determined a valuation factor on such transactions and intersections, the researcher can calculate quantitative expectations with focused attention for improvements.

Drawing upon the relationships shown in Figure 6.9 for tracing a portion of the economic value-producing path, additional research on performance and impact on overall satisfaction ratings can be captured and ranked. The researcher examines these results to identify the best opportunities for greatest leverage and necessary changes in product offerings or delivery of service.

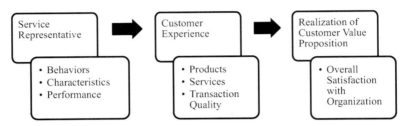

FIGURE 6.9 Drivers of Performance.

Scaling and related critical ratios can be used to help quantify potential impact and return on investments, as shown in Figure 6.10.

Nearly Loyal Customers (Broader Interpretation)
- Non-loyal customers who missed the defined satisfaction and loyalty criteria on one of the measures, irrespective of the score.

Nearly Loyal Customers (Tighter Interpretation)
- Non-loyal customers who missed the defined satisfaction and loyalty criteria on one of the measures by only one point below the cutoff for qualifying as a loyal customer.

Best Opportunity for Conversion to Loyal Customer Relationship
- Applying the tighter interpretation noted above and attitude ratings, these nearly loyal customers represent the strongest potential for movement to loyalty, high levels of satisfaction, and likelihood to make positive recommendations to others.
- Each loyal customer represents a valuation of at least X dollars to the organization per year.

FIGURE 6.10 Value of Loyalty.

The researcher seeks out trigger points within the customer experience that can be traced to specific processes, practices, behaviors, or performance levels. A sample customer experience appears in Figure 6.11.

Stage Four – Analysis and Observation Development 119

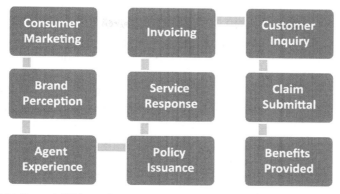

FIGURE 6.11 Potential Trigger Points in Customer Choice Analytics.

For example, as revealed in Box 6.5, the Rapid Due Diligence diagnostic process was used to highlight incisive customer intelligence and leverage its intentional application in the delivery of service and quality audits.

BOX 6.5 INSIGHTS ON CUSTOMER PREFERENCES

A financial organization had experienced a series of financial difficulties, employee downsizing, and serious diminution of its shareholder value. New business models and approach to the marketplace were urgently being explored by the new management team. A complete market study had been completed, and a lucrative underserved market was identified. New strategic initiatives were being launched to change the portfolio mix, achieve a desirable sales to payments ratio, reduce charge-offs, stabilize a favorable account base, and secure and retain profitable member relationships.

In preparation for the launch of a strategy to pursue this newly uncovered market opportunity, the management team decided to deploy the Rapid Due Diligence diagnostic method to identify insights to achieving a more consistent customer service strategy. The research team conducted considerable preparatory investigation, probing deeply within the findings of the market study. The initial findings included key market descriptions, detailed definitions, measures, and specific behavioral implications of the desired customer relationship and probable decision/loyalty migration triggers. Working alongside the organization's performance engineering function, the research team examined the business impact connections of consistent customer service behaviors. The organization itself, as noted above, was at a particularly key point in its own customer migration path, where its own business needs

(*Continued*)

120 Stage Four – Analysis and Observation Development

produced a high level of readiness to listen to relevant recommendations and take immediate action.

As part of the discovery process, the research team conducted a working session with twenty-five members of the management group to pursue a clarified and aligned strategy to better serve the newly identified strategic dimensions for the organization. Among the findings from the earlier Rapid Due Diligence diagnostic work, the research team had uncovered some details that could bring significant value with the proper connections to customer service. Some of those findings included the following:

- The market would find strong appeal in a product offering based on respect and recognition of the potential buyer. The effects of this type of appeal were measured in detailed surveys.
  - o Research indicated that forty-eight percent of prospects would definitely or quite probably seek more information.
  - o Another thirty percent of prospects would definitely or probably make application for the product.
  - o Of existing customers, fifty-nine percent would definitely or probably seek information.
  - o The remaining forty-one percent definitely or probably would make application.
- The definitions of respect and recognition in this market opportunity were clarified with specific behaviors during the entire proposed set of customer experiences.

The research team worked with the members of the management group to pinpoint explicitly how the pursuit of a new brand based on the respect and recognition promise to existing customers and prospects in the targeted market space could deliver the strategic results they were fervently seeking. The key elements are outlined below:

- Set the new direction.
  - o Engage strategy best practices and alignment.
  - o Review vision, mission, and values strategic dimensions.
  - o Integrate the success review with the enterprise scorecard.
  - o Review customer data and benchmarks.
  - o Define a newly differentiated customer value proposition.
- Design the new customer experience.
  - o Validate the customer requirements and preferred experience.
  - o Design the customer relationship process.
  - o Identify critical competencies to match the new definitions.
  - o Analyze the cycles of service in current processes.
  - o Enhance the customer experience to fit the preferred experience.
  - o Align processes and systems.

Stage Four – Analysis and Observation Development **121**

- Develop the implementation plan.
  - o Connect the training to the strategy and specific goals.
  - o Determine drivers and barriers to the desired training outcomes.
  - o Involve key stakeholders in the process.
  - o Communicate the purpose of service skill training and the impact on the business.
  - o Launch the implementation and accompanying training plan.
- Capture the results.
  - o Monitor and measure the impact.
  - o Recognize changes in skills, knowledge, and behaviors that drive the targeted results.

The facilitated working session of the management group produced a key turning point. With this hands-on discovery process, the management group deepened its involvement, pushed for acceleration of all the steps outlined above, and demanded measurement of results. The acceptance of the full set of findings and management group discoveries prompted expansion of the approach to other business units.

The performance engineering function started to track the impact of the strategy. Meticulous, quantifiable data were shared with the management group on a weekly basis. The metrics were moving positively within four to six weeks after completion of the launch of implementation and the accompanying training plan. Other business units followed a similar path.

The executive team took note of the inflection point in the performance of the organization and gave credit to the entire process. The strategy was adopted throughout the organization, including the opening of new call centers in India.

Findings from such rigorous examination and analysis, as referenced in Box 6.5, can be critical to designing the full spectrum of customer experiences that leverages the key drivers and triggers of customer choice-making. The details of qualitative and quantitative factors for process steps and performance competencies (skills, knowledge, abilities, and motivations) can be intentionally built into the strategy, its execution, and supporting systems. These insights ideally are used to inform strategic decision-making about product offerings and development, business development, marketing, distribution channel preparation, sales force and service provider behaviors and performance, and all sources of service and support. The customer value proposition and branding can be more directly driven by inference engine principles extracted from the customer intelligence.

122 Stage Four – Analysis and Observation Development

BOX 6.6 MULTINATIONAL BUSINESS DEVELOPMENT PROCESS

The Rapid Due Diligence diagnostic method was deployed to identify opportunities to develop and implement a comprehensive, strategic model for superior multinational sales performance.

Using the findings from in-person interviews, telephone interviews, direct observations of business development visits with a variety of customers in several countries, and examination of significant market studies, the researcher crafted a panel discussion experience with business development managers. The panel provided deeper background information to identify a number of steps commonly deployed across all countries in Europe and Asia, plus Australia, in developing business opportunities. These findings were compared with research and evidence from customer visits on the customer buying process.

The full set of findings was combined into a single, enterprise-wide business development process. This output was accompanied by sets of competencies and suggested metrics of progress. The findings were mirrored in the automated sales tracking system to ensure that business development managers were focused on the behaviors and process steps that fit the customers' preferences in the buying cycle.

In another example in Box 6.6, the Rapid Due Diligence diagnostic process was engaged by a multinational organization that required examination of the unique variances of the business development process in a number of countries. Extensive on-site discovery with all organizational levels and types of customers in each country produced significant findings. Guided country manager discussions produced new insights about the nature and steps of the customers' buying processes. These findings were integrated with the activities and roles supporting the progressive business development process.

Enterprise goals and performance standards were reconciled with customer expectations at the respective intersections of the business development and customer buying processes. The supporting details included performance competencies by role, quantitative and qualitative performance metrics, and system support definitions designed to produce more predictable and positive results. A simplified summary of such an enterprise business development process appears in Table 6.18.

TABLE 6.18 Enterprise-Wide Business Development Process

Process Steps	STEP 1 Identifying Opportunities	STEP 2 Qualifying Opportunities	STEP 3 Analyzing Situation and Preparing Solution(s)	STEP 4 Presenting Solution(s) and Resolving Concerns	STEP 5 Reaching Agreement and Closing	STEP 6 Implementing Solution(s)	STEP 7 Monitoring Performance	STEP 8 Leveraging Success
Key Activities and Roles SP = Sales Professional SM = Sales Manager UW = Additional Underwriting Support	• Prepare territory and key account plan to set targets (SP) • Focus search for best opportunities (SP) • Investigate resources to discern potential opportunities (SP) • Identify initial contacts (SP)	• Make and complete appointment (SP) • Probe to establish need (SP) • Support need with solution (SP) • Agree organization can provide a viable solution (SP) • Secure request for quote (SP) • Affirm buying process + decision criteria (SP)	• Analyze situation and confirm our solution (SP) • Involve other resources (SP + UW + SM) • Determine best approach for solution and quote (SP and team) • Prepare quote (SP)	• Submit quote (SP) • Uncover and resolve any concerns (PS) • Confirm customer's understanding of benefits (SP) • Check if ready to close (SP)	• Summarize, affirm customer agreement, and close the business. (SP) • Validate contract detail (SP) • Complete contract documents (SP + ?) • Notify internal team (SP)	• Monitor administration, implementation, and service processes (SP + ?) • Organize payment and support processes (SP + ?)	• Monitor solution and service performance (SP) • Check for satisfaction (SP) • Arrange for any adjustments (SP + ?) • Notify internal team of feedback and results (SP)	• Affirm end customer's willingness to be a reference (SP) • Complete arrangements for reference (SP) • Inquire about new opportunities (SP)
Performance Standards	* Identify opportunities that can produce revenue target	* Confirm needs and solutions for qualified opportunities	• Prepare quote within X days of qualifying visit .	• Present quote within X days of qualifying visit. • Customer expresses preference for proposed solution.	• Attain close rate of at least X %. • Aggregate deals ≥ territory target.	• Signed acceptance document .	• 100% satisfaction with solution + service	• Complete follow-up plan for every satisfied customer.
Enterprise Goals	• Identify potential opportunities with sufficient potential to meet target	• Identify need we can solve • Secure data for quote	• Complete understanding of need • Set quotation strategy	• Present best solution • Resolve concerns • Prepare to close	• Close the business • Confirm contract details	• Complete implementation • Complete acceptance and authorize invoice	• Establish customer confidence and satisfaction	• Secure customer as a reference * Earn right for future business opportunity
Customer Expectations	• Explore how to address a need	• Crystallize a specific need • Explore our capabilities	• Explain needs and goals	• Receive clear information • Opportunity to present concerns	• Determine whether to buy our solution • Confirm contract details	• Prepare to accept solution and accept invoice	• Affirm results • Validate the decision	• Build financial, image, and performance success • Place future business with confidence
Customer Buying Process	STEP 1 Plan and Prioritize	STEP 2 Identify Options		STEP 3 Evaluate Options	STEP 4 Select the Best Option STEP 5 Contract	STEP 6 Implement Solution and Track Performance		
Sales Relationship			**Problem-Focused Solution Provider**					
	Customer-Focused, Strategic, and Trusted Business Advisor							

124 Stage Four – Analysis and Observation Development

Engaging in Innovative Product Development

Tracing the economic value-producing path can include a focus on the business issue of engaging in more effective and innovative product development. In this case, the researcher needs to do preparatory investigation into the organization's new product development process prior to conducting on-site discovery. The new product development process should have a specific framework for each of the typical stages of development, with roles, responsibilities, qualitative and quantitative inputs and outputs at progressive stage-gates, approval requirements, and schedule guidelines. The typical stages are listed below:

- Knowledge acquisition
- Concept investigation
- Fundamental design
- Prototype creation
- Pilot production
- Initial manufacturing

It is important for the researcher to understand the perspective of the owner of the business issue with respect to new product development, its current contributions, and any new strategic targets. In those situations where the difference between current and future contributions is more than twenty percent acceleration in schedule or in revenue stream, the researcher needs to be seeking evidence of opportunities that can yield highly innovative or breakthrough results. Less aggressive improvements can be achieved through a more incremental set of improvements in the existing new product development process.

During the preparatory investigation, the researcher needs to verify the description of the new product development process to ensure that it represents a complete and logical framework for each of the development stages. Some specific fields of inquiry can then be crafted for the on-site discovery work, including the following:

- Description and rationale for any deviation from the classic new product development process framework
- Amount of management time and attention during each stage of the new product development process
- Capability for adaptation to unplanned changes in the market's requirements
- Clarity of roles and authority among functional areas during each stage
- Capabilities and environmental support for innovation
- Sufficiency of resources for each stage
- Policy issues among functional areas
- Teamwork and collaboration throughout all the stages

Stage Four – Analysis and Observation Development   **125**

- Results of any previous product development audits
- Compliance with the design of the new product development process

With the findings from both the preparatory investigation and the on-site discovery, the researcher seeks to uncover any gaps between current and targeted results in the fields of inquiry noted above. The most frequent findings tend to pinpoint weakness in the execution of a new product development framework rather than flaws in the framework itself. These weaknesses are most often evident at the intersection of activities among functional areas of marketing, development, and manufacturing or operations. Another frequent gap is the management's desire for significant and frequent innovative product development from a culture that does not intentionally nurture all of the environmental factors for creativity and the risk of failure.

An example of the application of the Rapid Due Diligence diagnostic process for the purpose of improving new product development appears in Box 6.7. In this situation, the new product development process framework was sound. The best opportunities for improvement were revealed in the actual execution of that process.

BOX 6.7 SEEKING PRODUCT DEVELOPMENT IMPROVEMENTS

The Rapid Due Diligence diagnostic method was applied to study the roles, contributions, and skill levels of project teams involved in new product development for a major consumer products organization. Following the preparatory investigation of the documented new product development process and related financial performance expectations, the researcher interviewed twenty management members, directors, group managers, and project leaders on-site.

Following the analysis and synthesis, the researcher concluded that the current new product development system and the organizational culture were quite capable of producing a continuing stream of incremental products within the core business. The new product development process was a classic system that can function very well and produce good results. By design, it tends to produce incremental improvements more easily than breakthrough ideas. However, with its announced aggressive business goals, management was seeking home-run ideas to occur more frequently. The researcher found that potential home-run ideas appeared to develop more often from outside the formal new product development system. Persistent,

(Continued)

126 Stage Four – Analysis and Observation Development

insightful individuals were exercising personal initiative and developing home-run ideas without the full sanction of an internal governing committee.

The researcher observed that the management committees and project teams tended to struggle through the new product development process to commercialize sponsored ideas. The process was viewed by many as a strait-jacket that prompts compliance rather than full pursuit of innovation. The long-standing, functional stovepipes and resulting politics were impeding the intended impact of the new product development process and delivery of home-run ideas. Potentially worthy ideas were being stifled. Some unworthy ideas with political sponsorship appeared to be absorbing precious resources.

The researcher observed that the culture was unsafe for people to bring unwanted messages. As a result, project teams were often searching for less time-consuming paths and knowingly delivering mediocre, over-compromised results. The researcher also observed that project leaders tended not to have sufficient organizational savvy and business experience to effectively lead the projects and stimulate the depth and breadth of inquiry required for success.

A series of recommendations were offered to the senior management members to constructively address systemic challenges and opportunities that can either impede or drive the desired aggressive growth strategy of the organization. Principal recommendations included the following:

- Engage in an integrated deliberation of the strategic focus required for both the near and long-term growth of the business.
- Address the cultural reality of the competitive, functional orientation and its affect on the growth aspirations of the organization. Foster an environment that invites professional perspectives, concerns, and differing points of view into the deliberation process. Demonstrate unanimity of purpose and keep commitments.
- Establish a portfolio management or funnel process at the front end of the current new product development process. Draw upon constant vigilance on market and competitive conditions. Use clear assumptions, priorities, and guidelines. Identify potential areas for accelerated breakthroughs.
- Consider an innovation hub in tandem with the new product development process. Focus on quickly identifying and generating potential breakthrough ideas. Consider accelerated commercialization to secure fast-cycle, consumer acceptance. Deep organizational, business, and cross-functional savvy is required for the hub team.
- Build understanding, appreciation, and disciplined application of the new product development process. Apply more explicit senior management focus in the early gates. Do not skip gates.
- Consider a full-time new product development champion to manage and guide the full new product development effort. Affirm the importance of access to market data.

Stage Four – Analysis and Observation Development **127**

- Select new product development project leaders on the basis of the appropriate skills and depth of expertise required for solid results. Draw leaders from any functional area, not just marketing.
- Adopt a jumpstart approach to accelerate new project teams. Include a full array of practical tools and techniques, including disciplined use of the new product development process, project management, team effectiveness, creativity, innovation, and collaboration across boundaries.
- Create easy, simple, low-cost knowledge sharing mechanisms to facilitate the natural flow of key learning, potential big ideas, and best practices. Focus on building an energetic, non-competitive culture that values this practice.

Focusing on Effective and Efficient Operations

The Rapid Due Diligence diagnostic process can also be applied to a business issue that focuses on the effectiveness and efficiency of operations in delivering value to the organization's customers. In these cases, the researcher typically needs to allow more time for engaging in on-site discovery with multiple levels of management, supervision, and individual or team member participation in the operational processes. The preparatory investigation also requires the gathering of process descriptions, flow charts, operational plans, playbooks, value-stream analyses, and corresponding metrics to gauge current and targeted levels of qualitative and quantitative attributes.

Rapid Due Diligence diagnostic process work may be positioned prior to or following the adoption of operations review processes, such as business process reengineering, Lean 6s, Six Sigma, or some combination of effectiveness, efficiency, or quality improvements. The fields of inquiry will include the following:

- Degree of linkage between strategic goals and on-site expectations for performance
- Logical work flow design, process steps, availability of resources, and condition of environmental work areas
- Leadership behaviors and practices in guiding the performance of operations
- Cultural adaptation to any required changes
- Alignment of performance metrics and reward systems

The researcher is encouraged to engage in direct observations of individuals and team members during actual production activities as well as any planning or review meetings. In this type of Rapid Due Diligence diagnostic process, the opportunities for improvement more frequently appear in the actual day-to-day work production or operational review meeting discussions.

An example of a complex Rapid Due Diligence diagnostic process within a very large operation appears in Box 6.8. Several initiatives were well underway,

128 Stage Four – Analysis and Observation Development

BOX 6.8 IMPROVING OPERATIONAL QUALITY AND EFFICIENCY

A military organization had already invested heavily in implementing a combination of Lean 6s and Six Sigma initiatives to improve both the quality and efficiency of delivery of essential equipment to troops in combat zones. The Rapid Due Diligence diagnostic method was dispatched to investigate why the results to date had not matched expectations.

The research team conducted considerable on-site discovery work with direct observations and interviews with multiple shifts of production operations, all levels of authority, and process improvement initiative events.

The massive set of findings was analyzed with careful attention to protocol for behavioral analysis, competency comparison, and process integrity. The findings revealed inconsistencies from expected application of both competency skill sets and process guidelines. There was little evidence of full supervisory support for demonstrating such skills. There was cultural aversion to risk-taking in conjunction with process improvement and rejection of new ideas. The culture was found to be non-conducive to an environment for long-term successful application and realization of Lean 6s and Six Sigma results. A thorough cultural transformation and skill-building plan were warranted in order to achieve the targeted results.

---

yet the month-to-month production and financial results were not delivering the desired improvements. The expected return on investment in the planned operational efficiencies was not yet being realized.

The nature of the business situation and the scope of the inquiry may require further analytical techniques to gain deeper insight into the crevasses and edges of opportunities for improvement or new frontiers. The techniques and tools described in this chapter are the ones that are more commonly applied.

Unlike formal scientific behavioral or social research studies, the Rapid Due Diligence diagnostic method, with its scope and time boundaries, rarely needs to incorporate complex tests of statistical significance, multiple regression analyses, analysis of variances, or other multivariate computational methods. In most cases, any behavioral, values-oriented, or attitude indicant expressions are labeled, classified, compared, and contrasted with defined or research-based constructs.

Discussion Questions

- How does the researcher determine which analytical techniques are appropriate in stage four of the Rapid Due Diligence diagnostic process?
- Why are data management techniques so important to this step?

How does the researcher maintain a Triple Win perspective throughout the complexity of this stage?

- How can analytical questions and techniques be applied without introducing bias?
- What does a researcher do when the initial analysis reveals a need for additional or clarifying evidence?
- What other unique analytical techniques or tools may be useful in the Rapid Due Diligence diagnostic process?

Notes

1 Joyce A. Thompsen, *Achieving a Triple Win: Human Capital Management of the Employee Lifecycle* (London: Routledge, 2010), 31.
2 ————, *A Case Study of Identifying and Measuring Critical Knowledge Areas as Key Resource-Capabilities of an Enterprise* (Ann Arbor, MI: UMI Dissertation Services, 2000).
3 E. Jaques, S. D. Clement, C. Rigby, and T. O. Jacobs, "Senior Leadership Requirements at the Executive Level," *ARI Research Report Number 1420* (Alexandria, VA: U.S. Army Research Institute for the Behavioral and Social Sciences, 1986).
4 Mark Clare and Arthur W. Detore, *Knowledge Assets: Professional's Guide to Valuation and Financial Management, 2000 Edition* (San Diego, CA: Harcourt, 2000), 68–72.
5 Alexander Osterwalder and Yves Pigneur, *Business Model Generation* (Hoboken, NJ: John Wiley & Sons, Inc., 2010), 16–19.

References

Clare, Mark, and Arthur W. Detore. 2000. *Knowledge Assets: Professional's Guide to Valuation and Financial Management.* San Diego, CA: Harcourt.
Jaques, E., S.D. Clement, C. Rigby, and T.O. Jacobs. 1986. "Senior Leadership Requirements at the Executive Level," *ARI Research Report Number 1420.* Alexandria, VA: U.S. Army Research Institute for the Behavioral and Social Sciences.
Osterwalder, Alexander, and Yves Pigneur. 2010. *Business Model Generation.* Hoboken, NJ: John Wiley & Sons, Inc.
Thompsen, Joyce A. 2000. *A Case Study of Identifying and Measuring Critical Knowledge Areas as Key Resource-Capabilities of an Enterprise.* Ann Arbor, MI: UMI Dissertation Services.
————. 2010. *Achieving a Triple Win: Human Capital Management of the Employee Lifecycle.* London: Routledge.

Selected Bibliography

Listed below are a number of works and sources that have been useful in writing this textbook. The list is intended as a convenience for those who wish to pursue additional study in the selected fields covered in this chapter. In view of the number of resources, this section has been organized into four categories:

- Capabilities and Capacity to Perform and Achieve Targets
- Critical Knowledge Areas©
- Employee Value Proposition
- Measuring the Impact of Learning

130 Stage Four – Analysis and Observation Development

Capabilities and Capacity to Perform and Achieve Targets Resources

Badaracco, J. *Leading Quietly: An Unorthodox Guide to Doing the Right Thing.* Boston: Harvard Business School Press, 2002.

Bartlett, C., and S. Ghoshal. "The Myth of the Generic Manager: New Personal Competencies for New Management Roles." *California Management Review* 40 (Fall 1997): 92–116.

Basford, Tessa, Bill Schaninger, and Ellen Viruleg. "The Science of Organizational Transformations." *McKinsey Quarterly* (September 2015).

Bazigos, Michael, and James Harter. "Revisiting the Matrix Organization." *McKinsey Quarterly* (January 2016).

Bergmann, H., K. Hurson, and D. Russ-Eft. *Everyone a Leader: A Grassroots Model for the New Workplace.* New York: John Wiley & Sons, 1999.

Bossidy, Larry, and Ram Charan. *Execution: The Discipline of Getting Things Done.* New York: Crown Business, 2002.

Collins, J. *Good to Great: Why Some Companies Make the Leap ... and Others Don't.* New York: HarperBusiness, 2001.

Doherty, Rebecca, Oliver Engert, and Andy West. "How the Best Acquirers Excel at Integration." *McKinsey Quarterly* (April 2015).

Fulmer, R., and M. Goldsmith. *The Leadership Investment: How the World's Best Organizations Gain Strategic Advantage Through Leadership Development.* New York: AMACOM, 2000.

Greenleaf, Robert, and Larry Spears. *Servant Leadership: A Journey into the Nature of Legitimate Power and Greatness.* New York: Paulist Press, 2002.

Hamel, G., and C. K. Prahalad. *Competing for the Future: Breakthrough Strategies for Seizing Control of Your Industry and Creating the Markets of Tomorrow.* Boston: Harvard Business School Press, 1994.

Handy, C. *Understanding Organizations: How Understanding the Ways Organizations Actually Work Can Be Used to Manage Them Better.* New York: Oxford University Press, 1993.

Hope, J., and T. Hope. *Competing in the Third Wave: The Ten Key Management Issues of the Information Age.* Boston: Harvard Business School Press, 1997.

Howard, A. *Diagnosis for Organizational Change: Methods and Models.* New York: The Guilford Press, 1994.

Imparato, N., and O. Harari. *Jumping the Curve: Innovation and Strategic Choice in an Age of Transition.* San Francisco: Jossey-Bass Publishers, 1996.

Kanter, R. *E-volve! Succeeding in the Digital Culture of Tomorrow.* Boston: Harvard Business School Press, 2001.

Kaplan, R., and D. Norton. *Translating Strategy into Action: The Balanced Scorecard.* Boston: Harvard Business School Press, 1996.

Kerr, S. "How to Create and Maintain a Learning Organization." The Chief Learning Officers Conference, Boston, 1998.

Kotter, John, and Dan Cohen. *The Heart of Change: Real-Life Stories of How People Change Their Organizations.* Boston: Harvard Business School Publishing, 2002.

Koulopoulos, R., R. Spinello, and W. Toms. *Corporate Instinct: Building a Knowing Enterprise for the 21st Century.* New York: Van Nostrand Reinhold, 1997.

Leifer, R., C. McDermott, G. O'Connor, L. Peters, M. Rice, and R. Veryzer. *Radical Innovation: How Mature Companies can Outsmart Upstarts.* Boston: Harvard Business School Press, 2000.

Markides, C. *All the Right Moves: A Guide to Crafting Breakthrough Strategy.* Boston: Harvard Business School Press, 2000.

Matheson, D., and J. Matheson. *The Smart Organization: Creating Value through Strategic R & D.* Boston: Harvard Business School Press, 1998.

Maynard, Jr., H., and S. Mehrtens. *The Fourth Wave: Business in the 21st Century.* San Francisco: Berrett-Koehler Publishers, 1993.

Michaels, E., H. Handfield-Jones, and B. Axelrod. *The War for Talent.* Boston: Harvard Business School Press, 2001.

Mintzberg, H., B. Ahlstrand, and J. Lampel. *Strategy Safari: A Guided Tour through the Wilds of Strategic Management.* New York: The Free Press, 1998.

Mitroff, I., and E. Denton. *A Spiritual Audit of Corporate America: A Hard Look at Spirituality, Religion, and Values in the Workplace.* San Francisco: Jossey-Bass Publishers, 1999.

O'Reilly, III, C., and J. Pfeffer. *Hidden Value: How Great Companies Achieve Extraordinary Results with Ordinary People.* Boston: Harvard Business School Press, 2000.

Pfeffer, J., and R. Sutton. *The Knowing-Doing Gap: How Smart Companies Turn Knowledge into Action.* Boston: Harvard Business School Press, 2000.

Rasiel, E., and P. Friga. *The McKinsey Mind: Understanding and Implementing the Problem-Solving Tools and Management Techniques of the World's Top Strategic Consulting Firm.* New York: McGraw-Hill, 2002.

Schaubroeck, Ruben, Felicita Holsztejn Tarczewski, and Rob Theunissen. "Making Collaboration Across Functions a Reality." *McKinsey Quarterly* (March 2016).

Schrage, M. *Serious Play: How the World's Best Companies Simulate to Innovate.* Boston: Harvard Business School Press, 2000.

Slater, R. *The GE Way Fieldbook: Jack Welch's Battle Plan for Corporate Revolution.* New York: McGraw-Hill, 2000.

Smart, B. *Topgrading: How Leading Companies Win by Hiring, Coaching, and Keeping the Best People.* Paramus, NJ: Prentice Hall Press, 1999.

Thompsen, J. "Leading Virtual Teams." *Quality Digest,* September 2002.

———. "Management and Leadership Issues for the Information and Knowledge Era: Integrated Strategic Focus for Knowledge-Intensive Enterprises." *Futurics: A Journal of Future Research* (February 1999).

Thompsen, J., and K. Wright. "Building the People's Capacity for Change." *The International Review of Organizational Improvement* 9 (1997): 36–41.

Tichy, N. *The Leadership Engine: How Winning Companies Build Leaders at Every Level.* New York: HarperBusiness, 1997.

Ulrich, D. *Human Resource Champions: The Next Agenda for Adding Value and Delivering Results.* Boston: Harvard Business School Press, 1997.

Ulrich, D., J. Zenger, and N. Smallwood. *Results-Based Leadership: How Leaders Build the Business and Improve the Bottom Line.* Boston: Harvard Business School Press, 1999.

Vicere, A., and R. Fulmer. *Leadership by Design: How Benchmark Companies Sustain Success through Investment in Continuous Learning.* Boston: Harvard Business School Press, 1997.

Wenger, E., R. McDermott, and W. Snyder. *Cultivating Communities of Practice: A Guide to Managing Knowledge.* Boston: Harvard Business School Press, 2002.

Zook, C. *Profit from the Core: Growth Strategy in an Era of Turbulence.* Boston: Harvard Business School Press, 2001.

Critical Knowledge Area© Resources

Barney, J. "Firm Resources and Sustained Competitive Advantage." *Journal of Management* 17 (1991): 99–120.

Grant, R.M. "The Resource-Based Theory of Competitive Advantage: Implications for Strategy Formulation." *California Management Review* 33 (1991): 114–135.

132 Stage Four – Analysis and Observation Development

Hall, R. "A Framework Linking Intangible Resources and Capabilities to Sustainable Competitive Advantage." *Strategic Management Journal* 14 (1993): 607–618.

Jaques, E., S. D. Clement, C. Rigby, and T.O. Jacobs. "Senior Leadership Requirements at the Executive Level," ARI Research Report Number 1420. Alexandria, VA: U.S. Army Research Institute for the Behavioral and Social Sciences, 1986.

Kamoche, K. "Strategic Human Resource Management within a Resource-Capability View of the Firm." *Journal of Management Studies* 33 (1996): 213–233.

Mahoney, J.T. "The Management of Resources and the Resource of Management." *Journal of Business Research* 33 (1995): 91–101.

Penrose, E. *The Theory of the Growth of the Firm*. New York: John Wiley & Sons, 1959.

Porter, M.E. "Toward a Dynamic Theory of Strategy," article in *Fundamental Issues in Strategy: A Research Agenda,* by R. P. Rumelt, D. E. Schendel, and D. J. Teece, eds. Boston: Harvard Business School Press, 1994.

Spender, J.C. "Making Knowledge the Basis of the Dynamic Theory of the Firm." *Strategic Management Journal* 17 (1996): 45–62.

Thompsen, Joyce. *A Case Study of Identifying and Measuring Critical Knowledge Areas as Key Resource-Capabilities of an Enterprise.* Minneapolis, MN: Walden University, 1999.

———. "A Case Study on Achieving Return on Critical Talent in Technology-Intensive Organizations." Presentation to the Portland International Conference on Management of Engineering and Technology, Portland, OR, 2003.

———. "Achieving Return on Critical Knowledge." *Technology and Innovation Management: Setting the Pace for the Third Millennium,* Proceedings of the Portland International Conference on Management of Engineering and Technology, Portland, OR, 1999.

———. "Achieving Return on Critical Knowledge and Talent." Presentation to the American Society of Training and Development, Houston, TX, September, 2001.

———. "Achieving Return on Critical Talent in Technology-Intensive Organizations." IEEE International Engineering Management Conference Proceedings, Cambridge University, Cambridge, England, August 2002.

———. "Critical Knowledge Areas: The Seeds for Survival and Growth." *Innovation in Technology Management: A Convergence of Communications, Computing, and Energy Technologies.* Proceedings of the International Conference on Engineering and Technology Management, Vancouver, British Columbia, Canada, 1996.

Zaccaro, S. *The Nature of Executive Leadership: A Conceptual and Empirical Analysis of Success.* Washington, D.C.: American Psychological Association, 2001.

Employee Value Proposition Resources

Bell, Andrew. "The Employee Value Proposition Redefined." *Strategic HR Review* 4, no. 4 (2005).

Chambers, Elizabeth G., Mark Foulon, and Helen Handfield-Jones. "The War for Talent, Attracting and Retaining the Best Talents." *The McKinsey Quarterly* 1, no. 3 (1998): 44.

Evans, Scott R., Jenny Gonzalez, Stephen Popiel, and Terry Walker. "Whose Capital Is It? Trends in Human Capital; Statistical Data Included." *Ivey Business Journal,* January 1, 2000.

Gakovic, Anika, and Keith Yardley. "Global Talent Management at HSBC." *Organizational Development Journal* 25, no. 2 (2007): 201–05; 231.

Halloran, Lisa. "Attracting and Retaining the New Generation of Leaders." *Human Resources Magazine,* September 25, 2003.

Stage Four – Analysis and Observation Development **133**

Harper, Rebecca. "Hanging on to What You've Got." *Money Management*, November 9, 2006.

Harvie, Jeni. "Look at Employee Value Propositions on Offer." *Weekend Australian*, November 18, 2006.

Ingham, Jon. "Closing the Talent Management Gap." *Strategic HR Review* 5, no. 3 (2006): 20.

Jex, Steve M. *Organizational Psychology: A Scientist-Practitioner Approach*. New York: John Wiley & Sons, 2002.

Kanter, Rosabeth Moss. *Men and Women of the Corporation*. New York: Basic Books, 1993.

Kiger, Patrick J. "Employment Branding: More Than a Catchphrase." Special advertising section produced in partnership with *Forbes* magazine, 2007.

Kirsch, Christina. "Loyalty and Disengagement – Taming the Retention Monster." *Australian Management Magazine*, October 1, 2007.

Lawrence, Stewart D., and Joel Rich. "Pensions Law Changes Require Deliberate Response: As Plan Sponsors Grapple with Greater Volatility, They Also Should Consider Where Their Pension Fits within the Broader Context of Their Employer Value Proposition." *Employee Benefit News*, September 15, 2006.

Medcof, John. "Total Rewards: Good Fit for Tech Workers." *Research Technology Management*, September 9, 2006.

Scofield, Leah. "Attract Talent by Focusing on Company Values." *Sioux Falls Business Journal*, October 24, 2007.

Measuring the Impact of Learning Resources

Becker, B., M. Huselid, and D. Ulrich. *The HR Scorecard: Linking People, Strategy, and Performance*. Boston: Harvard Business School Press, 2001.

Becker, G. *Human Capital: A Theoretical and Empirical Analysis with Special Reference to Education, Third Edition*. Chicago: The University of Chicago Press, 1993.

Brinkerhoff, R. *The Success Case Method: Find Out Quickly What's Working and What's Not*. San Francisco: Berrett-Koehler Publishers, Inc., 2003.

"Business Transformation and Operational Excellence." Economist Intelligence Unit and Marakon Associates, Corporate Strategy Board Research, 2005.

Clare, M., and A. DeTore. *Knowledge Assets: Professional's Guide to Valuation and Financial Management*. London: Harcourt Professional Publishing, 2000.

Courtney, H. *20/20 Foresight: Crafting Strategy in an Uncertain World*. Boston: Harvard Business School Press, 2001.

Davenport, R. "In God We Trust: All Others Bring Data." *Training and Development* magazine, April, 2006.

Ernst and Young LLP, "Measures that Matter." 2000.

Fitz-enz, J. *The ROI of Human Capital: Measuring the Economic Value of Employee Performance*. New York: American Management Association, 2000.

Kaplan, R., and D. Norton. *Alignment: Using the Balanced Scorecard to Create Corporate Synergies*. Boston: Harvard Business School Press, 2006.

Kirkpatrick, D. *Evaluating Training Programs, Second Edition*. San Francisco: Berrett-Koehler Publishers, Inc., 1998.

Low, J. "Gauging Results: What Measures Matter." *Harvard Management Update*, 1999.

Mankins, M., and R. Steele. "Turning Great Strategy into Great Performance." *Harvard Business Review*, July-August 2005.

134 Stage Four – Analysis and Observation Development

Pfeffer, J., and R. Sutton. *Hard Facts: Dangerous Half-Truths and Total Nonsense, Profiting from Evidence-Based Management*. Boston: Harvard Business School Press, 2006.

Phillips, J., *Return on Investment in Training and Performance Improvement Programs*. Houston, TX: Gulf Publishing Company, 1997.

Raden, N. "BI Megatrends." *Intelligent Enterprise* 9, no.9 (September 2006).

Russ-Eft, D., and H. Preskill. *Evaluation in Organizations: A Systematic Approach to Enhancing Learning, Performance, and Change*. Cambridge, MA: Perseus Publishing, 2001.

Scott, M. *Value Drivers: The Manager's Framework for Identifying the Drivers of Corporate Value Creation*. West Sussex, England: John Wiley & Sons, 1998.

Sisk, M. "Are the Wrong Metrics Driving Your Strategy?" *Harvard Management Update*, 2003.

Sugrue, B., O'Driscoll, T., Vona, M. "C-Level Perceptions of the Strategic Value of Learning Research Report." ASTD and IBM joint research, January 2006.

Swanson, R., and E. Holton, III. *Results: How to Assess Performance, Learning, and Perceptions in Organizations*. San Francisco: Berrett-Koehler Publishers, Inc., 1999.

Thompsen, J. "Aligning Content Strategies with Workforce Competencies." *CLO Magazine*. April, 2006.

———. "Strategy to Results: Achieving Greater Return on Critical Talent." AchieveGlobal research paper, 2004.

Welborn, R., and V. Kasten. *Get It Done! A Blueprint for Business Execution*. Hoboken, NJ: John Wiley & Sons, Inc., 2006.

7

STAGE FIVE – SYNTHESIS AND FORMULATION OF RECOMMENDATIONS

Learning Objectives

- To acquire an understanding of several synthesis techniques used in the Rapid Due Diligence diagnostic method.
- To learn how to prepare observations, conclusions, and recommendations for action.

In the fifth stage of the Rapid Due Diligence diagnostic process, the researcher and any team members engage in a more complex, holistic, systems thinking approach to the complete set of findings. Discoveries from the application of analytical techniques in the earlier stage are also examined from the perspective of synthesis, or fusion of the separate elements to form a coherent whole system. For reference, the description of the fifth stage has been excised from the full six-stage table in Chapter Two and appears in Table 7.1.

TABLE 7.1 Rapid Due Diligence Method of Diagnostics: Stage Five – Synthesis and Formulation of Recommendations

Players Involved	• Principal researcher
	• Research team (if any)
Process Steps	• Conduct more complex analyses & synthesis of all sources of data.
	• Capture gaps.
	• Record conclusions.
	• Formulate specific steps to move from current to targeted outcomes.
Outcomes	• Conclusions
	• Recommendations for action
Timeline	3–5 days

136 Stage Five – Synthesis and Formulation of Recommendations

Execution of this stage requires the researcher to envision the business issue under the Rapid Due Diligence diagnostic review as more than a single problematic event that requires a simple decision to produce improved results. A broader systems thinking perspective is required to see the situation as a complex set of intersected, interdependent constituents framing the whole.

System Dynamics

Adaptations of system dynamics are required to help the researcher better understand the complexity of the situation, commence to reach better conclusions, and design effective recommendations. In its nature, system dynamics is an interdisciplinary synthesis method that draws upon nonlinear dynamics and environmental feedback from the physical sciences, as well as cognitive and social sciences and economics.

The field of system dynamics is supported by a number of tools, formal models, simulation methods, and other techniques designed to identify mental model barriers and sharpen scientific reasoning. The intent is to introduce a few key techniques of integrative synthesis that most often lead to discovery of hidden opportunities for specific improvements within the Rapid Due Diligence diagnostic method.

Iterative Feedback Loops

From a systems thinking perspective, the dynamics emerge from the interaction of multiple loops of feedback, each delivering either positive or negative reaction to any form of change. The researcher needs to be cognizant of the risk of reliance on a single feedback loop which long-standing research shows does not sufficiently alter embedded mental models, or beliefs about causes and effects, to achieve the required and sustained change in behavior. Any premature or incomplete conclusion and recommendation, as informed by a single feedback loop, is confronted by an environment of existing mental models, supported by decision rules, policies, practices, cultures, and institutional momentum or inertia designed to resist the intended change. On the other hand, nonlinear, double-loop or multiple-loop feedback can reframe a situation, stimulate a new level of understanding, and be used to craft new decision rules.

Moving from the simplified event-oriented perspective to system dynamics requires the researcher to recognize patterns of behavior and avoid common misperceptions of feedback. Sample patterns over time horizons that may emerge include exponential growth, S-curve cycle, oscillation, and overshot or overcompensated growth followed by the collapse of growth. Similar to the requirement of the researcher to ensure discovery integrity without the introduction of bias, in this synthesis stage the researcher needs to remain cognizant of the potential consequences and limitations of bounded rationality, constraints to attention, memory recall, and human capability for information processing.

Even with comprehensive, strong evidence and complete knowledge about the relationships and parameters of the strategic dimensions, it can be difficult for a researcher to make reasonable inferences about the complex dynamics of the system in motion. Errors in the heuristics that are used to judge causality can lead to faulty cognitive maps, ignorant of multiple-loop feedback, time delay impact, non-linearity, spatial distance, and unknown or unknowable consequences.

The researcher can affect some of these potential errors in reasoning and judgment by conscientiously engaging in rigorous, disciplined rules of scientific inference in interpreting feedback loops. The researcher needs to intentionally seek possible contradictory evidence and test for the intrusion of faulty mental models into the synthesis and insight development process.

Causal Loop Diagramming

Causal or consequence loop diagrams are useful tools in capturing the feedback structure within multiple loops of a system. Causal loop diagrams depict the variables, feedback loops, and influences among the variables. The drawing process itself facilitates the identification of mental models, potential causation of specific dynamics, eventual formation of patterns, and clarity in communicating the impact factors and results of the synthesis of many variables and elements.

As shown in Figure 7.1, causal links show the connections between variables and are portrayed as directional arrows. Either positive (+) or negative (-) polarity is assigned to each causal link to identify how the dependent variable changes when the independent variable changes. In addition, the more important feedback loops are marked to note either positive (reinforcing) or negative (balancing) feedback. Thus, when the researcher finds that the cause increases and the effect also increases, a positive link exists. A positive link also exists if both the cause and effect decrease. This sample is deliberately simplified to illustrate the basic structure.

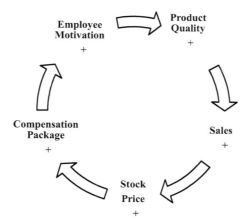

FIGURE 7.1 Sample Causal Loop Diagram.

138 Stage Five – Synthesis and Formulation of Recommendations

By contrast, a negative link means that if the cause increases, the effect decreases further below what it otherwise would have decreased and vice versa. In cases where there are more positive than negative links, those loops illustrate drivers for growth. The presence of more negative links or balancing loops can produce oscillation, potential overshot, or overcompensation and collapse within the system dynamics.

The researcher is seeking to capture the genuine causation links within the structural dynamic system. Data from the on-site discovery stage can be effectively used to draft causal or consequence loop diagrams. The accumulation of rich, thick descriptions of decision rules, decision-making processes, cultural practices, attributions of motives, and rationale can be confusing or unfounded; and the triangulation of findings and causal loop diagramming helps clarify actual causation. Other archival data, both qualitative and quantitative, from the preparatory investigation of documentation may be required to verify causal links. Care is required to avoid mistaking simple correlations as relevant causation when preparing the causal loop diagrams.

With more complicated sets of causal loops and links, the researcher is advised to use neutral numbers and labels to avoid the perception of bias or preferential attitude in any level of communications. A few iterations of the causal loop diagram may be necessary to achieve the best layout and to gain clarity in an impactful portrayal of system structures, causation, and polarity. These causal loop diagrams may be used for joint inquiry or testing recommendations among only the members of the research team, with the organizational key contact, or with the owner of the business issue.

The findings at this level of synthesis can yield significant, even unexpected or counterintuitive insights into the aggregate feedback loops among the strategic dimensions and variable factors. The diagrams also distinguish between actual and perceived conditions and can be used to test hypotheses for potential recommendations.

Effects of Cognitive and Behavioral Limitations

A challenging task for the researcher is the discovery of organizational decision rules and how well those are applied within decision-making processes. The decision rules are the guiding policies or procedures that specify how decision-makers process information and apply judgment to a variety of factors to arrive at a conclusion or decision. These decision rules embody assumptions about the degree of rationality of both the decision-makers and the decision-making process. The researcher needs to realize that human decision-making typically falls between the extremes of rote behavioral response and the perfect rationality of economic theory.

The decision-makers unconsciously apply mental models to select the types of information or cues that they endeavor to process. For some organizations, these decision rules and supporting assumptions have become autonomic; and decision-makers tend to ritually engage in stochastic conjecture about the most salient factors or rote response to a set of commonly recognizable cues. Such situations can preclude the discovery of insights from unexpected sources. Other organizations or decision-makers may operate at the other extreme, insisting on vast amounts of information, the full range of assumptions, and decision-testing rationale that filter out the perceived potential for decision error. Applying behavioral economics, ideally the decision-makers apply decision rules and assumptions to maximize the utility of the information and secure optimal decisions, thus investing their time and energy only to the degree that further effort fails to yield higher quality deliberations.

During the synthesis stage, the researcher is testing the explicit or implicit application of any decision rules and assumptions to support the decision-making processes. The researcher notes the degree of robustness, rationality, potential for realistic outcomes, and follow-through in actual practice.

The researcher also looks for evidence of interpersonal or political dysfunctionality as an overt or hidden driver within the decision rules. Evidence of unusual or unstable behavior among decision-makers may provide indications of unresolved conflict, political intrigue, or unaccepted disagreement on decision rules, assumptions, or information sources. The presence of persistent difficulties can introduce irrationality and strain the level of sophistication, innovation, and discipline in the application of decision rules, as well as skew the quality of the decision-making process.

The researcher needs to be aware that some findings may reveal early evidence of an individual decision-maker suffering from any form of cognitive dysfunction, such as chronic fatigue syndrome, depression, or difficulty with intellectual functionality such as verbal recall, level of concentration, memory, or orderly reasoning capabilities. At any time that the researcher finds sufficient evidence to suspect the presence of cognitive dysfunction, the individual situation must be handled with the greatest respect for privacy and not be referenced in any concluding commentary. Discreet, confidential conversation with the organizational key contact is advised to ensure proper handling of any such situations.

Bounded rationality accounts for limitations on human cognitive capabilities to absorb and process vast amounts of information within brief timeframes. Combining this factor with selective perceptions, governed by individual mental models, incomplete or imperfect knowledge, and weak powers of rational deduction, there are numerous ways in which cognitive limitations can interfere with rational decision-making, according to optimization theory. Instead, decision-makers may consciously or unconsciously apply heuristics as guides or proxies for decision rules. The researcher needs to identify the use of any such habits or rules of thumb to understand the potential for systematic or persistent errors in setting strategic direction, goals, or priority application of resources, all of which can confound the ambition for targeted results.

In those situations where the researcher discovers potential flaws due to any form of cognitive or behavioral limitations, the use of causal loop diagramming can be helpful in identifying and illustrating the consequences, any form of

140 Stage Five – Synthesis and Formulation of Recommendations

bounded rationality, or how intentionally rational decision rules can create dysfunctional system dynamics and unintended consequences.

The example in Box 7.1 describes a situation where the Rapid Due Diligence researcher uncovered both subliminal and conscious, yet hidden, disagreement with the assumptions and consensual strategy development of an organization. The discovery was required to understand the frustrating yield of the strategy.

BOX 7.1 EFFECTS OF HIDDEN DISAGREEMENT

A regional insurance organization decided to pursue a more effective customer service strategy as measured by increases in both customer loyalty and financial growth. The Rapid Due Diligence diagnostic method was deployed to gain deeper perspective and insights on opportunities for improvement.

Following the preparatory investigation, the researcher completed multiple in-person and telephone interviews with executives and managers of all functional areas and business groups.

A number of observations emerged from the analysis and synthesis of the findings. The organization enjoyed a reputation for exceptional levels of service. A clear, comprehensive, and deliberately focused strategy to manage the entire customer relationship process could yield the targeted growth. This approach would require deep resolve and unified, unequivocal conviction, at least among the management group members. While the most senior executive was adamantly convinced the entire leadership team was already committed to the customer service strategy, the researcher uncovered that thirty percent of the discovery respondents voiced concern about surface levels of commitment, lip service, or acquiescence on the part of at least some of those same senior leaders.

During a facilitated meeting of the organization's senior leadership team, the researcher diplomatically raised this finding without revealing identities. All those in this meeting who had provided the clear feedback in private chose to publicly deny their responses.

Other findings revealed cues of organizational patterns of strong reluctance to change, prevalent comfort with long-standing processes and pace, excessive flexibility in managing work/life balance issues without any supervisory imposition, and tolerance of poor performance.

The executives held the conclusions of the Rapid Due Diligence report suspect, declaring that these findings did not reflect their perceptions. At the time, the executive team chose to take no new action to verify or reset their strategy.

Three months later, the key executive acknowledged the hidden dissension and a heightened resolve to proceed with remedial strategic actions.

Oscillations and Amplifications in Key Processes

In the earlier stages of the Rapid Due Diligence diagnostic method, the researcher will have identified specific key organizational processes that present symptoms of the original business issue under review. Examples of key processes include at least the following:

- Market research
- Product development
- Product pricing and positioning
- Manufacturing
- Product distribution
- Employee recruitment and selection
- Business development
- Customer service and support

Each one of these processes has a defined structure to acquire inputs, conduct a set of transforming procedures, and deliver an output to a customer inside or outside the organization. In many cases, these processes reach beyond the controllable boundaries of an organization.

As the researcher conducts any on-site discovery about a specific key process, the findings may reveal variations from the prescribed set of procedures and practices, which in turn can yield unintended qualitative or quantitative results. In those situations, the researcher conducts deeper inquiry into the conscious or unconscious rationale and behavior that produces such variances or discovers other physical or timing factors that interfere with the intended process outputs. The discovery of such variances and causal loop diagramming to trace unintended consequences can reveal insights and opportunities for impact.

In other situations, during the integrative synthesis, the researcher may uncover evidence of oscillation and amplification occurring within or outside the organization's key processes. In ideal circumstances, the flow of inputs and outputs through key processes is timely and smooth. However, with the introduction of any change, the responses governing the flow take corrective action, may consciously or unintentionally over-compensate or under-compensate, and simultaneously stimulate swings in outputs and inventory levels. Combined with time delays or phase lags, even minor oscillations can become amplified to extremes, producing unforeseen fluctuations, deleterious customer impact, and undesirable counteractions.

When the researcher encounters evidence of such cycles, chronic oscillation, amplification, or time lags, it is helpful to construct causal loop diagrams or a variation in stock and flow maps to illustrate the structure of the key process, its inputs, decision points responding to changes from any sources, and the effects of actual outputs compared to the targeted results. These synthesis techniques can be used to illustrate the business issue in motion, expose hidden assumptions, flaws in decision rules, and broaden the view of the full effect of cyclicality. The diagrams

142 Stage Five – Synthesis and Formulation of Recommendations

and maps can be used to summarize the findings from preparatory investigation of archival documents, on-site discovery in personal interviews, panel interviews, and direct observations of operations. These modeling techniques can highlight the consequences and instability derived from decisions taken throughout the key process. These techniques can also reveal opportunities for changing decision rules, assumptions, or response behaviors.

Where appropriate, the researcher calculates or estimates the effects on key metrics and critical ratios to provide additional qualitative and quantitative evidence. Whenever possible, the researcher is advised to provide evidence in metrics that are already accepted by the organization's decision-makers.

Geographic Dispersion

In this synthesis stage, the researcher seeks to identify how and why the organization may conduct its business across significant geographic distances in ways that fit the unique local environment and contribute to the viability of the whole. This is an area of investigation that is especially important when the business issue under review involves any degree of geographic dispersion. The dispersion may be limited to several offices or operations within a single metropolitan area, spread in regional centers across a country, or multinational in nature.

In any situations where there is geographic dispersion, the researcher seeks to understand the definitions of each strategic dimension and how those definitions are interpreted into strategy and localized execution. The location of the organization's headquarters which houses the principal executive decision-makers is a significant governing factor in the organization's approach to its business model, the nature of its mission and vision, and core values.

The researcher may find that the core values remain intact throughout all locations while granting accommodation for unique local labor and customer market perspectives and locally applied behavioral economics. These differences become evident in the distinctive descriptions of customer and employee value propositions for the various geographic areas.

For example, a North American organization's headquarters was seeking to determine whether it could craft a common business development approach within offices serving several countries across Europe. The researcher did extensive on-site discovery with individual interviews, panel discussions, and visits with customers at several types of facilities. While the findings revealed definite differences in the detail of the way the customers and sales executives engaged in their business relationships, a common underlying process eventually became evident. The researcher was able to assist the broad group of people serving several countries to arrive at a consensus on how to effectively match business development activities with the preferred approach of their targeted customers. Further, the findings from this on-site discovery were incorporated into the automated sales management system. The automated system was populated with key questions which matched the customers' choice analytic triggers.

Stage Five – Synthesis and Formulation of Recommendations **143**

In another example, an organization based in Asia espoused an approach which emanates from its intimate understanding of how business can thrive in the Asian culture, including the distinctions that vary from country to country, regional sectors within those countries, and other demographic slices of the targeted markets. In contrast, an organization based in a Western European country will likely hold a somewhat different world view that informs its business model, mission, vision, and core values. The same is expected to be true for an organization based in the African continent, the Middle East, or the Americas.

It is the researcher's responsibility to gain a sufficient understanding of the central set of strategic dimensions from the originating country, then to identify whether, why, and how there are any specific, intentional differences among any geographically dispersed locations of operation.

The example that appears in Box 7.2 summarizes some of the findings and recommendations for an Asian-based organization that was seeking improvement in its North American operations. Significant differences in leadership style among multiple levels of management were discovered and required a degree of reconciliation to improve business results.

BOX 7.2 EXAMPLE OF INTEGRATING DIFFERING GEOGRAPHIC CULTURES

As an Asian-based organization was preparing to execute a new transnational strategy, the key organizational contact expressed a need to understand more clearly the subtle differences in how the Asian managers were driving performance in North American operations. In the preparatory investigation and early in the on-site discovery, the researcher uncovered underlying cultural differences among the multiple levels of management, their countries of origin, and the practices that they engaged in leading and communicating among themselves and with those of other cultural origins and backgrounds.

In panel interviews, the researcher also uncovered significant differences of opinion about the rationale for any potential erosion of realizable strategic value. People in higher levels of authority stated unequivocally their firm conviction that strategic goals had been clearly communicated and expectations for performance were indisputable. The reality for those who received those instructions was different. Furthermore, there were few opportunities for lower level managers to engage in constructive conversation about those dictated goals or to provide input based upon their direct operational experience.

As an area of opportunity for improvement, the researcher introduced all parties to new tools that were compatible with both the Asian and North

(Continued)

144 Stage Five – Synthesis and Formulation of Recommendations

> American cultures of this organization. These included techniques for enlisting others in constructive dialogue, new ways of communicating to more expressly invite potentially good ideas, and how to self-identify situations where individual or culturally-driven communication styles had been discouraging input and innovation. Both Asian and North American managers at multiple levels were provided with a form of critical incident assessment that they could privately use in more clearly identifying opportunities for self-improvement and in providing feedback to others. The managers were invited to describe situations in which they were principal players, the behaviors and actions they actually undertook, the results for the business that were derived from those actions, and the impact on the relationships with their work colleagues.
>
> The researcher also recommended that future managers from the Asian headquarters who were being assigned to North American operations sites be exposed to more intensive intercultural relationship studies with specific applications in the overarching, corporate-wide performance management system.

In another situation, the researcher was asked to use the Rapid Due Diligence diagnostic process to identify a set of leadership practices and behaviors that could be universally acceptable to multiple branch operations across North America. In this case, the owner of the business issue was insisting upon a uniform application of such practices and behaviors throughout the system. The findings were significantly informed by research into the unique and distinctive requirements for leadership attention in virtual project team or remote management situations, where individuals who share responsibilities for common goals reside in geographically dispersed locations.

The researcher needs to understand these distinctive requirements in order to recognize opportunities for improvement in conducting Rapid Due Diligence diagnostics with a geographically dispersed business issue. While there may be commonality in the business model, mission, vision, and core values of a geographically dispersed organization, the findings that often reveal difficulties and thus opportunities for improvement are uncovered in the day-to-day operating relationships among people at different locations. The following research addresses specific behavioral cues and preferences that can yield greater effectiveness and employee engagement in dispersed or distant working relationships.

To participate efficiently in a rapidly-changing economy, research confirms that leaders must be effective at managing technical and support teams whose members are scattered across many geographic boundaries. The research reveals a core set of essential leadership skills that meet the needs of dispersed, out-of-sight people while achieving targeted results. [1]

Key findings from both research and best practices across many industries reveal that effective leadership from a distance includes the typical fundamentals for leading

Stage Five – Synthesis and Formulation of Recommendations **145**

people and managing resources in a traditional office environment. Difficulties in the traditional environment, however, can be magnified significantly in virtual or remote situations. Difficulty in communications, working together and producing high-quality on-time results typically is heightened by distance. Effective leaders need to quickly, confidently and competently diagnose such issues themselves and take deliberate actions to keep project team relationships, productivity and outcomes on track. There is even more emphasis on the use of appropriate communications skills to fit the needs of both the people and the situation.

The research also reveals a profile of employees who operate well in virtual project team situations. When possible, it is advisable to select team members who already demonstrate these characteristics or who are willing and able to quickly develop them. Employees tend to be more comfortable and effective if they are:

- Able to perform the core task for their roles
- Self-disciplined
- Goal-directed
- Flexible
- Collaborative
- Willing to share and exchange information
- Open to feedback, change, differences in people and culture, ways of thinking, discipline models, signature skills, and alternative approaches to processes
- Committed and connected to the business
- Competent in using the technology required for their roles

A model of effective leadership from a distance or with a virtual project team can be demonstrated as a visual image of a camera with a telephoto lens. Similar to the mechanics of operating such a camera to secure a clear image of a distant situation, effective leaders adjust their communications and method of technology to bring situations into focus. Deliberately applying the five categories of essential leadership skills for leading from a distance (outlined below) gives leaders an enlarged and clearer image of a distant situation.

Virtual project team leaders typically get brief situational snapshots via communication such as voice mail, e-mail, and text messages. Effective leaders need to quickly and skillfully diagnose what is happening, determine what action is required, and adjust how they communicate and what technology they use to achieve the desired results.

The five categories of effective leadership skills in virtual project team or distance management situations are listed and described below.

- Communicating effectively
- Building community
- Establishing a clear and inspiring shared purpose
- Leading by example with a focus on visible, measurable results
- Coordinating and collaborating across boundaries

146 Stage Five – Synthesis and Formulation of Recommendations

Effective communication is key with virtual project teams. It requires careful attention to listening, how to present our own thoughts and ideas, a clear focus on positive and constructive intent, choosing the right technology to quickly and sensitively communicate a clear message, and taking extra steps to respectfully ensure understanding and expectations for action. It includes important feedback loops and networking and often requires daily contact during fast-changing times.

Effective communication also requires careful diagnosis of any given situation to discern not only the task or work objective in question, but also the obvious or hidden emotional content within the situation. It requires deliberate attention to the needs of project team members and their desire for timely, sensitive action. An especially effective technique is to establish communications ground rules that meet the needs of the project team and the leader.

Following are observable leadership behaviors for communicating effectively with a virtual project team:

- Model the organization's values and members' ground rules in all communications.
- Choose a communication method that meets the needs of members as well as the situation.
- Apply communications technology that best fits the situation, and help all members apply available technology for communication with confidence.
- Formulate specific objectives and an organized delivery plan for communication.
- Link messages to the members' shared purpose, goals and performance contributions to results.
- Encourage all members in a conversation to participate fully.
- Listen proactively.
- Verify understanding of the message and expectations for action.
- Guide communications to achieve positive and constructive outcomes.
- Coach and offer feedback with respect and support.

Once the leader determines which communication method is appropriate for the situation, the technology, if any, which best fits or is preferred by team members can be selected.

Face-to-face communication has its place, especially when addressing issues of high emotional content. Such issues include anxiety, loss of cohesion in the group, self-doubt, over-sensitivity to an issue, under-performance, alienation from other team members, restlessness, distrust, dissatisfaction, paranoia, indecision, confusion, toxic worry, disconnection, mental fatigue, ambiguity, burnout, and social isolation.

Face-to-face communication also helps develop sensitivity to diversity and is important for social contracting, bonding, and realizing the benefits of human

Stage Five – Synthesis and Formulation of Recommendations   **147**

contact on performance. When properly positioned and managed, this type of communication builds community and strengthens connections to the business.

Research shows a sense of community is based on mutual trust, respect, fairness and affiliation among members. It includes sensitivity to differences, plus establishing and adhering to ground rules on how the team will work together.

Mutual trust must be established at the beginning of a work relationship. Trust is fragile, requiring clarity of intent. Over time, actions that fulfill commitments solidify the trust. This is especially important for virtual project team members who have diverse skills or represent different technical disciplines. Effective leaders should consider an initial face-to-face meeting to orient members toward constructive intent built on community and trust.

As an example, an international privately held software development firm with multiple virtual product development and project support teams began to miss critical development deadlines with key customers. Once the organization uncovered and addressed specific roadblocks to their mutual sense of community and trust, it quickly got back on schedule.

Trust also is essential to social contracting, especially among knowledge workers. It often begins or grows when knowledge is willingly shared. Consistent, positive, respectful interactions among members create a strong bond of trust that serves as glue for the community.

The perception of fairness is another important element. As team members observe day-to-day activity, they naturally form opinions about the fairness of any given situation. An action or situation that prompts a member to perceive bias, cultural insensitivity, unethical, or unbalanced treatment of others can directly affect that member's desire to support the project team and its goals.

The need for affiliation, for belonging, for identifying with a respected group, for pursuing a worthy objective or noble purpose with colleagues, for some level of bonding, is important for overcoming social isolation, alienation, and disconnection.

All of these elements are typically portrayed in the unique ground rules a virtual project team establishes for itself. These ground rules demonstrate attention to building community. They often include keeping commitments, providing feedback in preferred ways, giving everyone an equal voice, sharing important information, acknowledging preferences for type and frequency of communications, and other unique points for how the project team wants to work together. Observable behaviors that promote and build community are listed below:

- Model the behaviors expected of all members.
- Maintain the self-confidence and self-esteem of others.
- Demonstrate respect for all members and their opinions.
- Encourage all members to participate fully.
- Focus on the situation, issue or behavior, not on the person.

148 Stage Five – Synthesis and Formulation of Recommendations

- Confront issues with others directly.
- Take initiative to make things better.
- Keep confidences.
- Maintain constructive relationships.
- Keep commitments.
- Admit mistakes.

The importance of establishing a clear and inspiring shared purpose, a common vision, accompanying goals, and expectations for performance has received a great deal of attention in recent years. This category of leadership skills is another essential area that requires deliberate attention in effectively leading from a distance. This leadership skill requires taking initiative to ensure all members are involved in creating or understanding the purpose and vision of the group or a specific project. It is important for all members to have sufficient opportunity to voice their respective opinions.

This full involvement in creating a shared purpose or common vision serves as a foundation for unified project team commitment. When coupled with clear expectations for contributions and measurable performance, this combination of elements can be an effective driving force for self-discipline and motivation. Combined with a sense of community, there can be a reduced need for continuous monitoring and control mechanisms in order to achieve team goals. This category can become one of the effective secrets for shifting from control to member self-management. Day-to-day, moment-to-moment, or transaction-to-transaction, the members can self-coach on the organization's vision, the project team's vision, its sense of purpose, specific goals, and expectations for contribution. This common vision is essential for virtual project teams that are purposefully undertaking highly creative or innovative approaches. The observable leadership behaviors for this category include the following:

- Share information about the organization's mission, vision, strategies, and goals.
- Clarify the rationale and intent of strategies and goals.
- Provide clear expectations for contributions and measurable results.
- Ensure members are involved in decisions that affect their work.
- Seek ideas and opinions from all members.
- Ensure consideration of customer needs when planning work.
- Use the organization's core values to guide the members' planning, decisions, and actions.
- Promote creativity and innovation in undertaking new goals or opportunities.
- Help members develop positive approaches to the needs of the organization.
- Challenge assumptions that may inhibit progress.
- Demonstrate flexibility in adapting to changes in goals and expectations.

Leading by example with a focus on visible, measurable results is a natural extension of the previous category. The clear and inspiring shared purpose, vision, and resulting project team's goals and expectations become targets for establishing individual and team contributions.

The important distinction for virtual project teams is the need to make out-of-sight contributions as visible as possible. Individual members need to know how their roles and tasks directly contribute to achieving group and organizational goals. They need to understand how customer needs are met by their contributions. On a day-to-day basis, they need to self-direct and self-discipline their work on clear priorities. They need to deliver visible, measurable outputs, transactions, or next steps in key processes. Preferably, they are able to self-track their contributions and measurable progress toward specific goals.

This often means the project team needs to ponder the critical path for achieving a specific goal. Deliberate attention is focused on how each member contributes content and/or key process transactions each step of the way. Particular attention is paid to the interdependencies among members' contributions. There are detailed discussions about what information or output needs to be delivered by when and in what condition in order for the next member to take action. One way to describe this activity is managing intersections of mutual accountability or handoffs.

In adopting this approach for day-to-day activity, group members engage in goal-directed self-discipline for completing essential tasks and making visible, measurable contributions to results. In essence, the locus for control subtly shifts from the traditional manager role to group members. Personal responsibility and ownership for results set in; and members tend to deliver more energy, creativity and innovation, and greater achievement.

For example, a virtual project team with a variety of signature skills was brought together for the first time to turn around a disappointing situation with a major customer. Each member needed a clear understanding of performance expectations and how their respective, visible contributions fit into a complex, critical path of product development activity. The project team leader decided to set even more aggressive schedules to renew customer confidence and provided more frequent opportunities for the team to come together electronically with the customer to demonstrate progress. The actions were akin to joint innovation to restore the business relationship while meeting product requirements.

In this category of effective leadership, each opportunity for communication on an individual or project team basis includes clear focus on the visible, measurable contributions that produce high-impact results. Effective leaders inspire members to reach and exceed performance expectations. They understand the capabilities required for such achievement and ensure all members have the necessary skills and knowledge. They also ensure team members have the equipment and tools to make their critical contributions.

150 Stage Five – Synthesis and Formulation of Recommendations

Effective leading from a distance also means asking the right questions, staying alert for early coaching opportunities, providing constructive feedback, and reinforcing contributions. The observable leadership behaviors for this category include the following:

- Link work contributions to the organization's goals.
- Ensure all members know how their contributions affect customers.
- Help all members understand their roles and responsibilities.
- Emphasize identifying visible contributions and setting verifiable goals.
- Track contributions and measurable progress on goals.
- Ensure members complete appropriate planning to achieve results.
- Inspire members to reach or exceed expectations for performance and results.
- Emphasize the need for goal-directed self-discipline in completing daily work.
- Use performance contributions and results to guide communications and agendas.
- Seek opportunities to recognize members' contributions to results.

The fifth category involves coordinating and collaborating across boundaries. This includes extending the same level of mutual trust and respect, teamwork and collaboration, and focus on visible contributions that appears within your own project team to other individuals or groups within your organization, as well as customers and suppliers. This set of behaviors includes smooth coordination of a key process or a project that may cross a number of natural organizational boundaries. Information or technical assistance outside the project team's capabilities may be needed.

While coordination and collaboration across boundaries can be uncomfortable or difficult in the traditional organizational structure, it magnifies when complicated by distance. In many cases, a project team leader needs to remove protective firewalls that have been constructed at those boundaries. There also is often a need to diagnose and handle differences, challenge assumptions, and defuse the potential for conflict.

The observable behaviors which are effective in coordinating and collaborating across boundaries are shown below:

- Seek ways to build teamwork and collaboration across groups and functions.
- Establish mutual involvement in situations that cross organizational boundaries.
- Link the need for coordination and collaboration to the needs of the customer and the organization.
- Help members identify opportunities for improvement in projects and processes that cross organizational boundaries.

Stage Five – Synthesis and Formulation of Recommendations **151**

- Help members plan, coordinate and implement projects and processes across boundaries.
- Help members diagnose and solve problems.
- Help members track progress in projects and processes across boundaries.
- Promote information sharing in situations of mutual interest.
- Ask for specific support you will need and what you will do in return.
- Challenge unnecessary barriers to collaboration across boundaries.
- Help members move constructively from conflict to collaboration.

In summary, research and best practices reveal that the five categories of effective leadership skills for virtual project teams serve as a sound basis for achieving business and technical results, while simultaneously meeting team member needs.

The researcher who learns that geographic dispersion and potential leadership skills may be included within the scope of inquiry of a Rapid Due Diligence diagnostic process may choose to use an assessment tool to determine the degree of effective application of the behaviors from this research as part of the on-site discovery. Responses to the assessment tool may identify explicit opportunities for improvement. The tool appears in Table 7.2.

TABLE 7.2 Discovery Tool: Leadership from a Distance

Instructions: Put an "X" in one category for each statement.

	Almost Never	Seldom	Sometimes	Usually	Almost Always
Segment One: Communicating Effectively and Using Technology that Fits the Situation Do you make a conscious effort to:					
1. Model the organization's values and members' ground rules in all communications.					
2. Choose a method of communications that best fits the mutual needs of members and the situation.					
3. Apply a communications technology that best fits the needs of the situation.					
4. Help all members apply available technology for communication with confidence.					
5. Formulate specific objectives and an organized delivery plan for communications.					
6. Link messages to the members' shared purpose, goals, and performance contributions to results.					

(Continued)

7. Encourage all members in a conversation to participate fully.
8. Engage in proactive listening.
9. Verify understanding of the message and expectations for action.
10. Guide communications to achieve a positive and constructive outcome.
11. Conduct coaching and feedback in ways that convey respect and support.

	Almost Never	Seldom	Sometimes	Usually	Almost Always

Segment Two: Building Community among Team Members, Based on Mutual Trust, Respect, Fairness and Affiliation
Do you make a conscious effort to:

1. Model the behaviors expected of all members.
2. Maintain the self-confidence and self-esteem of others.
3. Demonstrate respect for all members and their opinions.
4. Encourage all members to participate fully.
5. Focus on the situation, issue, or behavior, not on the person.
6. Confront issues with others directly.
7. Take initiative to make things better.
8. Keep confidences.
9. Maintain constructive relationships.
10. Keep commitments.
11. Admit mistakes.

	Almost Never	Seldom	Sometimes	Usually	Almost Always

Segment Three: Establishing a Clear and Inspiring Shared Purpose, Vision, Goals, and Expectations
Do you make a conscious effort to:

1. Share information about the organization's mission, vision, strategies, and goals.
2. Clarify the rationale and intent of strategies and goals.
3. Provide clear expectations for contributions and measurable results.

4. Ensure that members are involved in decisions that affect their work.
5. Seek ideas and opinions from all members.
6. Ensure consideration for the needs of customers in planning work.
7. Use the organization's core values to guide the members' planning, decisions, and actions.
8. Promote creativity and innovation in undertaking new goals or opportunities.
9. Help members develop positive approaches to the needs of the organization.
10. Challenge assumptions that may inhibit progress.
11. Demonstrate flexibility in adapting to changes in goals and expectations.

	Almost Never	Seldom	Sometimes	Usually	Almost Always

Segment Four: Leading by Example with a Focus on Visible, Measurable Results

Do you make a conscious effort to:

1. Link work contributions to the organization's goals.
2. Ensure all members know how their contributions affect customers.
3. Help all members understand their roles and responsibilities.
4. Help members identify work priorities that support the organization's goals.
5. Emphasize identifying visible contributions and setting verifiable goals.
6. Track contributions and measurable progress on goals.
7. Ensure members complete appropriate planning to achieve results.
8. Inspire members to reach or exceed expectations for performance and results.
9. Emphasize the need for goal-directed, self-discipline in completing daily work.

(Continued)

154 Stage Five – Synthesis and Formulation of Recommendations

10. Use performance contributions and results to guide communications and agendas.
11. Seek opportunities to recognize members' contributions to results.

	Almost Never	Seldom	Sometimes	Usually	Almost Always

Segment Five: Coordinating and Collaborating across Organizational Boundaries
Do you make a conscious effort to:

1. Seek ways to build teamwork and collaboration across groups and functions.
2. Establish mutual involvement in situations that cross organizational boundaries.
3. Link the need for coordination and collaboration to the needs of the customer and organization.
4. Help members identify opportunities for improvement in projects and processes that cross organizational boundaries.
5. Help members plan, coordinate, and implement projects and processes across boundaries.
6. Help members diagnose and solve problems.
7. Help members track progress in projects and processes across boundaries.
8. Promote sharing of information in situations of mutual interest.
9. Ask for specific support you will need and what you will do in return.
10. Challenge unnecessary barriers to collaboration across boundaries.
11. Help members constructively move from conflict to collaboration.

Opportunities for New or Unusual Strategies

During this fifth stage of the Rapid Due Diligence diagnostic method, the researcher may recognize cues that portend potential opportunities for decision-makers to consider new or unusual strategies. For example, in reflection upon the preparatory investigation information found within management discussion and analysis segments in annual reporting documents, the examination of market and competitive

Stage Five – Synthesis and Formulation of Recommendations **155**

forces, technological capabilities, risk areas, and mitigation processes, the researcher may uncover specific cues which are later addressed in on-site discovery. Developing those initial, tentative cues within the fields of inquiry deployed in interviews and interactive panel interview discussions can yield additional observations and open speculation about potential strategies that can create new markets, products, or organizational schemes to address either markets or products.

As the researcher synthesizes any such cues and observations with the organization's strategic dimensions, opportunities or potential ideas for break-out, disruptive innovation, co-opting, or cooperation strategies may begin to emerge.[2] These insights most often appear in the examination and comparison of the organization's mission, vision, business model, Critical Knowledge Areas©, customer value proposition, and competitive distinctions, together with the discovery cues.

The researcher can intentionally seek out such opportunities by applying a series of speculative questions to the elements of the business model, in particular. Sample questions may include the following:

- What could be the potential effect of a radical, disruptive innovation that creates a new business model, market, or a new customer value proposition?
- What disruptive or displacement innovations could this organization produce, based on its Critical Knowledge Areas©, such as unique technology applications, market or customer knowledge, product development, and production capabilities?
- How could this organization engage digital disruption to reframe the competitive arena from either an offensive or defensive posture?
- How could this organization engage in unexpected competitive incursions on an adjacent market space?
- What outside resources could be assimilated to engage in a co-option, not necessarily merger or acquisition, strategy that yields greater capability or an opening for disruptive innovation?
- Reflecting on the existing functional residence of Critical Knowledge Areas© within different segments of the organization, what opportunities for intentional knowledge sharing and cooperative competition or intra-organizational coopetition can be realized?
- What outside organizations deploy Critical Knowledge Areas© that could be effectively enjoined with this organization's capabilities to explore opportunities for greater value creation and disruptive innovation?
- How could this organization engage disintermediation as a means of redefining the value chain, the supply side structure, and attendant costs?
- How could this organization enlist hyperscaled information platforms as the basis for market opportunities or barriers?
- How would any of these opportunities change any of the elements of the organization's business model, especially the market structure, customer value proposition, distribution channels, cost structure, or revenue and value streams?

156 Stage Five – Synthesis and Formulation of Recommendations

Dependent upon the answers to such questions, the researcher may choose to draft causal loop diagrams or stock and flow maps, chart potential outcomes within the customer choice analytics, define unique characteristics of new distribution channels and business development processes, or model changes in key metrics or critical ratios.

The researcher may also choose to formulate these questions and answers into either offensive or defensive strategies. The organization may take the overt action to exercise any of these strategic moves from an offensive strategy perspective or prepare to defend itself from similar moves by other organizations.

Applying a Behavioral Economics Perspective

Reflecting on behavioral economics as maximizing behavior in the presence of scarce resources, competing ends, and stable preferences, the researcher may also seek patterns of behavior which mimic certain behavioral economic principles.[3]

For example, the behavioral economics approach to the optimal or rational accumulation of costly information suggests greater investment in securing information when undertaking significant decisions. The researcher can observe the degree to which organizational decision-makers, whether governed by mental models or intentional formal decision rules, seek to accumulate information in preparation for strategic decision-making. Rational accumulation suggests gathering more explicit information to the point where the decision-makers can maximize the utility of that investment. The same principle applies in investigating the opportunity costs of decisions not taken.

An assumption is that the decision-makers are engaging in rational behavior by consistently seeking to maximize a well-ordered function such as utility or profitability. The decision-makers may hold assumptions about market rationality or irrationality in response to its offering of products and services, for example, purposes of utility or preferences driven by impulse satisfaction or inertia. The same principles apply to not-for-profit organizations and government units. Where there are sets of opportunity and limited resources, the decision rules will reflect economic theory, whether rational or irrational.

In those cases where the researcher finds evidence of market or customers responses that differ substantially and consistently over time from the predictions of the organization, a recommendation may be in order to examine greater amounts of empirical evidence with the aim to understand the underlying behavioral economics and driving forces of the customers' choices. These more extensive analytics may have a significant influence on the decision rules for future decision-making and may require changes to the business model, the customer value proposition, and descriptive points of competitive distinctions.

Examining the Organization's Decision Analysis Process

Another area of examination in this synthesis stage of the Rapid Due Diligence diagnostic method is the decision analysis performed within the organization's

Stage Five – Synthesis and Formulation of Recommendations **157**

decision-making processes, recognizing that decision analysis is a methodology with probabilistic frameworks for facilitating a logical investigation of information to reach decisions. While normative decision analysis describes how organizations should make decisions, there is also descriptive analysis which explains how decision-makers actually go about the process. The researcher is seeking cues of the descriptive analysis as the basis for identifying opportunities for improvement at the desirable discipline of normative analysis level.

Within the organization's decision analysis model or cycle, the researcher seeks to clarify which factors, likely including all of the classic strategic dimensions, are considered of value. The researcher learns how the decision-makers structure their approach to decision-making, how they clarify and crystallize the business issues and decisions to be secured, how they acquire information of each type and depth, how they engage in the evaluation of information, how they apply decision rules to develop alternatives, and how they come to agreement on their preferred course of action.

Depending upon the degree of complexity, uncertainty, and ambiguity of the issue, the organization may choose to deploy a favored set of tools to engage, for example, in sensitivity analysis, influence charting, causal or consequence loop diagramming, decision trees, tornado diagrams, multiple-point comparative radar charting, or staging sets of sequential decisions. While many of these analysis techniques may be used with regularity, the researcher needs to detect the pattern of how the decision-makers actually engage the findings to arrive at decisions. The critical questions will include at least the following:

- To what degree do the decision-makers widen their view beyond event-driven situations to broader system dynamics?
- How well are decision rules and assumptions formed and on what basis?
- What criteria are consistently used to filter information and guide the decision-making process?
- How well are analytical tools used in the decision analysis process? Are the findings interpreted accurately and completely?
- What characteristics or habits of evaluation and making choices are practiced by either specific individuals or the decision-making group?
  - o Mental models
  - o Functional expertise
  - o Life experience
  - o Conscious or unconscious biases
  - o Economic rationality or irrationality
  - o Intuitive types
  - o Emotional propensity
  - o Tolerance for risk
  - o Need for higher levels of certainty
  - o Desire for fact-based or evidence-based data
- How does the decision analysis process look differently for various types of situations or decisions?

158 Stage Five – Synthesis and Formulation of Recommendations

- Who plays the typical roles in the decision-making process?
  - o Decision-maker with the responsibility of the decision
  - o Member who carries accountability for results
  - o Contributor or consultant to the decision-making process
  - o Others who need to be informed about the deliberation and decision
- How do the decision-makers engage in any probability factoring?
- What types of evidence tend to hold more sway with the decision-makers?
- How do the decision-makers engage in conversation to complete the decision analysis and arrive at a course of strategic action?

Responses and insights to at least these questions are important to the researcher for a number of reasons. The descriptive reality of the decision analysis process may have a number of opportunities for improvement in the quality of the process and the decision choices. The researcher may choose to pinpoint specific changes to bring the actual decision analysis process closer to a constructive, normative level.

The researcher also benefits from this deeper level of understanding as the Rapid Due Diligence diagnostic process moves through synthesis to preparing conclusions, formulating recommendations, and delivering the results to the decision-making group. To the degree possible and desirable, the researcher will want to frame the conclusions and recommendations in a way that best appeals to the natural, descriptive approach already in use by the decision-makers. The researcher may also choose to shape the conclusions, recommendations, and delivery process to demonstrate the contrast and any significant differences in the actual decision analysis process from the normative approach.

With the application of these analysis and synthesis techniques, the researcher has been testing degrees of alignment between the stated strategy and the reality of its execution, pinpointing specific misalignments, uncovering granular details within market and customer analytics that reveal how to trigger greater loyalty and revenue streams, identifying behaviors, actions, decision rules, policies, processes, or practices that interfere with intended results, and potentially discovering hidden opportunities for specific improvements in the stated strategy, the organization's execution, and decision-making process. With all of these findings at hand, the researcher is now at the step for preparing observations and conclusions about the evidence set.

Preparing Observations and Conclusions

Depending upon the mass of data gathered from the entire process, the amount of coding and categorization required, the complexity of the central issue, the competence and sophistication of the researcher, and the established timeline, the observations and conclusions from the findings will emerge with varying degrees of ease. An experienced researcher will begin to identify items of meaning from the beginning of the Rapid Due Diligence data collection. These items

Stage Five – Synthesis and Formulation of Recommendations **159**

may include recognition of regularities or irregularities, specific recurring patterns, causal flows and relationships, explanations, alignments, or misalignments. A competent researcher will make notes of such items while maintaining an open mind to new findings as the data collection progresses.

As those observations and conclusions become manifest, the researcher needs to conduct additional tests to affirm the sturdiness or plausibility of those meanings. This may require further comparison with system dynamics, business models, customer analytics, or behavioral and values constructs.

The researcher can choose either an inductive or deductive approach to building causal networks. Within the inductive or generative approach, the researcher discovers recurring themes, patterns, and relationships progressively throughout the Rapid Due Diligence data collection process. The linkages naturally emerge. With the deductive or enumerative approach, the researcher begins the Rapid Due Diligence process with some orienting constructs or propositions, and then matches findings to that front-end concept. The inductive researcher ends up with a causal network while the deductive researcher begins with one.

The inductive researcher tends to focus on a broader domain of data and, while dealing with a potentially more massive data set, tends to be open to more unlikely or unexpected insights. The deductive researcher, by contrast, will deliberately seek out relevant data and must apply personal discipline to ensure that unexpected findings are not ignored.

In preparing observations and conclusions about the full set of evidence, the researcher commences to assemble a list of key observations and principal themes that have emerged from any of the earlier stages and steps. These observations include summaries of qualitative commentary and any quantitative data that relate to the business issue under review. The commentary is accompanied by either a tally of frequency or a percentage of respondents without acknowledgment of individual identity. The themes are derived from analysis of interviews, panel discussions, and online survey responses to open-ended questions. An example of a display of principal themes appears in Table 7.3.

Box 7.3 includes an example of the written assembly of observations for this same organization.

In the case of this Rapid Due Diligence diagnostic process, the researcher completed an additional review of external research (see Box 7.4) to provide relevant comparative data that would be of keen interest to the owner of the business issue and other key decision-makers. Citations were provided separately in the accompanying resource bibliography in the final written report.

Upon completion of the assembly of observations, the researcher can choose either the deductive or inductive approach, as noted earlier in this chapter, to draw meaning from these observations and begin to form conclusions.

Given the intent of the Rapid Due Diligence diagnostic method to discover opportunities for a Triple Win, the researcher seeks to form conclusions that produce positive outcomes for the organization, its customers, and employees.

160 Stage Five – Synthesis and Formulation of Recommendations

TABLE 7.3 Principal Themes from Commentary

Several principal themes emerged from the commentary and findings. The eight themes that appeared with the greatest prevalence are shown in the table below in descending order with the number of comments, percent of respondents, and aggregate frequency of mention.

Principal Themes	Number of Categorized Comments	Percent of Categorized Comments	Aggregate Frequency	Percent of Total Applicable Comments
Performance management to make mission	26	7.0	392	17.0
Better work-life balance and stress reduction	23	6.2	334	14.8
Change capability and buy-in	15	4.1	229	10.1
Communications	14	3.8	68	3.0
Adjustment from operations	13	3.5	49	2.7
Accountability	8	2.2	108	4.8
Selection of people for better fit with the role	8	2.2	59	2.6
Demonstrating trust and respect	7	1.9	40	1.8

BOX 7.3 SAMPLE OF PRELIMINARY OBSERVATIONS

Examining the content and frequency of comments within the findings, the following observations have surfaced that relate to the business issue under review at a military organization.

- Most respondents indicated a desire for improving the culture and experiences for both recruiters and families.
- Recruiters enjoy the gratification of helping build the force, helping people choose a military career, and see people's lives change.
  - o Twelve percent of participants referenced the opportunity to help people change their lives.
  - o Ten percent noted the gratification of helping people choose a military career.
  - o Ten percent also noted recruiting is the best thing an experienced soldier can do to help build the force.

Stage Five – Synthesis and Formulation of Recommendations **161**

- In joining the military recruiting organization, soldiers are seeking stability and a break from deployment and repetitive rotations.
  - o Thirty-four percent of participants referenced this primary decision criterion, whether selected or volunteering.
  - o Fifteen percent indicated they want to be at home with the family each night.
  - o Nine percent want the ability to be assigned to a desirable location, often near home.
- Today, this organization does not enjoy a reputation as being a desirable place for soldiers to serve. The constant attention and pressure to making the mission numbers frequently requires long working hours and produces significant stress for recruiters and their families.
  - o Thirty percent of participants responded about the sole focus on production and the pressure to make numbers every month.
  - o Thirty percent also referenced micromanagement to achieve mission.
  - o Twenty-six percent cited constant long hours and the resulting stress and burn-out.
  - o Twenty-three percent spoke about the need for better work-life balance for recruiters and families, while twelve percent requested time for important family events, and ten percent requested more predictability with work schedules.

BOX 7.4 EXTERNAL RESEARCH COMPARISON

There is a host of external research related to high-performing organizations which conduct recruiting, selling, or influencing behavioral activities that is worthy of consideration. These include leadership or managerial skill sets, performance management practices, and selection and development policies that can be critical to improving productivity, efficiency, and effectiveness, similar to the goal of creating more compelling interactions with targeted audiences to produce more commitments.

- People who receive at least three hours of direct coaching per month perform fifteen to seventeen percent better than their peers.
- The combination of training and coaching improves return on investment four-fold.
- Systematic interventions (training, coaching, and reinforcement) focused on performance-based human resource development deliver a two to eight times return on investment within the first year.
- Successful organizations formally allocate approximately forty percent of their managers' time to coaching and mentoring people.

(Continued)

- While conventional wisdom suggests coaching should be focused on star performers or poor performers, research shows that greater leverage or lift occurs when coaching is targeted at the middle core. Good coaching drives people to work harder and stay with the organization. Poor coaching demoralizes people and stimulates defection or, at best, compliant and reluctant performance.
- Superior people who have been hired and trained using a competency-based focus can be expected to produce 123 percent more than average people.
- Highly effective organizations on average provide ongoing training as follows: thirty percent ongoing and on-the-job coaching; twenty-nine percent in class; fourteen percent each online and through seminars or workshops; and thirteen percent through external training groups.
- Training without systematic coaching wastes eighty-seven cents of every training dollar.
- Coaching from a manager inside the organization has the greatest impact on performance, more so than peer mentors or others outside the organization.
- Of the twenty-two top processes and systems that drive the highest level of impact in an organization, coaching yields the greatest set of results.
- People managed in a contingent-reward style (continuing monitoring and modification of behaviors) have greater levels of job satisfaction, satisfaction with manager, and commitment, than those who are managed by exception (intervention only when goals are missed).
- People in recruiting or sales positions most often look for the following sources of job satisfaction:
    o Challenging and varied tasks
    o Increased involvement
    o Role clarity
    o Recognition and approval
    o Feedback and coaching
    o Engaged supervision
    o Shared organizational values
    o Training to build skills
    o Higher pay
- Employees want leaders they can trust, whose humanity shines through, who demonstrate courage, step up in difficult moments, and can confidently make risky decisions.
- Organizations that use employee-involvement practices and build collaborative environments have twenty percent higher return on investment in assets.
    o Nineteen percent (nearly one in five) employees declare themselves to be disengaged or marking time on the job.

> o Excellence in all four of the following practices contributed to a ninety percent chance of being an outperforming organization in a ten-year study.
> o Strategy: Devise and maintain a clearly stated, focused strategy.
> o Execution: Develop and maintain flawless operational execution.
> o Culture: Develop and maintain a performance-oriented culture.
> o Structure: Build and maintain a fast, flexible, flat organization.

Ideally, the achievement of the representative value propositions of each segment produces a convergent Triple Win (see Figure 7.2). This means the researcher engages the findings, observations, and framework of strategic dimensions to secure valid conclusions that close any type of gaps between the current reality and the desired future state of the value propositions for all three perspectives.

The researcher prepares conclusions as specific statements of gaps or opportunities from at least the following conditions emerging from the observations and sources of evidence.

- Incomplete or misaligned strategic dimensions
- Weak valuations of critical ratios
- Metrics that do not bring meaning or fulfillment to the mission
- Metrics that take the organization off track
- Disconnected links within the organization's economic value-producing stream
- New insights into customer choice analytics and triggering decision points
- Inadequate performance management systems that do not fully support the strategy
- Failure to commit sufficient and timely resources to the strategy
- Insufficient organizational engagement to make necessary changes
- Failure to identify, leverage, protect, or appropriately propagate Critical Knowledge Areas©

FIGURE 7.2 The Triple Win.

164 Stage Five – Synthesis and Formulation of Recommendations

- Incomplete attention to any aspects of the Integrated Strategic Human Capital Alignment Framework
- Undervaluing the importance of cultural fit to new organizational combinations
- Misalignment or inconsistency among the elements of the organization's business model
- Incompatible business development and customer buying processes and requirements
- Stifling practices that inhibit innovation
- Unfinished plans or contradictory positions in pursuing quality, efficiency, or effectiveness improvement initiatives
- Unintended or exacerbating consequences uncovered in causal loop diagrams
- Application of unhelpful or irrational mental models, decision rules, assumptions, or decision analysis habits
- Chronic self-inducted extreme oscillations and amplifications in key processes
- Unorganized or misfit application of unique differences and needs across geographically dispersed organizations
- Failure to seize opportunities for break-out, disruptive innovation, co-opting, or cooperation strategies

In situations where the researcher has sufficient quantitative data to fit the organization's preferred critical ratios and other measures used to gauge progress, this is the time to prepare any estimates of the potential economic impact supporting the conclusions. The researcher is advised to use data, ratios, and analytical formulas with which the organization is already familiar and accepts as valid. If other types of calculations or estimates are introduced, the researcher needs to support those conclusions with credible, verifiable proof sources that can be readily accepted by decision-makers. References to formal or longitudinal research conducted by unbiased resources such as institutional research organizations are preferable.

In some cases, the nature of the conclusions can only be supported by comparative results achieved in organizations which have dealt with similar circumstances and taken specific remedial actions. Examples of such comparative results are listed below.

- Loyalty drivers
  - o Relationship (twenty-five percent)
  - o Product/service differentiation (twenty-five percent)
  - o Customer experience (twenty-three percent)
  - o Image (twenty-two percent)
  - o Price (five percent)

Stage Five – Synthesis and Formulation of Recommendations **165**

- Consumer service expectations
  - o Elevated year-over-year expectations
  - o Poor service as a primary reason for switching
  - o Break-out strategy
    - o Know your customers and what they value most.
    - o Make improvements they will value and notice.
- Outside-in approach to customers
  - o Organizations are still inside-out (seventy-five to eighty percent).
  - o Manage all customer touch points.
  - o Focus on top customer service processes.
- Strategy execution
  - o Strategy potential achieved (sixty-three percent)
  - o Value lost due to ineffective people management issues (thirty-seven percent)
    - o Ineffective performance management and coaching
    - o Unavailable, capable resources
    - o Failure to engage required changes
- Sales managerial skills critical to productivity and effectiveness
  - o Salespeople who get more than three hours of coaching per month perform fifteen to seventeen percent better.
  - o Training plus coaching multiplies return on investment by four times.
  - o Systemic training, coaching, and reinforcement deliver two to eight times the return on investment within the first year.
  - o Focus coaching on the middle core of the organization for greatest lift.
  - o Sales training without systematic coaching wastes eighty-seven cents of every dollar invested.
  - o Coaching yields the greatest impact of the top twenty-two development processes.
  - o Coaching from the manager has more impact than peer mentoring.
  - o Turnover can be reduced through effective training.
  - o Best ways to drive skill application
    - o Sales manager communications before any training
    - o Coaching and reinforcement after training

In all cases, the researcher needs to apply evidence-based knowledge to craft any estimates for potential impact.

Preparing Recommendations for Action

Upon completion of the conclusions, the researcher commences the formulation of specific recommendations for action. Considering the situation, all forms of

166 Stage Five – Synthesis and Formulation of Recommendations

evidence, the observations, and conclusions, the researcher needs to determine the overarching best opportunity to make a significant difference and measurable progress in capitalizing upon any gaps or new opportunities. This means identifying the highest level opportunity with the furthest practical reach and determining which course to take to chart a path between the current reality and the promise of the best opportunity.

Given the nature of the original business issue under review in the Rapid Due Diligence diagnostic method, a hierarchy or sequence of recommendations will flow from the conclusions. The recommendations include specific action statements that stitch together a comprehensive, cohesive set of actions to produce remedies for the principal gaps or opportunities embodied in the conclusions. These recommendations typically begin with overarching statements about the strategy under review and how it can be refined or redirected to achieve the targeted results. From this overarching statement, the researcher constructs a series of actions embracing the strategic dimensions. In sequence, the actions need to address characteristics or valuations that improve the results and conditions for the organization, its customers, and employees.

As these recommendations take shape in a cascading outline, the researcher completes the supporting sets of tasks and responsibilities by role to achieve the targeted outcomes. Where possible, the recommendations insert timelines that are naturally complementary to the business cycle of the organization. When the acquisition of any level of skills, knowledge, abilities, or shift in motivation is required, the researcher incorporates these elements of competency, capability, or capacity to support the actions and tasks.

In the example shown in Table 7.4, the organizational key contact had requested a compact reporting format to set forth three progressively more intensive options for pursuing the recommended actions for a training and development remedy to an organization-wide set of efficiency and quality issues. The table summarizes the following elements for each option:

- Business focus
- Implementation planning on the strategic and tactical levels
- Communications planning
- Training process and participants
- Reinforcement techniques
- Progress evaluation
- Expected impact
- Comparative advantages and disadvantages of each option

This summary document accompanied the more comprehensive written report with the full supporting detail.

TABLE 7.4 Implementation Options

	Minimum	Standard	Aggressive
Business Focus	• Effectiveness of people in new roles • Initial identification and development of potential future leaders • Instill and sustain Leadership Competencies and cultural transformation • Targeted Lean work on selected, high-impact areas of the Vehicle Value Stream	• Effectiveness of people in new roles • Identification and development of potential future leaders • Instill and sustain Leadership Competencies and cultural transformation • Targeted Lean work on all projects for the Vehicle Value Stream • Non-manufacturing/Support Areas	• Effectiveness of people in new roles • Identification and development of potential future leaders • Instill and sustain Leadership Competencies and cultural transformation • Teaming to training just-in-time for all projects in all work areas. • Non-Manufacturing/Support Areas
Implementation Planning Strategic Level	• A checklist will be provided outlining decisions to be made and actions to be taken by the senior team to assure the success of all training activities.	• Face to face session with the senior leadership team to identify and address key components of a successful training rollout • Included in the output is a comprehensive communications plan that clarifies content of all senior leader communications as well as identifies who will deliver various messages. • Critical components of the communications plan include clarity around purpose of the various training activities, how each component integrates with overall objectives and accountabilities attached to training outcomes.	• Face to face session with the senior leadership team to identify and address key components of a successful training rollout • Included in the output is a comprehensive communications plan that clarifies content of all senior leader communications as well as identify who will deliver various messages. • Critical components of the communications plan include clarity around purpose of the various training activities, how each component integrates with overall objectives and accountabilities attached to training outcomes.

(Continued)

	Minimum	Standard	Aggressive
Implementation Planning Tactical Level	• Continued support for the implementation team • Support begins with development of an effective training rollout schedule, considering the work and production schedules. • Included are comprehensive logistics discussions and assignments, as well as planning all facets of training class management. Plans include all actions to take to assure maximum participation in each class. Also included will be arrangements for opening and/or closing speakers for each class. These speakers lend credibility and importance to the Leadership Competencies and Team training content.	• Decisions will be made about the appropriate vehicles for evaluating the effectiveness of the training. • Continued support for the implementation team • Support begins with development of an effective training rollout schedule, considering the work and production schedules. • Included are comprehensive logistics discussions and assignments, as well as planning all facets of training class management. Plans include all actions to take to assure maximum participation in each class. Also included will be arrangements for opening and/or closing speakers for each class. These speakers lend credibility and importance to the Leadership Competencies and Team training content. • Additional support is available upon request.	• Decisions will be made about the appropriate vehicles for evaluating the effectiveness of the training. • Continued support for the implementation team • Support begins with development of an effective training rollout schedule, considering the work and production schedules. • Included are comprehensive logistics discussions and assignments, as well as planning all facets of training class management. Plans include all actions to take to assure maximum participation in each class. Also included will be arrangements for opening and/or closing speakers for each class. These speakers lend credibility and importance to the Leadership Competencies and Team training content. • Additional support is available upon request.

| Communications Planning Tactical Level | • Prepare and facilitate a conference call that will discuss all facets of an effective communications plan whose goal is to create maximum receptivity for the training. Additionally an effective communications plan provides support for training participants as they develop their skills and integrate the Leadership Competencies and Team tools into their work life. | • On site meeting with Implementation Team including: Training Manager, Administration Manager, Communications Specialist, representatives from the population to be trained
• Outcome: comprehensive plan to create messages that facilitate understanding about the purpose of each program and how it fits with the overall mission.
• Outcome: develop messages that maintain interest in the training for those not yet scheduled for training
• Outcome: create plan for multiple communications that support and reinforce the Leadership Competencies, change management and team skills
• Outcome: support mid- levels of management and supervision by providing specific talking points that can be used in one on one or small group meetings that will demonstrate support for the training and accountability for the manager and participant | • On site meeting with Implementation Team including: Training Manager, Administration Manager, Communications Specialist, representatives from the population to be trained
• Outcome: comprehensive plan to create messages that facilitate understanding about the purpose of each program and how it fits with the overall mission.
• Outcome: develop messages that maintain interest in the training for those not yet scheduled for training
• Outcome: create plan for multiple communications that support and reinforce the Leadership Competencies, change management and team skills
• Outcome: support mid levels of management and supervision by providing specific talking points that can be used in one on one or small group meetings that will demonstrate support for the training and accountability for the manager and participant |

(Continued)

	Minimum	Standard	Aggressive
Training: Identification and Number of Participants	**Leadership Competencies Foundation** • Senior leaders – quarterly review and coaching • Leadership Competencies – 5 day class – 4 • Power Training (2 days) – 1 class – 30 participants • Turbo training 9 (1 day) – 9 classes – 3 classes delivered every two months – 400 participants **Just-in-time** • Teaming training (2 days) – 8 teams per month/2 classes – 60 participants per month • Leading Change (1 day) – 1 class – 30 participants	**Leadership Competencies Foundation** • Senior leaders – quarterly review and coaching • Leadership Competencies – 5 day class – 4 • Power Training (2 days) – 1 class – 30 participants • Turbo training (1 day) – 9 classes – 3 classes delivered every two months – 400 participants **Just-in-time** • Teaming Training (2 days) – 12 teams per month/3 classes – 90 participants per month • Leading Change (1 day) – 1 class – 30 participants	**Leadership Competencies Foundation** • Senior leaders – quarterly review and coaching • Leadership Competencies – 5 day class – 4 • Power Training (2 days) – 1 class – 30 participants • Turbo training (1 day) – 9 classes – 3 classes delivered every two months – 400 participants **Just-in-time** • Teaming Training (2 days)– 20 teams per month/5 classes – 150 participants per month • Leading Change (1 day) – 1 class – 30 participants
Training: Identification and Number of Participants	**Leadership Competencies Foundation** • Turbo training – 9 classes – 3 classes delivered every two months – 400 participants • Power Training – TBD • Senior leaders – quarterly review and coaching	**Leadership Competencies Foundation** • Turbo Training – 9 classes – 3 classes delivered every other month – 400 participants • Power Training – TBD • Senior leaders – quarterly review and coaching	**Leadership Competencies Foundation** • Turbo Training – 9 classes – 6 classes month one and 3 classes month two – 400 participants • Power Training – TBD • Senior leaders – quarterly review and coaching

	Just-in-time	**Just-in-time**	**Just-in-time**
Reinforcement Toolkits and Techniques for Managers, Supervisors, Team Leaders, and Lean Facilitators to Apply on the Job to Assure Use of the Newly Learned Skills	<ul><li>Teaming training – 8 teams per month/2 classes – 60 participants per month</li><li>Leading Change – 1 class – 30 participants</li><li>Organize reinforcement toolkit and coach managers on how to apply tools.</li><li>Provide reinforcement for RIE team members who have been previously been in JIT sessions.</li><li>Day-to-day tools for coaching, giving and receiving feedback, identifying opportunities for improvement and recognition.</li><li>Website Resource Center</li><li>Reminders (quizzes, posters, quotes)</li><li>Scripted 20 minute Leadership Competencies reviews that can be incorporated in team meetings</li><li>Involvement pages for managers (who have attended the 5–day session) to introduce key Leadership Competencies concepts to their work group</li><li>Refreshers to address current and/or critical Leadership Competencies topics.</li></ul>	<ul><li>Teaming Training – 12 teams per month/3 classes – 90 participants per month</li><li>Leading Change – 1 class – 30 participants</li><li>Organize reinforcement toolkit and coach managers on how to apply tools.</li><li>Provide reinforcement for RIE team members who have been previously been in JIT sessions.</li><li>Day-to-day tools for coaching, giving and receiving feedback, identifying opportunities for improvement and recognition.</li><li>Website Resource Center</li><li>Reminders (quizzes, posters, quotes)</li><li>Scripted 20 minute Leadership Competencies reviews that can be incorporated in team meetings</li><li>Involvement pages for managers (who have attended the 5–day session) to introduce key Leadership Competencies concepts to their work group</li><li>Refreshers to address current and/or critical Leadership Competencies topics.</li></ul>	<ul><li>Teaming Training – 20 teams per month/5 classes – 150 participants per month</li><li>Leading Change – 1 class – 30 participants</li><li>Organize reinforcement toolkit and coach managers on how to apply tools.</li><li>Provide reinforcement for RIE team members who have been previously been in JIT sessions.</li><li>Day-to-day tools for coaching, giving and receiving feedback, identifying opportunities for improvement and recognition.</li><li>Website Resource Center</li><li>Reminders (quizzes, posters, quotes)</li><li>Scripted 20 minute Leadership Competencies reviews that can be incorporated in team meetings</li><li>Involvement pages for managers (who have attended the 5–day session) to introduce key Leadership Competencies concepts to their work group</li><li>Refreshers to address current and/or critical Leadership Competencies topics.</li></ul>

(Continued)

	Minimum	Standard	Aggressive
Progress Evaluation	• Set baseline metrics and conduct semi-annual reviews. • Complete After Action Review – Training Experience. • Link to the Production Performance Scorecard • Track Incident Reports and production impact of chokepoints in targeted Vehicle Value Stream areas. • Track number and duration of amber and red categories related to human performance in the Vehicle Value Stream only. • Compare annual Climate Survey results. • Seek proof of concept and simple cost/benefit analysis and qualitative evidence.	• Set baseline metrics and conduct quarterly reviews. • Complete After Action Review – Training Experience. • Link to the Production Performance Scorecard. • Track Incident Reports and production impact of chokepoints in entire Vehicle Value Stream areas. • Track number and duration of amber and red categories related to human performance in the Vehicle Value Stream only. • Compare annual Climate Survey results. • Seek proof of concept with cost/benefit analysis and qualitative evidence. • Prepare and analyze evaluation data, plus facilitate a senior team discussion of results, concerns, and related issues that have emerged at the site or during training.	• Set baseline metrics and conduct detailed quarterly evaluation. • Complete After Action Review – Training Experience. • Link to the Production Performance Scorecard and any other ROI data. • Track Incident Reports and production impact of chokepoints in all Lean project areas. • Track number and duration of amber and red categories related to human performance in all Lean project areas. • Track sustained Lean Six Sigma efficiencies to fixed price analyses and decisions. • Track man-hour metrics attributable to human performance in all Lean project areas. • Conduct pre and post team assessment and Lean Six Sigma impact. • Compare annual Climate Survey results. plus complete targeted segment analysis • Seek proof of concept with more detailed cost/benefit analysis and qualitative evidence.

| Expected Impact | • Reduce Incident Reports and production impact of chokepoints in targeted Vehicle Value Stream areas.
• Reduce number and duration of amber and red categories related to human performance in the Vehicle Value Stream only.
• Produce more and broader ideas for improvements and stronger ROIs from targeted Vehicle Value Stream RIEs.
• Sustain Lean Six Sigma results in specific project areas (compared to mixed variances in FY Lean scorecard to date).
• Accelerate effectiveness of new supervisors.
• Begin to identify potential future leaders. | • Reduce Incident Reports and production impact of chokepoints in all Vehicle Value Stream areas.
• Reduce number and duration of amber and red categories related to human performance in the Vehicle Value Stream only.
• Produce more, broader, and collaborative ideas for improvements and stronger ROIs from all Vehicle Value Stream RIEs.
• Sustain Lean Six Sigma results in specific project areas (compared to mixed variances in FY Lean scorecard to date).
• Accelerate effectiveness of new supervisors and managers.
• Begin to identify and develop potential future leaders. | • Create and rate cultural transformation scorecard.
• Prepare and analyze evaluation data, plus facilitate a senior team discussion of results, concerns, and related issues that have emerged at the site or during training.
• Reduce Incident Reports and production impact of chokepoints in all Lean project areas.
• Reduce number and duration of amber and red categories related to human performance in all Lean project areas.
• Produce more, broader, and collaborative ideas for improvements and stronger ROIs from all Lean project areas.
• Sustain Lean Six Sigma efficiencies in a longer timeframe for favorable fixed price analyses and decisions.
• Improve man-hour metrics attributable to human performance in all Lean project areas.
• Improved post-team assessment and Lean Six Sigma impact. |

(Continued)

	Minimum	Standard	Aggressive
	• Sustain FY Climate Survey results, in spite of influx of new employees/ supervisors.	• Climate Survey results show continuing progress, in spite of influx of new employees/supervisors.	• Sustain Lean Six Sigma results in specific project areas (compared to mixed variances in FY Lean scorecard to date). • Secure proof of concept with more detailed cost/benefit analysis and qualitative evidence. • Accelerate effectiveness of new supervisors and managers. • Begin to identify and develop potential future leaders. • Achieve positive cultural transformation scorecard. • Climate Survey results show strong indication of cultural transformation, in spite of influx of new employees/ supervisors.
Comparative Advantage of Each Option	• Smaller scale, limited to most urgent needs and paced to fit the Vehicle Value Stream schedule • Improved, immediate results with selected RIE projects for Vehicle Value Stream only • Accelerated effectiveness of people in new supervisory roles	• Broader, mid-level scale and moderate pacing to accommodate production schedule • Increased effectiveness and collaboration with non-manufacturing and support areas • Improved, immediate results on ALL RIE projects tied to the Vehicle Value Stream	• Broader scale and faster pacing to accelerate the impact of Leadership Competencies on the business • Increased effectiveness and collaboration with non-manufacturing and support areas • Improved, immediate results on ALL RIE projects in all areas (not only the Vehicle Value Stream)

	• Potential future leaders are spotted and development begins • Lesser time and budget investment now	• Accelerated effectiveness of all people in new managerial and supervisory roles • Solid approach to sustain Leadership Competencies	• Greatest opportunities to identify and develop potential future leaders • Best way to achieve cultural transformation • More detailed, frequent progress tracking and evaluation
Comparative Disadvantage of Each Option	• Impact limited to specific, targeted pockets of high need (highest impact Vehicle Value Stream RIEs and only new supervisors) • Limited opportunities for reinforcement by managers, supervisors, team leaders, and Lean facilitators • Delayed critical mass for cultural transformation	• Slower achievement of critical mass for cultural transformation and broad-scale impact on business results • Impact limited to all RIE projects tied only to the Vehicle Value Stream	• Greatest time and budget investment now

176 Stage Five – Synthesis and Formulation of Recommendations

Continuing the use of the same example noted earlier for preparing observations and conclusions, the excerpt appearing in Box 7.5 provides a partial set of recommendations.

BOX 7.5 PARTIAL SET OF SAMPLE RECOMMENDATIONS

As a result of the findings, observations, and conclusions of the Rapid Due Diligence diagnostic process, a number of key recommended actions are listed below.

- Consider a reset of the strategic plan to pursue an even more diligent, disciplined, and determined dual course of operational efficiency and effectiveness to achieve mission critical production and cultivating a positive climate that demonstrates care for military members, families, and civilians.
- Identify specific steps of accountability within this dual strategy to make measurable progress with current leadership and in the presence of leadership transitions toward achieving the strategy under review.
- Create tightly integrated alignment between the recruiter value proposition (both the current reality and the future state) with the strategy statement.
- Pursue the full application of the recruiter value proposition to begin building a new, appealing reputation for the military organization. Implement the recruiter value proposition appropriately within all stages of the human capital cycle or recruiter lifecycle.
    - o Infuse the recruiter value proposition in the early stages of the human capital cycle.
    - o Conduct communications on expectations for application of the recruiter value proposition within the organization and how leaders at all levels will be held accountable for knowing and performing their roles in ways that positively deliver the recruiter value proposition throughout the recruiter lifecycle.
- Complete a comprehensive communications matrix strategy map to capture and track dynamic messaging.
    - o Audience
    - o Message
    - o What are we asking the audience to do
    - o Benefit to audience (what's in it for them; what to expect)
    - o Audience expected reactions and ways to manage those reactions
    - o When to be delivered or how frequently
    - o Who does the delivery
    - o Vehicle or media choice
    - o Technical support for the delivery
    - o Audience feedback and measures of success

Stage Five – Synthesis and Formulation of Recommendations **177**

For further examples, the researcher may look to the recommendations contained with each of the cases included in Chapter Ten.

Discussion Questions

- How does the researcher determine which synthesis techniques are appropriate to use in stage five?
- Why is the application of system dynamics important to the synthesis stage?
- How can cognitive and behavioral limitations affect strategic decision-making and execution?
- Why does the researcher investigate in more depth the unique needs of geographically dispersed organizations?
- Why is it important to understand the organization's strategic decision analysis and decision-making process and practices?
- Why are inductive or deductive approaches to managing evidence preferable?
- Why is it important to identify observations and conclusions prior to formulating recommendations?

Notes

1 Joyce A. Thompsen, "Leading Virtual Teams: Five Essential Skills that Help You Lead Any Project – No Matter How Distant," *Quality Digest,* September 2000: 42–46.
2 "Disruptive Innovation," *Wikipedia,* last modified January 19, 2016, *https://en.wikipedia.org/w//index.php?title=Disruptive_innovation&oldid=700523878.*
3 Gary S. Becker, *The Economic Approach to Human Behavior* (Chicago: The University of Chicago Press, 1976), 3–14.

References

Becker, Gary S. 1976. *The Economic Approach to Human Behavior.* Chicago: The University of Chicago Press.
Skinner, David C. 2001. *Introduction to Decision Analysis, Second Edition.* Gainesville, FL: Probabilistic Publishing.
Sterman, John D. 2000. *Business Dynamics: Systems Thinking and Modeling for a Complex World.* Boston: McGraw Hill.
Thompsen, Joyce A. 2001. "Achieving Return on Critical Knowledge and Talent." Presentation to the American Society of Training and Development, Houston, TX.
———. 2000. "Leading Virtual Teams: Five Essential Skills That Help You Lead Any Project – No Matter How Distant." *Quality Digest,* September 2000: 42–46.
Wikipedia. 2016. "Disruptive Innovation." Last modified January 19, 2006. *https://en.wikipedia.org/w//index.php?title=Disruptive_innovation&oldid=700523878.*

Selected Bibliography

Listed below are a number of works and sources that have been useful in writing this textbook. The list has been segmented by topic for convenience in pursuit of further study in selected fields.

178 Stage Five – Synthesis and Formulation of Recommendations

Leading From a Distance Resources

Adler, T., and B. Zirger. "Organizational Learning: Implications of a Virtual Research and Development Organization." *American Business Review* 16 (1998): 51–60.

Angus, J., and S. Gallagher. "Virtual Team Builders." *Information Week* (May 4, 1998): 83–86.

Brown, S., and K. Eisenhardt. *Competing on the Edge: Strategy as Structured Chaos.* Boston: Harvard Business School Press, 1998.

Burton, T., and J. Moran. *The Future-Focused Organization: Complete Organizational Alignment for Breakthrough Results.* Englewood Cliffs, NJ: Prentice Hall, 1995.

Center, J., and J. Thompsen. "The Virtual Enterprise Framework and Tool Box." *Proceedings of the International Engineering Management Conference,* Vancouver, BC, Canada. July 1996.

Chase, N. "Learning to Lead a Virtual Team." *Quality* 38 (August 1999): 76.

Cohen, S. "On Becoming Virtual." *Training and Development* 51 (May 1997): 30–35.

Cole, J. "The Art of Long Distance Management." *Getting Results for the Hands-On Manager* 41 (November 1996): 1.

Davenport, T., and K. Pearlson. "Two Cheers for the Virtual Office." *Sloan Management Review* 39 (Summer 1998): 51–65.

Davidow, W., and M. Malone. *The Virtual Corporation: Structuring and Revitalizing the Corporation for the 21st Century.* New York: HarperBusiness, 1992.

Davis, S., and C. Meyer. *Blur: The Speed of Change in the Connected Economy.* Reading, MA: Addison-Wesley, 1998.

Davison, S., D. Hambrick, S. Snell, and C. Snow. "Use Transnational Teams to Globalize Your Company." Parts I, II, III, and IV. *Organizational Dynamics* (Spring 1996): 50–67.

Dinnocenzo, D. *101 Tips for Telecommuters: Successfully Manage Your Work, Team, Technology, and Family.* San Francisco: Berrett-Koehler Publishers, 1999.

Duarte, D., and N. Snyder. *Mastering Virtual Teams: Strategies, Tools, and Techniques that Succeed.* San Francisco: Jossey-Bass, 1999.

Eom, S., and C. Lee. "Virtual Teams: An Information Age Opportunity for Mobilizing Hidden Manpower." *Advanced Management Journal* 64 (March 22, 1999): 12.

Fisher, K., and M. Fisher. *The Distributed Mind: Achieving High Performance through the Collective Intelligence of Knowledge Work Teams.* New York: American Management Association, 1998.

Flatley, M. "Net Meeting 2.0: A Tool for Virtual Collaboration." *Business Communications Quarterly* 60 (December 1997): 101–103.

Gilmartin, R. "Innovation, Ethics, and Core Values: Keys to Global Success." *Vital Speeches of the Day* 65 (January 15, 1999): 209–215.

Goldman, S., R. Nagel, and K. Preiss. *Agile Competitors and Virtual Organizations: Strategies for Enriching the Customer.* New York: Van Nostrand Reinhold, 1995.

Grenier, R., and G. Metes. *Going Virtual: Moving Your Organization into the 21st Century.* Upper Saddle River, NJ: Prentice Hall, 1995.

Hallowell, E. "The Human Moment at Work." *Harvard Business Review* 77 (January–February, 1999): 58–66.

Henry, J., and M. Hartzler. "Virtual Teams: Today's Reality, Today's Challenge." *Quality Progress* 30 (May 1997): 108–109.

Hope, J., and T. Hope. *Competing in the Third Wave: The Ten Key Management Issues of the Information Age.* Boston: Harvard Business School Press, 1997.

Hornett, A. Dissertation. "Power and a Virtual Team: Modernist and Postmodernist Perspectives." George Washington University, 1998.

Stage Five – Synthesis and Formulation of Recommendations **179**

Kitchell, S. "CEO Characteristics and Technological Innovativeness: A Canadian Perspective." *Canadian Journal of Administrative Sciences* 14 (June 1997): 111–125.

Knutson, J. "Cohesive, Productive Distance Teams." *Network* 12 (October 1998): 14–16.

Kostner, J. *Virtual Leadership: Secrets from the Round Table for the Multi-Site Manager.* New York: Warner Books, 1994.

Lipnack, J., and J. Stamps. *The TeamNet Factor: Bringing the Power of Boundary Crossing into the Heart of Your Business.* Essex Junction, VT: Oliver Wight Publications, Inc., 1993.

———. *Virtual Teams: Reaching Across Space, Time, and Organizations with Technology.* New York: John Wiley & Sons, Inc., 1997.

———. "Virtual Teams: The New Way to Work." *Strategy & Leadership* 27 (January 1, 1999): 14.

Maynard, Jr., H., and S. Mehrtens. *The Fourth Wave: Business in the 21st Century.* San Francisco: Berrett-Koehler Publishers, 1993.

McKnight, D., L. Cummings, and N. Chervany. "Initial Trust Formation in New Organizational Relationships." *Academy of Management Review* 23 (July 1998): 473–490.

Nirenberg, J. *The Living Organization: Transforming Teams into Workplace Communities.* Homeword, IL: Business One Irwin, 1993.

Owen, H. *The Millennium Organization.* Cabin John, MD: Abbott Publishing, 1994.

Platt, L. "Virtual Teaming: Where is Everyone?" *Journal for Quality and Participation* 22 (September–October 1999): 41–43.

Quinn, J., J. Baruch, and K. Zien. *Innovation Explosion: Using Intellect and Software to Revolutionize Growth Strategies.* New York: The Free Press, 1997.

Slack, K. "Virtual Teamwork: Tale of Two Approaches." *Training Media Review* 6 (November 1998): 5–7.

Solomon, C. "Sharing Information Across Borders and Time Zones." *Workforce Magazine* 3 (March 1998): 12–18.

———. "Global Teams: The Ultimate Collaboration." *Personnel Journal* 74 (September 1995): 49–54.

Stamps, D. "Lights! Camera! Project Management!" *Training* 34 (January 1997): 50–56.

Tapscott, D. A. Lowy, and D. Ticoll. *Blueprint to the Digital Economy: Creating Wealth in the Era of E-business.* New York: McGraw-Hill, 1998.

Tullar, W., P. Kaiser, and P. Balthagard. "Group Work and Electronic Meeting Systems: From Boardroom to Classroom." *Business Communications Quarterly* 6 (December 1998): 56–65.

Ulrich, D., M. Losey, and G. Lake, eds. *Tomorrow's HR Management: 48 Thought Leaders Call for Change.* New York: John Wiley & Sons, Inc., 1997.

———. "Virtual Work: Real Results." The Interactive Manager Series, CD-Rom. Boston: Harvard Business School Publishing, 1998.

Waldman, D., and F. Yammarino. "CEO Charismatic Leadership: Levels-of-Management and Levels-of-Analysis Effects." *Academy of Management Review* 24 (April 1999): 266–285.

Wardell, D. "The Art of Managing Virtual Teams: Eight Key Lessons." *Harvard Management Update* (November 1998): 4–5.

Warkentin, M., S. Sayeed, and R. Hightower. "Virtual Team vs. Face-to-Face Teams: An Exploratory Study of a Web-Based Conference System." *Decision Sciences* 28 (Fall 1997): 975–996.

8
STAGE SIX – DELIVERY OF PROCESS RESULTS

Learning Objectives

- To learn how to organize and prepare documentation of results from the Rapid Due Diligence diagnostic method.
- To understand how to facilitate the delivery of the results to an organization's decision-makers.

In the sixth and final stage of the Rapid Due Diligence diagnostic method, the researcher and any team members commence the preparation of all documentation to present the results to the organization. For reference, the description of the sixth stage has been excised from the full six-stage table in Chapter Two and appears in Table 8.1.

At this stage, the researcher and any supporting team members prepare the findings, observations, conclusions, and recommendations for action in appropriate

TABLE 8.1 Rapid Due Diligence Method of Diagnostics: Stage Six – Delivery of Process Results

Players Involved	• Owner of situation
	• Organizational key contact
	• Principal researcher
	• Research team (if any)
Process Steps	• Prepare written report & supporting documents.
	• Present summary of key findings.
	• Facilitate discussion with designated decision-makers.
Outcomes	• Deliverables completed
	• Organization prepared for strategic decision-making
Timeline	2 days

and effective frameworks for decision-making. Typically, the researcher will prepare at least the following three specific deliverables:

- A written report of findings, observations about those findings, conclusions based upon multiple analyses and synthesis of data, and recommendations for action
- A visual project or implementation map
- A facilitated discussion with support documents with the owner of the business situation, organizational key contact, and other designated decision-makers

Additional figures, tables, summaries, and external research may be assembled to support the written report or the facilitated discussion.

The primary researcher bears the responsibility for determining the most effective framework which will best match with the organization's decision-making process and preferences for communication of complex information. In preparing to create each of these deliverables, the researcher confers with the organizational key contact to elicit specific preferences about the decision-making process and communications style of the group of people who will ultimately receive the information. Some organizations have a clearly expressed preference for receiving only abbreviated executive summaries in written reports or in limited numbers of bullet-point charts. Some organizations prefer to learn of the final recommendation at the very beginning of either written reports or in facilitated discussions, followed by supporting arguments and information. Some decision-makers prefer to have all information presented in quantitative impact terms, such as specific financial ratios, customer satisfaction or loyalty measures, competitive benchmark data, or comparative market standing. Still others request access to the full set of findings plus an executive summary.

The structure of a written report with the full set of findings typically flows in the following sequence:

- Introductory remarks with the identity of the organization, a description of the business issue and presenting symptoms, the desired strategic outcomes, roles and responsibilities of key players, and expected deliverables
- Details from the opening scope of inquiry discussion
- List of all documents and websites that were reviewed in the preparatory investigation stage
- Organization and methods used in the on-site discovery stage with the names, roles, and locations of all individual and group participants
- Description of the fields of inquiry, including primary questions
- Summary of responses provided to each of the primary questions, organized in order of frequency of repetition, without attribution to individual identity
- Observations about the on-site discovery process and findings from the perspective of the researcher

182 Stage Six – Delivery of Process Results

- Articulation of any specific areas that may require further investigation, clarification, or perhaps more direct observation, in order to develop an even deeper and mutual understanding of relevant circumstances associated with the scope of the inquiry
- Conclusions reached from a variety of analyses and syntheses conducted on all sources of findings
- Recommendations for addressing the business situation
- Identification of resources with capabilities that can best assist the organization in fulfilling the recommendations, as desired by the decision-makers

The researcher may choose to organize the written report to begin with an executive summary, followed by an expanded appendix with the details of the preparatory investigation, on-site discovery, and responses to each of the primary questions. The executive summary focuses on a brief description of the business situation, stages of the Rapid Due Diligence diagnostic process, abbreviated set of the most salient findings, conclusions, and recommendations for action. Supporting commentary for each of these sections follows in an appendix that is organized for ease in finding specific information.

The written report does not reveal the identity of specific individuals for any responses given throughout the on-site discovery process. Responses in the findings are stated in the words of the subject matter experts when possible or in abbreviated language that represents the intent of the response. Such abbreviations are often created by the researcher in the actual conduct of the interview and offered to the subject matter expert for agreement as a more concise description. The researcher is duty-bound to deliver the full range of responses to the fields of inquiry, including those that are most likely to be expected, as well as those that may be considered contradictory or quite unexpected. As borne out through the observations and conclusions, the best solutions and recommendations can occasionally be revealed in unexpected commentary. These perspectives can potentially contain important clues for highly innovative, efficient, and effective solutions.

The researcher chooses whether to include the identity, process steps, and detailed results of any specific analysis or synthesis techniques, depending upon the analytical preferences of the organization's decision-makers. The results are incorporated within the conclusions and recommendations portions of the written report. Where possible, the specific recommendations are supported by evidence of impact achieved with application of recommendations in similar business situations elsewhere. Some decision-makers request such proof sources to provide persuasive data to aid the decision-making process.

Upon completion of the written report, the primary researcher conducts a preview of the key content with the organizational key contact. The purpose is to provide the key contact with the opportunity to consider the content and ponder the likely reaction by the owner of the business situation and other designated decision-makers. In this conversation, the researcher points out the conclusions and recommendations with supporting rationale. Contradictory points of view or findings which may cause concern are also raised. The organizational key contact may suggest a simultaneous preview with the owner of the business situation. Occasionally, either the owner of the business situation or the organizational key contact may suggest the addition of an abbreviated executive summary, if it were not previously requested, or the movement of supporting detail into a summary and appendix format.

During this preview, the players organize for the concluding presentation and discussion with other designated decision-makers. Together, they craft the agenda, confirm the participants, clarify roles, set the schedule and allotted time for portions of the agenda, and identify all documents and formats for the presentation of results from the Rapid Due Diligence diagnostic process. They also jointly determine how and when the written report is distributed to the participants and prepare messaging about the meeting.

These players also pinpoint segments of the results that may become sources of disagreement or controversy with the designated participants. When this occurs, the researcher guides the discussion to determine the source of contention, underlying factors, areas for potential agreement, and facilitation techniques that can be applied during the meeting to mitigate the risk of hostile participation.

In preparation for the facilitated discussion, the researcher uses the recommendations from the written report to populate a visual representation of a proposed implementation plan. The intent is to capture the key roles, actions, and timeframes onto a single chart to provide a visual overview of the implementation process recommended for achievement of a set of specific strategic outcomes.

The project map or implementation plan can become a significantly complex document. The researcher builds in all the necessary steps or tasks for each active player or group of players, intersections of collaborative effort, communications flow, required skill building, multi-level performance management techniques, relationships among critical strategic dimensions, support mechanisms, and impact measurement. As the researcher constructs this complex project map, a number of questions guide the formulation and sequence of the content.

- What is the ultimate outcome from this course of action?
- What is the timeframe?
- How does the outcome link with the business strategy, vital objectives, and other strategic dimensions?
- Who are the players involved in the implementation process?
- What are the new behaviors or performance expectations by targeted groups?
- How are targets integrated into the performance management process?
- What are the baseline metrics?

184 Stage Six – Delivery of Process Results

- How will the organization gauge progress?
- What risks may exist, and what mitigation strategies are needed?
- What processes need attention?
- Who needs to know and use what new sets of information or skills?
- What training or orientation is required?
- How will any training or orientation be implemented? In what order? How far across the organization? How quickly does it need to be completed?
- What needs to happen for both current and any new employees?
- What needs to happen for the organization's customers?
- What are the responsibilities of the project implementation team?
- What is the supporting communications strategy for any actions or events?
- How will the organization deal with people who resist the implementation and any required changes?
- What feedback, coaching, reinforcement, and recognition steps will accompany the implementation?
- How will the organization conduct after action reviews, feedback loops, random audits, or trace any causal loops?
- How will the organization verify continuing alignment with the current or new business strategies and targets?
- What other resources and budget support are needed?

A template for the implementation project map is shown in Table 8.2.

A sample of a completed implementation project map is shown in Table 8.3. The very small print exemplifies why the project map is typically presented in a size large enough to cover a conference table or to post on a wall.

The primary researcher serves as the facilitator of the presentation and guides the group's discussion of the results. Following appropriate introduction of participants and any opening remarks by the owner of the business issue, the researcher manages the flow of the discussion. The meeting is typically supported by a set of visuals, such as a presentation deck of slides. An example of a slide deck appears in Figure 8.1.

The researcher introduces the agenda which had been previously agreed upon with the owner of the business issue and the organizational key contact. In the figure, this agenda begins with conclusions, followed by an overview of the Rapid Due Diligence diagnostic process, key observations, and recommendations.

A variety of comparative data from external benchmarking resources was included in this presentation to meet a specific need of the decision-makers to receive relevant proof sources. The researcher chooses proof sources which the decision-makers are expected to respect and value as worthy and credible.

With each slide or agenda item, the researcher invites clarifying questions and promotes discussion among the decision-making members. Where questions arise about the veracity of the findings, the researcher is advised to let the data stand as the evidence. As needed, the researcher refers to the detail of the written report or supporting external resource documents to respond to inquiries. The researcher

TABLE 8.2 Project Map Template

Roles & Calendar	Making Ready						Launching Program					
	Month One	Month Two	Month Three	Month Four	Month Five	Month Six	Month Seven	Month Eight	Month Nine	Month Ten	Month Eleven	Month Twelve
Business Strategy Links												
Sponsors & Senior Leaders												
Managers												
First-Level Leaders												
Individual Contributors												
New Employees												
Learning & Development Leaders												
Human Resources Core Team												

TABLE 8.3 Sample Project Map

Roles & Calendar	Making Ready						Launching Program					
	Month One	Month Two	Month Three	Month Four	Month Five	Month Six	Month Seven	Month Eight	Month Nine	Month Ten	Month Eleven	Month Twelve
Business Strategy Links	Align initiative & strategic dimensions.				Compare initial results w/strategic dimensions. Affirm initiative value.							
Sponsors & Senior Leaders		Clarify roles & tasks. Intro & link initiative to performance objectives.					Affirm fit with strategic dimensions. Model, coach, review, measure, and reinforce new skills within performance management system.					
Managers												
First-Level Leaders				Begin pilot for specified roles. Complete pre-post evaluation.			Begin participation in initiative skill-building. Apply new skills on the job. Engage in leader and peer coaching & reinforcement. Complete pre-post evaluations. Link with objectives.					
Individual Contributors												
New Employees							Incorporate content in orientation process.					
Learning & Development Leaders	Charter core team. Set details of all tasks for initiative. Schedule pilot. Align with talent system.				Evaluate pilot results & report to sponsors.		Complete final prep for launch.	Complete implementation tasks. Support leaders & participants to ensure targeted results. Gather & report periodic evaluation results.				
Human Resources Core Team												

Agenda

- Executive Summary:
  - Conclusions
  - Rapid Due Diligence Process
  - Key Observations
  - Recommendations
- Preliminary Project Map
- Next Steps

Executive Summary: Conclusions	Executive Summary: Rapid Due Diligence	Executive Summary: Recommendations

- Overarching opportunity
  - Cultivation of high performing, customer-centered organization
  - Immediate emphasis on consistent, efficient, and effective sales and service performance
- Dual strategic course
  - Pursue both customer-centricity AND operational efficiency and effectiveness
- Reflects your brand
- Draws on best-in-class research and experience
  - Create mutually valuable, long-term relationships with customers
  - Earn the right to serve as trusted advisors
  - Align strategy, culture, infrastructure, highly skilled behaviors
  - Acquire and develop customers who give referrals
	- Purpose
	  - Gain a clear understanding of current field training and future goals
	  - Identify opportunities for achieving best-in-class efficiency and effectiveness in sales performance
	- Process
	  - Document review
	  - Site visits and interviews
	  - Findings report and project map
		- Consider a re-set strategy to pursue dual course
		  - Customer-centricity AND operational efficiency and effectiveness
		  - Impact on customers and the business
		  - Structural alignment
		  - Accountability for results: new balance point with today's focus on the numbers
		- Clarify or create a customer relationship process
		  - Take outside-in perspective
		  - Map all customer experiences
		  - Identify trigger points that highly influence customer choices and loyalty
		  - Determine how to manage the ones that matter most
		  - Match with skills and accountability

Executive Summary: Observations		- Create an employee value proposition (EVP)
		  - Why bright, ambitious people would want to invest their careers with your organization
		  - Include in recruitment, selection, development, career paths
		- Incorporate new dual strategy goals and metrics
		  - Add EVP and CVP in explicit, line-of-sight performance expectations for all
		- Reconcile and refresh all curricula to address 4 objectives
		  - Decrease time to proficiency
		  - Establish effective coaching culture
		  - Use more field action learning
		  - Improve performance, satisfaction, turnover
		- Pursue parallel paths for greatest impact
		  - Start with field management
		  - Then, veteran sales representatives
		  - Streamline new sales representative on-boarding to go on plan within 80 days
		- Prepare capable core of field development specialists
		  - Centralized cadre in one office
		  - Cohorts in key locations
		  - Collaborate with – not displace – field management
		- Surround with focused communications and evaluation strategies
		- Putting it all together in a project map
		  - Comprehensive, aligned, integrated, systemic with embedded best-in-class practices
		  - Principal roles
		  - Key actions
		  - Proven implementation process
		  - Designed to yield targeted results

- Positive, respectful, employee pride in the organization and their roles
- High degree of autonomy in implementing field training
- Questionable transfer and application of skills and knowledge
- Inconsistent evidence of management modeling, coaching, reinforcing, and monitoring critical skills
- Insufficient rigor in skill building and application on the job
- Separation of sales and service, plus ambiguous accountability
	- Obsession with prospecting
	- Deficiencies in customer relationship building and selling skills
	- No clear focus on trigger points of customers' choice migration path
	- Your research
	  - Key driver of customer behavior = preference for a personal relationship
	  - Service events are critical triggers
	  - Importance of trusting relationship, personalized service, effective claim handling, speed, convenience, ease of purchase	

Executive Summary: Comparative Data		

- Loyalty drivers
  - Relationship (25%)
  - Product/service differentiation (25%)
  - Customer experience (23%)
  - Image (22%)
  - Price (5%)
- Consumer service expectations
  - Elevated year-over-year expectations
  - Poor service = primary reason for switching insurers
  - Break-out strategy
    • Know your customers and what they value most
    • Make improvements they will value and notice
- Outside-in approach to customers
  - 75-80% of organizations are still inside-out
  - Manage all customer touch-points
  - Focus on top customer service processes
- Strategy execution
  - 63% of strategy potential achieved
  - 37% lost to people management issues:
    • Ineffective performance management and coaching
    • Unavailable, capable resources
    • Failure to engage required changes
	- Sales managerial skills critical to productivity and effectiveness
	  - Salespeople who get ≥ 3 hours of coaching per month perform 15-17% better
	  - Training plus coaching multiplies ROI 4X
	  - Systemic training, coaching, and reinforcement deliver 2:1 to 8:1 ROI within the first year
	- Sales managerial skills critical to productivity and effectiveness
	  - Focus coaching on the middle core for greatest lift
	  - Sales training without systematic coaching wastes 87¢ of every dollar
	  - Coaching yields greatest impact of top 22 processes
	- Sales managerial skills critical to productivity and effectiveness
	  - Coaching from manager has more impact than peer mentoring
	  - Turnover can be reduced through effective training
	  - Best ways to drive skill application
	    • Sales manager communications before training
	    • Coaching and reinforcement after training	

		Next Steps

		- Internal deliberations
		- Decisions to guide
		  - Development and implementation of field training sales and coaching system
		  - How far, how fast, who first

FIGURE 8.1 Slide Deck for a Rapid Due Diligence Discussion.

188 Stage Six – Delivery of Process Results

intentionally draws all participants into the discussion. In some situations, the researcher gives voice to a question or concern as a stimulus to group discussion on important influencing factors.

Upon completion of the central recommendations, the researcher presents the implementation project map. The project map now becomes a central point of interest and portrays the recommendations in motion for the decision-makers. The researcher presents either an overview of critical segments or a point-by-point review of each segment, depending upon the interest level and questions raised by participants. For purposes of readability during presentations, the project map is often shown in a very large size, often the size of a large desk or conference table. The project map is presented as a working draft, and the researcher welcomes questions and alternative suggestions. Typically, the researcher marks up the chart throughout the discussion to capture the group's input. If the decision-makers express sufficient interest, after the meeting the researcher then edits the project map accordingly and delivers one or more workable copies to the organization.

Following a review of the project map content which sufficiently addresses any questions and concerns of the group, the researcher frames the next steps for the internal deliberations of the decision-making group. These steps are derived from the earlier preview with the owner of the business issue and the organizational key contact to align with the group's natural or preferred decision analysis process.

After any decisions are made that endorse the recommendations and direction portrayed in the project map, the final version of the map is often displayed in the work area of the primary project manager for the initiative. The project map becomes a visible reminder to the organization and any assigned work group of the complete set of tasks required to fully implement the strategic decision.

In addition to the classic approach to the facilitated discussion, the researcher may choose to create more tools to illustrate important segments of the findings, conclusions, or recommended actions.

The researcher can complete a detailed implementation chart to support the large project map. In sequence, this project management tool lists all of the actions in detail, assigns accountability and due dates, and includes space for noting completion status and clarifying comments. An example appears in Table 8.4.

TABLE 8.4 Sample Implementation Chart

#	Action	Accountable	Date Due	Completion Status	Comments
1	• Effectiveness Check-in Conference Call – Person A provides a overview of the Assessment Center to Senior Leaders	Person A	7/22	7/22	

#	Action	Accountable	Date Due	Completion Status	Comments
2	• Confirming Assessment Design – Internal discussion: design & outcomes – Review of materials by Sponsors and Project Manager and Lead Facilitator	Team A	7/30		
3	• SME content (additional broker profiles and cases)	Person B	7/29		
4	• Development of Assessment Center tools: – Talking Points for Assessment Center – Frequently Asked Questions – Representative per Assessment Center Checklist – Market Manager per Assessment Center Checklist – Roles and Responsible for Assessment Center Participants, Observers and Reps	Team A	7/22 8/5 8/2 8/2 8/2		Completed
5	• Development of Scoring Criteria for Assessment Center and definitions for certification and provisional certification	Persons B and C	8/6		
6	• Content Development (writing)	Person D	8/6		
7	• Assessment Center Content Review	Persons A, E, and F	8/7–9		
8	• Publishing Assessment Center Materials including: – Facilitator Guide – Role Plays – Participant Instruction Packet – Scoring documents – Logistical instructions	Persons G and H	8/7–20		
9	• Delivery of Assessment Center materials to Person D	Person C	8/21		

(Continued)

190 Stage Six – Delivery of Process Results

#	Action	Accountable	Date Due	Completion Status	Comments
10	• Communications – Week 4, August 9th, Delivery of Assessment Center Talking points • Distribute on 8/9 Assessment Center Frequently Asked Questions (FAQ) document and Pre-Assessment center preparation checklist • Development of the Frequently Asked Questions document & Pre-Assessment communication checklist	Team A	8/9 8/9 8/9		
11	• E-mail Pre-Assessment preparation packet to Market Managers – Talking Points – Frequently Asked Questions – Pre-Assessment center preparation checklist – Market Manager – Reps	Person D	8/12		
12	• Market Managers review the Assessment center information with the reps				
13	• Confirm participants and their roles	Person E	7/31		Complete

Other charts can be used to illustrate and outline the impact of comparative courses of action. For example, Figure 8.2 in two parts shows the relative performance improvement from the current state to a future state over time with the application of new skills in a business transformation or merger opportunity. The benefits of taking action are summarized below.

- Critical opportunity to make ready on the human side
  - o Effectively handling all the changes
    - o Those affecting front-line employees
    - o Those affecting leaders
  - o Building and immediately applying skills to take great care of constituents (customers, channels, providers, brokers, regulators, or others) during the transformation process
    - o Providing consistent, high quality service

Stage Six – Delivery of Process Results 191

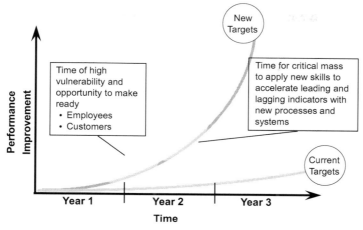

FIGURE 8.2 Comparative Course of Action.

- o Acquisition of new constituents
- o Retention of current constituents
- o Effectively handling hidden concerns
  - o All constituents' concerns about the business transformation and effect of the merger
  - o Special concern for employees
  - o Operating model shift, business transformation, process and system changes, new job roles
  - o Merger impact, job security, and future employability concerns

Other tools can be used to demonstrate the analysis of an important factor. The example shown in Table 8.5 shows the detail for calculating the full potential cost of employee turnover. The researcher may incorporate the actual data from the organization to show the impact or keep the chart open for the organization to apply data on its own.

The nature of the decision-making group's preferred decision analysis process may benefit from the revelation of any causal loop diagrams or stock-and-flow maps configured during the synthesis stage.

A draft chart of differing types of responsibilities for a series of tasks within key processes may be useful, especially in situations where role clarity is required. Also commonly described as a RACI Chart to delineate responsibility, accountability, communication linkages, or influence, an example appears in Table 8.6.

In situations where there is evidence of poor or incomplete communications patterns, the researcher may choose to create a set of communication plans to accompany the recommended course of action. In Table 8.7, there is a series of

192 Stage Six – Delivery of Process Results

TABLE 8.5 Potential Cost of Employee Turnover

Pre-Departure

a.	Average compensation for two weeks	$	
b.	Amount of decreased productivity (0% – 100%)	%	
c.	Cost of lower productivity	*(a x b)=*	$
d.	Compensation to manager to process separation		$
e.	Compensation to HR to process separation		$
f.	**Pre-departure costs**	*(c+d+e)=*	$

Vacancy

g.	Advertising the vacancy		$
h.	Payments to search firm		$
i.	Interview expenses (dollar value of time to interview)		$
j.	Interview expenses (travel & entertainment)		$
k.	Average number of weeks to fill vacancy	#	
l.	Average weekly overtime to compensate for vacancy OR weekly compensation to temp agency	$	
m.	Extra Compensation to cover vacant position	*(kxl)=*	$
n.	**Costs incurred during vacancy**	*(g+h+i+j+m)=*	

New Hires

o.	Average weekly compensation for filled position	$	
p.	Number of weeks in orientation & initial training	#	
q.	Compensation for orientation	*(oxp)=*	$
r.	Average sign-on bonus		$
s.	Moving allowance		$
t.	Compensation for 1st month following orientation (o) x(4.33)	$	
u.	Average performance level during 1st month following orientation (0% to 100%)	%	
v.	Value received with the 1st month's learning curve	*(txu)=*	$
w.	Value lost with the 1st month's learning curve (v-w)	*(t-v)=*	$
x.	**Costs incurred with new hires**	*(q+r+s+w)=*	$

Total Cost

POTENTIAL COST OF EMPLOYEE TURNOVER	*(f + n + x) =*	$

communications events of varying duration and depth of content. The purpose, key messages, and suggested communications techniques or tools are plotted for the organization's convenience.

Another tool the researcher may make available to the decision-making group applies a series of strategic thinking questions to a shared intersection of individuals or work groups in support of a key process or goal. While this tool

TABLE 8.6 Sample RACI Chart

(R=Responsibility; A=Final Accountability;

C=Communications to or from source; I=Influence or input)

Description of Day-to-Day Responsibilities	General Manager	Plant Manager	Team Leader	Floor Teams	Support Teams
Set process quality standards and measurements.					
Select or change work methods or procedures.					
Measure qualitative/quantitative progress.					
Take action to address quality/quantity issues.					
Set short-term output or process goals.					
Contact other functions for information or materials.					
Negotiate agreements with outside sources.					
Set own work hours or overtime.					
Approve vacation days or time off.					
Monitor time and attendance.					
Call in additional staff to get work done.					
Call meetings and set agendas.					
Set budgets within approved guidelines.					
Approve business expenses <$100.					
Approve business expenses >$100/<$500.					
Approve business expenses >$500/<$1000.					
Approve business expenses >$1000.					
Approve travel expenses.					
Take action to improve employee morale, cohesiveness and effectiveness.					
Provide feedback on performance.					
Conduct disciplinary action.					
Conduct formal evaluation for performance or development.					
Provide input on selection of others.					
Provide input on the dismissal of others.					
Evaluate others for compensation changes.					
Train or coach others in interpersonal skills.					
Train or coach others in technical skills.					

TABLE 8.7 Sample Communication Plans

Sales Performance Development Initiative – (Initiative Name or Tag Line)

Purpose:
- To equip Company name/logo employees with key messages and tools for selected internal communications opportunities about the Sales Performance Development Initiative tentatively entitled "(Initiative Name or Tag Line)."
- To outline the communications outcomes and key messages that can be matched to audience needs.
- Content will be refreshed and updated periodically as the initiative matures and moves through its phased implementation process.

Key Contact:
- (Point person name), (phone number)
- To secure:
  - o Guidance in the use of the communications kits
  - o Access to other communications resources
  - o Arranging other speakers for events
  - o Verifying currency of content and audience fit

Versions:
- 30-minute duration, very brief introduction
- One-hour duration, introduction
- Two or more hours' duration, introduction with facilitated discussion
- Three-four hours' duration, overview of core content with limited sample experiences
- Full-day duration, in-depth preview of core content with sample experiences

<table>
<tr><td colspan="3" align="center">30-Minute Duration</td></tr>
<tr><td>Purpose/Outcomes</td><td>Key Messages</td><td>Communications Tools</td></tr>
<tr><td>• Very brief introduction to the Sales Development Initiative</td><td>• What is the Sales Development Initiative – "(Initiative Name or Tag Line)"?
• Why is it important?</td><td>• PowerPoint slides
• Talking points</td></tr>
</table>

Purpose/Outcomes	Key Messages	Communications Tools
	• How does it align with our business?	
	• What are the benefits?	
	• Who is or will be involved? In what roles?	
	• What is the curriculum and core content?	
	• What's planned?	
	• What are the expectations for performance and results?	
	• What are any next steps for us?	
	• Questions	

One-Hour Duration

Purpose/Outcomes	Key Messages	Communications Tools
• Introduction to the Sales Development Initiative	• What is the Sales Development Initiative – "(Initiative Name or Tag Line)"? • How did we uncover the need? • Why is it important? • How does it align with our business? • What are the benefits? • What's been done to prepare? • Who is or will be involved? In what roles? • What is the curriculum and core content? • What have we learned so far? • What's planned? • What are the expectations for performance and results? • What are any next steps for us? • Questions	• PowerPoint slides • Talking points

(Continued)

Purpose/Outcomes	Key Messages	Communications Tools
• Introduction to the Sales Development Initiative • Facilitated discussion of expectations and impact for this audience	• What is the Sales Development Initiative – "(Initiative Name or Tag Line)"? • How did we uncover the need? • Why is it important? • How does it align with our business? • What are the benefits? • What's been done to prepare? • Who is or will be involved? In what roles? • What is the curriculum and core content? • What have we learned so far? • What's planned? • What are the expectations for performance and results? • What are potential challenges in our area? • How might we address these challenges? • What are any next steps for us? • Questions	• For any opportunities in excess of one hour, contact (Point person name) for guidance • PowerPoint slides • Talking points • Facilitating process

Three-Four Hours' Duration

Purpose/Outcomes	Key Messages	Communications Tools
• Overview of core content of the Selling model • Best practices for salespeople	• Reflection of your experiences as customers • Selling model and how it applies • Definition and sample experiences with primary skills within the selling model	• For qualified or certified facilitators to lead • Use PowerPoint slides • Mini-session leader's guide

Purpose/Outcomes	Key Messages	Communications Tools
• For audiences who may be scheduled for full training at a later date • For audiences who may play a support role to salespeople		• Selected wall charts • Group activity tools and directions

Full-Day Duration

Purpose/Outcomes	Key Messages	Communications Tools
• In-depth preview of core content of the Selling model • Key models, skills, and sample experiences • For audiences who may be scheduled for full training at a later date • For audiences who may play a support role to salespeople	• What is the Sales Performance Development Initiative – "(Initiative Name or Tag Line)"? • Why is it important? • How it aligns with our business? • What are the benefits? • What is the core content of the selling model and how it applies to our business • Deeper definitions of core skills • Sample experiences with core skills within the selling model • What is planned for this audience in the future? • What are the expectations? • Questions	• For certified facilitators to lead • Draw from the first day of facilitator kit and participant kit materials • PowerPoint slides + DVD • Wall charts

198 Stage Six – Delivery of Process Results

is particularly helpful to organizations that have adopted a matrix structure, it can also be applied in key areas where there are shared responsibilities for results without the formal matrix arrangement. This tool can assist the organization in clarifying situations and building the commitment or collaborative engagement at critical junctures or intersections that were uncovered during the Rapid Due Diligence on-site discovery. An example of this intersection tool appears in Table 8.8.

For situations where the Rapid Due Diligence diagnostic process uncovered a higher degree of tension or consistent difficulty in the business development process or relationships with critical or major customers, the researcher can provide a sample tool to help set and evaluate mutual expectations for performance. This is intended as a communications device to help identify sensitive areas and establish an improved relationship with major customers. An example appears in Table 8.9.

In situations where the organization's capability and capacity to engage in significant change is of high concern, the researcher may have conducted online surveys to gauge the current status of employees. Scatter grams, such as the one appearing in Figure 8.3, can be helpful to portray the survey results and generate evidence-based discussion with the key decision-makers.

TABLE 8.8 Managing Matrix Intersections

Our Common Goal: _____

	Names of People Sharing the Intersection
Questions	
Why is it important to achieve this goal?	
What do we need to do to contribute to this goal?	
What actions do we expect from others?	
What information is important? How would we prefer to receive it? When?	
What should stay the same? Why?	
What do we need more of? Why?	
What do we need less of? Why?	
How will we measure progress?	
What resources and support are required?	
How will we raise and resolve difficult issues among ourselves?	
How will we follow through on our mutual expectations and commitments?	

Stage Six – Delivery of Process Results **199**

TABLE 8.9 Mutual Expectations for Performance with Major Customers

The Customer			*Our Organization*	
Score	*Example*	*Expectations*	*Example*	*Score*
		Clear, complete planning and meeting preparation		
		Thorough follow-up and accountability		
		Clear and responsive communications within the next business day		
		Provide feedback, coaching, and direction		
		No surprises		

Scoring Legend
1 = Delighted with performance
2 = Performance exceeded expectations
3 = Meets expectations
4 = Caution: Pause to discuss
5 = Unsatisfactory: Stop action, conduct fact-finding, determine and engage recovery actions

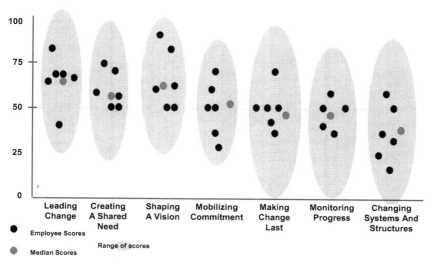

FIGURE 8.3 Snapshot of Change Capability.

Closure of the Rapid Due Diligence Diagnostic Process

When the decision-makers have reached a conclusion about the recommendations contained in the Rapid Due Diligence diagnostic process reports and review, the researcher may be invited to provide assistance in staging the implementation

200 Stage Six – Delivery of Process Results

of the decision. In a follow-up conference with the organizational key contact or a newly assigned manager for the initiative, the researcher may be asked to offer to create other supportive implementation techniques, change management tools, or communications devices to enable the implementation of the organization's decision. Some of these devices and techniques have been portrayed in the previous examples.

The researcher conducts a series of activities to bring closure to the Rapid Due Diligence diagnostic process. As soon as practical after the facilitated discussion, the researcher meets with the owner of the business issue and the organizational key contact to complete a post-project review. Four primary questions are addressed about the Rapid Due Diligence diagnostic method engaged in the situation.

- What worked well and why?
- What could have been done differently?
- What insights were gained?
- What additional work could be helpful?

Privately, the primary researcher and any team members also engage in a detailed review of the project, consider the input from the owner of the business situation and organizational key contact, and record any recommendations for future application or reflection.

Another key activity of closure is the organization of the full set of data and supporting documentation for ease of future inquiry. The archives should be sequentially ordered by stage and include all detailed findings, working papers, preliminary or draft observations, conclusions, recommendations, and presentation materials.

As any notice of future measurable impact is provided by the organization, those results need to be included with the archives. The intent is to create a complete and orderly record of the Rapid Due Diligence diagnostic method project for any future reference.

Discussion Questions

- How does the researcher determine the organization of the written report, supplemental documents, and the agenda for all preview conversations and presentation of results?
- How is the development of a project map helpful?
- Why does the researcher need to prepare carefully for the presentation of the results and facilitation of the discussion among key decision-makers?
- Why are after action reviews important?
- Why is the preparation of archives important for the Rapid Due Diligence diagnostic method?

9
IMPACT OF RAPID DUE DILIGENCE

Learning Objectives

- To acquire examples of results achieved upon implementation of recommendations from the Rapid Due Diligence diagnostic method.

This chapter is organized to provide specific examples of results achieved in real situations where the Rapid Due Diligence diagnostic method was applied and at least some of the recommendations were accepted and deployed. A variation of the critical incident methodology from applied social science research is used to set forth the context of each example. For each situation, the following information is revealed:

- Situation prompting the commencement of the Rapid Due Diligence diagnostic method
- Actions recommended upon analysis of all forms of discovery
- Results and impact achieved by the organization's acceptance and deployment of any recommendations

The examples include this three-part summary for each of the case studies appearing in Chapter Ten. In all situations, the identity of the organization remains anonymous. The examples are drawn from for-profit and not-for-profit organizations, some of which have operations in multiple geographic locations such as North America, Europe, Asia Pacific, India, and Australia.

Case Study One: Seeking an Enterprise-Wide Approach to Sales

A very large and financially successful insurance organization was exploring the potential for more innovatively representing itself both to independent agents and its customers. A number of new initiatives were underway across its dozens of business units. There were multiple marketing platforms, no common approach to business development, and incomplete metrics for measuring sales performance. The organization sought the assistance of Rapid Due Diligence diagnostic methodology to help define an enterprise-wide approach to fit its business model.

During the discovery stage, the researcher observed that many of the multiple initiatives in motion across the organization had the potential of producing results at cross-purposes. Unknown by many leaders in various business units, a new brand was about to be launched which depended upon precise execution of a new set of competencies within the sales and customer relationship segments of each business unit. This investment required integration with all strategic dimensions and focus upon building the necessary capability and capacity of the organization to actually deliver the promise of the new brand.

Findings from the Rapid Due Diligence diagnostic process were used to design a comprehensive, integrated, enterprise-wide approach to the organization's business development and multiple levels of customer relationships. This approach was supported by a cultural transformation design with development of new employee capabilities to more directly deliver the new brand and customer value proposition.

As a result, all business units have been building a common core of sales and service competencies to deliver the new brand. New metrics which match key customer analytics are being tracked.

A more robust, strategically aligned performance management system with communications, reinforcement, coaching, and evaluation is being practiced across all business units. A new value proposition for franchise agents is being redefined. The foundation for a Triple Win was set in place.

Case Study Two: Shifting Operating Models

A large, not-for-profit membership organization had conducted new market and member research to create a potential new operating model and chose to deploy the Rapid Due Diligence diagnostic method to help craft a process for implementing the model.

The researcher conducted a more granular examination of the market research data to trace leverage points within the economic value-producing stream across various functions of the organization. A more detailed operating model was designed, accompanied by a comprehensive approach to building a common relationship development process with new and current members. The organization's culture change process had stalled and required attention to more actively engage employees. With the findings of new specific trigger points for building member loyalty, new matching competencies and metrics were crafted to more intentionally leverage the new relationship-centered operating model. Hidden, unhelpful cultural dynamics among the layers of management were revealed.

Several weeks after the implementation of the new employee and leader development curriculum, now more directly aligned with the new operating model,

Impact of Rapid Due Diligence **203**

internal organizational analysts completed a thorough evaluation of results. Their findings showed that there was a significant and positive effect on gross new policy productivity. There was an immediate and high probability for sustainable productivity gain of at least four percent within the first month after commencement of the comprehensive new initiative. Change capability and employee engagement data were also improving.

The sales management role was redefined and restructured, reducing direct reports on average from twenty to eight. A clear shift in the operating model was underway and producing positive results.

Case Study Three: Improving Operational Quality and Efficiency

A military organization was seeking to provide the highest quality of equipment at the right time and in the most cost-efficient manner to soldiers in combat. A combination of Lean 6s and Six Sigma process improvement initiatives was well underway throughout the organization with mixed results. The Rapid Due Diligence diagnostic method was deployed to determine how to consistently improve and sustain both operational quality and efficiency.

On-site discovery included structured, direct observation of the application of leadership, teamwork, change management, problem solving, and process improvement skills in the Lean 6s and Six Sigma working sessions in multiple shifts of production operations and in off-line value-stream analysis meetings. Analysis of the findings provided evidence of gaps and hidden dynamics that were non-conducive to the desirable environment for long-term successful application and realization of Lean 6s and Six Sigma results. The research team designed a set of pilot training sessions to test a comprehensive set of skill development to improve results in pinpointed gaps. Upon completion of the pilot sessions, the research team returned to conduct a second round of comparative on-site behavioral observations.

Findings from the observations and critical incident interviews included considerable evidence of improvement in the quality of the project team meeting process and level of participation. There was evidence of a much higher frequency and degree of positive, confident application of leadership, teamwork, and process management skills.

The results from this multi-phase Rapid Due Diligence diagnostic process were sufficient to stimulate the consideration and approval of a command-wide, systemic leadership competency initiative with an expanded, comprehensive menu of services to support the broader cultural transformation. This included establishing a set of meaningful metrics to gauge progress and business impact, drawing upon the production performance, quality, and efficiency scorecards already in place.

Within six months of the expanded, more disciplined, organization-wide approach to combining the specified leadership competencies with Lean 6s, Six

Sigma, and related initiatives, there were quantifiable results from the comparison of the annual workforce climate surveys. The aggregate score improvements ranged from fifteen to sixty-one percent across twenty-nine locations. These results provided encouraging evidence of the potential for gaining significantly greater and longer lasting benefits from the process improvement initiatives.

Case Study Four: Creating a Post-Merger Talent Management Strategy

Following the acquisition of several additional properties, a very large hospitality organization deployed the Rapid Due Diligence diagnostic method to help gain a clear understanding of the human resources strategy currently in place and required for future business success across all the properties.

The on-site discovery required inclusion of a large number of participants from across the newly combined organization, representing multiple locations and layers of roles and responsibilities. A recent reduction in force process was having lingering, negative effects on the morale and turnover levels of the remaining population. With many hundreds of training courseware offerings across the new enterprise, there were significant redundancies, inconsistencies, gaps, and differences in both training designs and outcomes. The talent management processes were primarily supported in manual mode by outdated tracking systems. The acquisitions introduced many hidden dynamics in the highly fractured culture of the new enterprise.

On the basis of the evidence, the researcher recommended the adoption of a unified, competency-centered talent management system across all properties within the enterprise, the cultivation of a culture that demonstrates the value of the people to the business, and a more disciplined accountability for performance management tied to measurable business results and guest experiences. The researcher provided a draft set of core competencies that could be applied to all employees at all locations, plus an additional set of competencies for their leaders.

Specific recommendations were provided for restructuring the array of human resource professionals, reconciling and refreshing all curricula to provide more direct support to the talent management strategy, creating a new employee value proposition to build engagement and stem undesirable turnover, and align strategic dimensions within a comprehensive, integrated talent management system.

The recommendations were accepted by the organizational key contact and brought into the strategic development process for the newly combined enterprise.

Case Study Five: Pursuing an Effective Client-Focused Service Strategy

A large, successful financial services organization was seeking even greater efficiency and effectiveness in its relationships with financial advisors and clients. The Rapid Due Diligence diagnostic method was deployed to develop ideas for how these improvements might be achieved.

The on-site discovery revealed uncertainty about the exact role and balance of a client service strategy in conjunction with the long-held organizational focus on reducing cost and improving operational efficiency. Leaders and employees were experiencing difficulty in balancing these two apparently competing areas of focus. Without more clarity and line-of-sight connections among all strategic dimensions, the organization could expect to continue on its current service trajectory and not achieve the desired pinnacle of service reputation. Previous business process reengineering work had not been extrapolated with an enterprise-wide client relationship process that reflected on the reality of client and financial advisor experiences. A host of metrics and surveys were leading parts of the organization in conflicting and competing directions.

The recommendations of the Rapid Due Diligence diagnostic process included the crystallization of a much more precise client service strategy and all of its supporting strategic dimensions. An effective cultural shift from the current focus on operational efficiency to a balance of efficiency and client service required considerable evidence of conviction, clarity, and active involvement on the part of all leaders at all levels of the organization. Further data mining or new research was required to more accurately pinpoint specific triggers for developing client and financial advisor loyalties.

While the final strategic decisions and accompanying measurable results of this Rapid Due Diligence diagnostic process were ultimately not revealed to the researcher, listed below are sample results from other organizations which pursued a similarly focused, more effective and efficient client-service strategy.

- A sixteen percent increase in measurable service ratings
- At least a 4.5 rating (on a Likert scale of 1–5) on consistent demonstration of professionalism
- A twenty-five percent reduction in client complaints
- A fifteen percent increase in first-call resolution of difficulties
- A forty-four percent increase in employee job satisfaction
- At least a fifty percent improvement in call-handling efficiency
- At least a fifty percent decrease in call escalations
- An increase in client satisfaction scores from forty-eight to ninety-one percent

It is reasonable to conclude that at least one or more of these improvements would have been achieved with the careful formulation and precise execution of a focused client service strategy.

Case Study Six: Developing a Corporate University

The Rapid Due Diligence diagnostic method has been used in clarifying the need and shaping the infrastructure and learning processes within corporate universities, especially for organizations that are pursuing greater growth and profitability. In such situations, the learning and development function has been increasingly

206 Impact of Rapid Due Diligence

invited into the process of exploring ways to effective drive greater business success. The discussion among operations and learning development often includes topics such as how to engage in the effective replication of successful market initiatives and responding efficiently to addressing capability gaps across geographically dispersed organizations.

The combination of discovery, analysis, and synthesis deployed within the Rapid Due Diligence diagnostic method brings deeper investigation into the junctures within the strategic dimensions, especially the organization's business model and relationships with agents, clients, or customers. The discovery process can reveal the trigger points where specific critical knowledge, skills, abilities, or motivations can bring greater value to the intersections of employees or agents with clients or customers. In situations where the organization has not yet traced precisely the revenue generation stream throughout the execution of the business model, the discovery process has the capability of unlocking previously unknown opportunities for optimizing the realization of value in the strategy execution process.

In some situations, an organization is not yet fully convinced that any investment in learning and development on a significant scale can produce a real return. Therefore, the actual need for any corporate university approach is not yet established.

The preparatory investigation and discovery process of Rapid Due Diligence uses deeper investigation into the financial reporting statements and exchanges with the investment community to uncover important insights. For examples, these clues are often encased in commentary about ambitions for double-digit improvements in revenue streams, new market initiatives, optimizing competitive distinctions or opportunities, seeking greater efficiencies of effectiveness in operations, securing greater payback on invested assets, initiating compelling experiences for customers, and achieving consistent performance at point-of-contact or intersections with customers. The compilation and quantification of the value potentially realizable in all such opportunities from specific investments in human capital development can provide a compelling argument for organizing a central repository of learning and development resources with a one-stop, single point of contact for its leaders and employees at all levels and locations.

The researcher has also provided frameworks for establishing the central learning repository or university-like operations in ways that can directly contribute to the targeted business results.

On several occasions, the researcher has also been asked to prepare multi-year business plans with comprehensive sets of strategic dimensions, including the mission, vision, values, operating disciplines, value proposition, business goals for the early years of operation, key strategies, evaluation process, financial investment, and implementation plan recommendations that can accommodate significantly dispersed organizations across several continents.

Case Study Seven: Stabilizing a Software Development Startup Organization

The Rapid Due Diligence diagnostic process was completed with a software development startup organization, formed by a venture capitalist and technologist. As the organization slowly grew, insufficient market traction and revenue were being realized from the original business model. Funding was rapidly depleting. A highly lucrative potential market was identified in a previously unoccupied market niche, and the capability to seize the opportunity was fading. There was a high degree of turnover of key players. Even though the technical people declared the product development was on track, senior leaders eventually discovered the whole effort was seriously behind schedule.

The researcher was invited to conduct a Rapid Due Diligence diagnostic process to uncover insights into the complex set of business issues and organizational performance. The discovery revealed that no one in senior management had a clear grasp of the explicit Critical Knowledge Areas© required to realize the proposed new product platform. This vacuum impaired the organization's ability to manage the recruitment of new talent as well as the product development process. The organization also lacked clarity about their application of a product development process and a quality assurance practice.

These initial findings were used to design a comprehensive approach to define the organization's critical talent needs to drive the performance of the business. The findings of the study included a set of Critical Knowledge Areas©, definition of critical talent for the organization, a set of measures for calculating potential Return on Critical Talent, conclusions about those findings, and specific recommendations for applying the findings to the organization's management techniques, strategies, processes, and systems.

The senior management team took immediate action on several recommendations to gain prompt results. Within six months of the Rapid Due Diligence diagnostic process, a number of positive improvements occurred that the senior management has attributed in part to the influence of the study. These results included the following:

- Software engineers created an assessment tool for recruitment to discern the technical Critical Knowledge Area© capabilities with greater precision. Recent hires have been demonstrating greater capability to create additional product functionality and repair software malfunctions more rapidly.
- The turnover of critical talent has been significantly reduced from fifty to five percent.
- Key sources of organizational discontent have been constructively addressed.
- Product development has moved from a stall-out condition to produce customer acceptable product performance. A greater percentage of product development dates are being met on time.

208 Impact of Rapid Due Diligence

- The quality of communications and extent of feedback from customer have improved.
- Within twelve months of the study, additional results were reported and credited by management to their increased attention to talent:
  o Product version 2.0 was released for sale.
  o The organization closed another round of venture capital funding and reported a positive cash flow.
  o The customer base grew to number fifty-seven.

Case Study Eight: Applying Rapid Due Diligence to Not-for-Profit Organizations

The Rapid Due Diligence diagnostic method can be applied effectively for organizations that are classified as not-for-profit even though some of the motives and systemic forces may differ. In these situations, assets and resources can be constrained, limited, or highly dependent upon volunteers. As an example in this case study, a large religious congregation with a school chose to deploy Rapid Due Diligence to gain a deeper understanding of how it could adapt to a steady decline in its membership and assets.

The discovery stages revealed several incongruities that required attention. For example, the constitution of the congregation was out of date; and many clarifications and conflicting language required revision. There was no evidence of any form of long-range planning or intentional missional planning within the congregation, its governing council, or the school administration. There were limited amounts of financial information, forecasts, or analyses to assist in the existing decision-making process. There were no records of performance discussions, no set of administrative policies, and no level of community needs assessment to understand changing demographics and other influences on their viability as a congregation and school. A long-term pastor had recently retired, and the volunteer leaders were seeking direction.

Based upon these findings and observations, the researcher provided a series of detailed recommendations for updating the constitution, structure, and governance model, as well as engaging in strategic planning. Upon consultation with the senior leaders of the congregation and school, the researcher was invited to guide the planning process with the currently elected congregation council.

The outputs from the planning process included a set of congregation and leader goals, high-level definitions of key areas of mission and ministry, a strategy fulfillment map with descriptions and timelines of activity, a summary of the strategic direction, guiding principles, and assumptions, and a simple scorecard that could be using for communicating progress and measurable results.

Case Study Nine: Pursuing an International Business Development Strategy

A multinational pharmaceutical organization with reach across many countries in Asia Pacific, Europe, and North America, plus India and Australia, sought to increase its market share in existing and future markets to become a more formidable competitor in its product and market areas. The Rapid Due Diligence diagnostic method was engaged to identify a comprehensive, strategic model to support a new international business development strategy.

The significant diversity, geographic dispersion, and current degree of independence exercised within the international business development organization required a special level of sensitivity within all stages of the Rapid Due Diligence diagnostic process. It was essential to draw upon a wide variety of sources and levels of subject matter experts from around the world. These included preparatory investigation with review of a considerable customer and market research data from several countries, both in-person and telephone interviews, plus visits and interviews with customers with a diverse set of product portfolio needs.

The initial findings were used to shape the fields of inquiry into broad categories and strategic dimensions to support the pursuit of the overall business development strategy, key supporting processes, tools, and practices. The researcher intentionally incorporated a number of appropriate analysis and synthesis tools and techniques into a three-day, intensive working session with senior level subject matter experts from a number of country operations. Their involvement was facilitated to secure greater insights and details into the customer purchasing process, the business development process, and competency profiles for both business professionals and managers.

The intent was to simultaneously gather deep levels of rich data from a broad array of perspectives while building a foundation of potentially greater engagement and commitment to any findings and recommendations. This approach was important to establishing the credibility of the diagnostic process conclusions and recommendations in the minds of the executive owner and executive team members. It also served as an important springboard in the actual implementation of the international business development process, tools, and practices.

Within weeks of the facilitated executive team discussion of the diagnostic process conclusions and recommendations, nearly all of the recommendations were implemented in the international business development portion of the worldwide enterprise. Several months later, the organizational key contact reported that significant progress was being made on all fronts.

The way in which the Rapid Due Diligence diagnostic method had been deployed, with deliberate involvement of a wide swath of subject matter experts from multiple countries, was credited for producing a greater level of engagement

Impact of Rapid Due Diligence

and positive reaction to the new business development strategy. The organizational key contact also stated that a number of performance metrics were moving in desirable ways.

Discussion Questions

- Why does critical incident methodology provide a useful approach to gauging impact?
- What trends are revealed in the summaries of the case studies?

10
CASE STUDIES

Learning Objectives

- To examine in more detail the stages of the diagnostic process and outcomes from the Rapid Due Diligence diagnostic method deployed in a variety of real situations.

This chapter is organized to provide a series of case studies from real situations in which the Rapid Due Diligence diagnostic method was deployed. The identity of the organizations remains anonymous. The examples include for-profit and not-for-profit organizations, some of which have headquarters or operations in North America, Europe, Asia Pacific, India, and Australia.

To supplement the case studies, a number of illustrations have been incorporated, nearly all of which have not appeared in earlier chapters. Discussion questions are also included at the close of each case study.

Case Study One: Seeking an Enterprise-Wide Approach to Sales

A very large insurance company, writing both commercial and personal insurance through agents, scattered throughout North America and portions of Europe, had a well-established brand and considerable financial strength. Even so, this historically conservative management culture was now open to innovation and breakthrough thinking in how the company represented itself to both its agents and ultimate customers.

Leaders within the company were awakening to the potential of an enterprise-wide culture that provided consistency across all forms of agency and consumer experience. Some preliminary steps were taken to explore the potential of such an enterprise-wide approach. A sales and marketing task force was formed, including several bright, energetic leaders from across the many business units or divisions. Enterprise development was becoming more formalized.

A field needs assessment was conducted by these internal resources and revealed several potential areas for consideration and attention. The company would benefit by the use of a common language among the many business units. There was no common approach to sales performance. There were multiple marketing platforms which, if consolidated, could present much more leverage in the marketplace. Metrics for measuring sales and marketing performance were incomplete.

Upon review of these initial findings, the sales and marketing task force concluded that they needed a comprehensive, integrated, enterprise-wide approach that included the appropriate cultural transformation, consistent organizational performance, and reliable application of best-in-class sales skills and working knowledge of the various product categories. It was also clear that an outside resource would be helpful in verifying the findings, then crafting and implementing this enterprise-wide approach to sales.

The researcher was invited to meet with the designated executive from the company's enterprise development function. The initial agenda included a confirmation of the scope of the inquiry and outcomes, charter of a core project team, clarification of preliminary implementation plans, messaging to participants in the process, and scheduling of the Rapid Due Diligence diagnostic process.

The investigative research design included various techniques for discovery of each of the organizational strategic dimensions and how those were already manifesting across each of the many business units. Figure 10.1 highlights in black nodules those strategic dimensions that were known to be in place while those that were under development or questionable were subject to discovery during the diagnostic process.

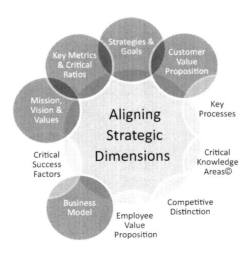

FIGURE 10.1 Strategic Dimensions Status.

Summaries of the findings from the sales and marketing task force were provided to the researcher for thorough review. The researcher also scoured the company's website for detailed definitions of the many products, services, business units, marketing platforms, financial performance, and reports to investment analysts. Even more granular investigation was done within the Securities and Exchange Commission reports and especially the management discussion and analysis sections to uncover distinctions and differentiations between the company and its many competitors. On the basis of this preview of available documentation, the researcher conferred with the designated executive contact to confirm the identity of people who should be interviewed in person. A set of interview questions and protocol for the interview process was also previewed.

Midway through the interviews, the researcher observed that there were multiple initiatives in motion across the company. Many of these initiatives were unknown to the various business units and had the potential of producing results at cross-purposes. The researcher posited that there could also be much greater potential within the enterprise-wide aspirations if there was specific effort to orchestrate and realize the power of deliberate convergence of these multiple initiatives.

A significant opportunity was uncovered in the planned launch of a new enterprise brand. Considerable effort and resources had been dedicated to identifying the market value of more distinctive differentiators between the enterprise and its competitors. To a large degree, this new brand required precision in execution of a fresh set of competencies, especially within the sales and customer relationship building segments of each unit. However, with several inquiries, the researcher learned that this intended launch of a new brand was unknown to many leaders across the various business units.

The situation begged the question of how the enterprise could immediately fulfill the expressed brand if there were no planned attention or changes to the competencies in the delivery of sales or services to customers. No one had been engaging in the granular examination of how well the current competencies could deliver on such a new brand. No one had described what the appropriate new set of competencies should become, or how to prepare the business units and specific players to consistently demonstrate such competencies. The brand, label, or tag line would be out in the public arena without intentional delivery of the purported service or any other required support. In other words, the equivalent of a new customer value proposition was about to be exposed without the necessary systemic inquiry of the capability and capacity of the organization to actually deliver on it. The researcher inquired about the degree to which this strategic opportunity and potential risk had been explored. Because the planned launch was imminent, the need to consider all such implications became urgent.

Within the remaining interviews and in group processing with members of the sales and marketing team, the researcher posed large-scale questions to inquire about any work that may have been done, as well as probing the proclivity of the

214 Case Studies

people to do so. Specific questions also plumbed the identity or description of specific competencies required to fulfill the new brand. These questions included:

- What do the people (whether employees or agents) need to know and do differently in order to deliver the promise of the new brand and ultimately the new customer value proposition?
- What economic or competitive power can be achieved with consistency in sales and service execution and performance across all business units?
- What brand-specific competencies (skills, knowledge, abilities, and motivations) would be required of people in various roles (for example, agents, customer service representatives, and underwriters) to fulfill such a scope and scale of enterprise-wide consistency?
- How would such an approach align with the overall strategic objectives of the company, such as:
  o Maximizing the potential of the franchise
  o Achieving the organic growth goals of the combined business units
  o Becoming the number one competitor in all market spaces
  o Differentiating the company from its competition
  o Living the new brand
  o Growing and more effectively applying the capabilities of people throughout the company

The results of the Rapid Due Diligence diagnostic process were delivered verbally in direct conversation with the designated executive, the core project team, and members of the sales and marketing team. A defined set of competencies for both sales and customer service was identified that matched the planned change in branding, or de facto the new customer value proposition. The degree of difference between the current practices and competencies across the various roles and business units was compared with the new set required to support the brand. These new competencies and the brand were posited as the core of the several strategies in motion. The market value and economic importance of a converged strategy justified immediate attention. The findings and recommended pursuit of a converged strategy were accepted.

A preliminary version of a project map to accomplish these objectives was prepared and presented. The intent was to capitalize upon the discoveries and prepare for enterprise-wide consistency of sales performance, as an important first step in fulfilling delivery of the brand. A make-ready period spanning five months was identified, followed by the first six months of the launch of the comprehensive approach.

Best practices for strategy implementation were incorporated in the map content. Specific roles were pointed out for maintaining links with the company's vital objectives, people who would serve as centers of influence or sponsors of the broad initiative, sales managers, account executives, the core project team, other internal partners such as underwriters, and outside resources.

The order and integration of specific tasks within the eleven-month period were visually portrayed across the very large, table-sized map. Every role and task was reviewed in detail to test the plan's completeness, sequence, and fit with the culture, ambition, and resources of the enterprise.

Upon acceptance of the project map content, a lift-off implementation plan with even more granular detail, timing sequence and duration, and traceable outcomes was provided to guide the day-to-day project management.

In keeping with its conservative reputation, the core project team determined to conduct more than a dozen test sessions of the primary learning experiences in the targeted sales performance skills. These were quickly conducted across several of the differing business units to gauge the relevance of the competencies, inherent business development model tied to the new brand, and customization of content to fit the enterprise. In-depth data and insights from each test session were analyzed and applied to the intended broader implementation plan. A number of critical factors for the successful broader implementation plan emerged.

- Communications planning with specific messaging and timing would be paramount.
- Performance expectations would require overt modeling, reinforcement, and coaching of the targeted skills and behaviors.
- Results would be measured, monitored, and compared.
- The broader launch would require attention to the participation level and logistics on the enterprise-wide scale.

Multiple communications plans were created for thirty-minute and sixty-minute briefings, longer two to four-hour sessions, and full-day experiential immersion in the purpose, key messaging, and samples of learning experiences. Executive overviews including senior field leadership were conducted in all geographic regions and across all business units. Skill development commenced.

Testimonials and leading indicator results began flowing and were routinely analyzed. Continual refinements were being made to the process to accommodate the sense of urgency in key pockets of the enterprise, to adjust to the massive scale, and manage the many moving parts of the process.

New needs were being uncovered, many of which had been identified in the Rapid Due Diligence diagnostic process and temporarily set aside to focus initially on building the skills and capabilities of the core players in the sales roles. There was a growing desire to move to a single business development or sales process. The researcher used all of the findings from the Rapid Due Diligence diagnostic process, as well as test process results, known customer choice analytics and decision-making process, and fresh metrics from the leading indicators to produce a sample enterprise-wide business development process. Table 10.1 illustrates this business development process.

The proposed business development process encompassed eight broad steps and laid out key activities and roles, plus aligned performance standards, and the company's goals. To optimize the effectiveness and efficiency of the process, plus

TABLE 10.1 Business Development Process

	STEP 1 Identifying Opportunities	STEP 2 Qualifying Opportunities	STEP 3 Analyzing Situation and Preparing Solution(s)	STEP 4 Presenting Solution(s) and Resolving Concerns	STEP 5 Reaching Agreement and Closing	STEP 6 Implementing Solution(s)	STEP 7 Monitoring Performance	STEP 8 Leveraging Success
Process Steps								
Key Activities and Roles SP = Sales Professional SM = Sales Manager UW = Additional Underwriting Support	• Prepare territory and key account plan to set targets (SP) • Focus search for best opportunities (SP) • Investigate resources to discern potential opportunities (SP) • Identify initial contacts (SP)	• Make and complete appointment (SP) • Probe to establish need (SP) • Support need with solution (SP) • Agree organization can provide a viable solution (SP) • Secure request for quote (SP) • Affirm buying process + decision criteria (SP)	• Analyze situation and confirm our solution (SP) • Involve other resources (SP + UW + SM) • Determine best approach for solution and quote (SP and team) • Prepare quote (SP)	• Submit quote (SP) • Uncover and resolve any concerns (PS) • Confirm customer's understanding of benefits (SP) • Check if ready to close (SP)	• Summarize, affirm customer agreement, and close the business. (SP) • Validate contract detail (SP) • Complete contract documents (SP + ?) • Notify internal team (SP)	• Monitor administration, implementation, and service processes (SP + ?) • Organize payment and support processes (SP + ?)	• Monitor solution and service performance (SP) • Check for satisfaction (SP) • Arrange for any adjustments (SP + ?) • Notify internal team of feedback and results (SP)	• Affirm end customer's willingness to be a reference (SP) • Complete arrangements for reference (SP) • Inquire about new opportunities (SP)
Performance Standards	* Identify opportunities that can produce revenue target	*Confirm needs and solutions for qualified opportunities	• Prepare quote within X days of qualifying visit.	• Present quote within X days of qualifying visit. • Customer expresses preference for proposed solution.	• Attain close rate of at least X %. • Aggregate deals ≥ territory target.	• Signed acceptance document.	• 100% satisfaction with solution + service	• Complete follow-up plan for every satisfied customer.
Enterprise Goals	• Identity potential opportunities with sufficient potential to meet target	• Identify need we can solve • Secure data for quote	• Complete understanding of need • Set quotation strategy	• Present best solution • Resolve concerns • Prepare to close	• Close the business • Confirm contract details	• Complete implementation • Complete acceptance and authorize invoice	• Establish customer confidence and satisfaction	• Secure customer as a reference • Earn right for future business opportunity • Build financial, image, and performance success
Customer Expectations	• Explore how to address a need	• Crystallize a specific need • Explore our capabilities	• Explain needs and goals	• Receive clear information • Opportunity to present concerns	• Determine whether to buy our solution • Confirm contract details	• Prepare to accept solution and accept invoice	• Affirm results • Validate the decision	• Place future business with confidence
Customer Buying Process	STEP 1 Plan and Prioritize	STEP 2 Identify Options		STEP 3 Evaluate Options	STEP 4 Select the Best Option STEP 5 Contract	STEP 6 Implement Solution and Track Performance		

Problem-Focused Solution Provider

Sales Relationship

Customer-Focused, Strategic, and Trusted Business Advisor

Case Studies **217**

proactively live the new brand and customer value proposition, this business development process also aligned specifically with the known expectations of consumers and their typical decision-making and purchase process.

This case study illustrates a practical example of how the deployment of Rapid Due Diligence can uncover much more valuable information about an organization than the original process was designed to do.

In this situation, it was in the midst of the interviews that the multiple, potentially competing initiatives were discovered, to the surprise of the cross-business unit team members who had already done considerable internal assessment. The researcher was the resource that identified the potential for much greater business impact by deliberate convergence of the many moving parts into a holistic system, in this case, to prepare the entire enterprise to deliver the new brand. The original investment in researching and creating the new brand was considerably more leveraged and more quickly recovered in the broader enterprise revenue stream.

Behind the scenes, the information gained from the Rapid Due Diligence diagnostic process continued to produce further insights as the initial stages of the implementation plan commenced.

- The findings provided content for compelling messages for the communications strategy, with differentiation as needed for the various business units and geographic areas.
- The need for an enterprise-wide approach to business development took shape, with granular details of the steps, performance standards, and links with the business objectives, plus the decision-making steps for consumers that arose from the findings.
- The data also informed the approach for communicating, reinforcing, and coaching within natural performance management cycles and measurement processes for employees at multiple roles and levels across the business units.

The Rapid Due Diligence diagnostic process also called for attention to the refinement of a value proposition for franchise agents plus making available the findings on the business development process and skill development.

The core project team and designated executive contact were gradually and deeply immersed in not only the findings and recommendations, but also the triangulation and rationalization of business system dynamics, strategic integration, and execution techniques. The entire Rapid Due Diligence diagnostic process de facto became the instigation of an executive development process for all the key players.

Discussion Questions

- Why was the discovery of the new branding initiative so important in this situation?
- How was the Rapid Due Diligence process able to discern the potential for convergence of multiple initiatives into a holistic, systemic strategy?

218 Case Studies

- How would this discovery affect other strategic dimensions and the strategic objectives of the organization?
- Why would a value proposition for franchise agents be useful?

Case Study Two: Shifting Operating Models

A large, not-for-profit membership organization had for decades provided a wide variety of products and services. The proliferation of internet services, fierce competition from existing and new sources, plus the application of new technologies challenged this organization's traditional operating and business development model.

Operations had previously centered on walk-in customers. Competitors were now promoting lower rates and rate comparisons to prospective customers through television advertising and online contact. Furthermore, the ubiquitous use of cell phones, geographic positioning system capabilities, quickly expanding online competitive sources, and other electronic services had disrupted the former need for sole reliance on in-person transactions.

The organization came to the conclusion that a fresh and consistent operating model, or sales model, was required in order to meet the new environment for their current and future members. This new strategy required the provision of services with higher quality, more consultative interactions, and the capability to more intentionally influence current members to cultivate stronger loyalty and discover their broader array of available products and services.

This intended shift would require a major transition from the long embedded attention to transactional operations to a new, consultative, relationship-building model. A significant cultural shift throughout the organization and its various business units was warranted. The long-held values of the organization needed to be further tested and updated to align with the proposed new operating model. A thorough change in the day-to-day mindset was in order, from the executive level decision-makers all the way throughout the entire population of associates who come in contact with current and potential new members.

This organization had a well-established and respected employee development function. Some recent reorganization of this function further elevated the interest level in ensuring that any development activities become directly aligned with the strategic focus expressed at the executive table. The executive conversation about the potential need to shift to a fresh operating model eventually brought attention to employee development. There were many questions to be asked and answered. Why was the organization convinced it needed to make any changes? What was the new operating model? What would it require of employees at all levels, especially associates on the front line? How would the deeply embedded culture embrace such changes? How would the results of the transition be measured?

From an earlier successful experience together at a previous employer, the new head of employee development chose to ask the researcher to engage in an exploratory conversation about the organization-wide situation. The Rapid Due

Diligence diagnostic process was a good fit for this strategic challenge, and the work began.

Deploying the background investigations and arranging an initial set of interviews, the strategic conversations eventually revealed the work that was already in hand. With the previous assistance of a capable outside consulting resource, the organization had completed significant market and member research. The data were used to help create a potential operating model, with a common process, clarity of roles in fulfilling the model, and the identity of fundamental skills that would address the needs of current and future members.

This research also revealed how the new model could potentially trigger members' interest in gradually becoming loyal members who would choose to utilize more products and services. The implementation of this new model was left to the devices of the organization.

All of this work developed into a broad initiative with the intent to clarify the new model and identify the required skill development to fulfill the new approach. The organization would eventually transition from its strong service reputation to a more intentional sales-oriented, member-driven, loyalty building focus. Some specific objectives were established.

- Establish a common process that would span all the business units and provide a consistent way for sales associates to consultatively engage and relate to members and potential member prospects.
- Provide a unique standard for sales excellence throughout the organization.
- Support the goal of providing a consistent experience for associates and members, related to the provision of all products and services.
- Develop a deeper understanding of the business and the rationale for such a change among all associates and their managers.

A team of associates had been collecting data from across multiple layers throughout the organization for a parallel purpose. They were attempting to define more specifically how the organization would measure any impact of a change in the operating model and which metrics they would use to evaluate progress.

The organization wanted to track progress on the application of the new operating model and supportive skills. They were interested in learning about any differences in the impact of both behavior and process changes. Particular attention was being paid to three specific metrics.

- Insurance and other service policy counts
- Revenue production
- Sales productivity by associate

Taking a much more granular look at the research data and tracing a probable set of leverage points within the likely economic value-producing stream throughout

220 Case Studies

the various functions of the organization, the researcher established a corollary to the proposed operating or business development model. Working alongside the organization's analysts who possessed expertise in performance metrics, a systemic approach was devised to provide trustworthy, organizationally credible data collection and interpretation that was more easily and naturally acceptable to senior executives, middle managers, and front line associates.

The executive level sponsors for the new operating model also brought together the key leaders in the sales performance area to openly participate in direct and candid dialogue. In this gathering, the researcher facilitated deep, engaging discussions among these key leaders to much more thoroughly understand the newly identified needs of the organization's members and how to more reliably match current products and services to those needs. Participants acquired more specific details about the new model, the comprehensive approach to its implementation throughout the sales function, the importance of this initiative to members, and refinements in the leaders' roles and responsibilities for the fulfillment of the new model. This depth of engagement was essential to cultivate and demonstrate true commitment to providing the ultimate service, well beyond the former transactional model.

The executive sponsors also realized the importance of their own direct involvement in the development of all levels of management and associates in the new skills inherent in the new model. The sponsors also knew the value of providing organizationally acceptable forms of evidence to prove why these skills were important to members. This action was essential to convince the many managers and associates who were naturally skeptical and would likely be resistant to the requirement to change their long-held, comfortable habits and behaviors.

With careful implementation and analysis of feedback from pilot experiences, the comprehensive skill development plan was conducted across nearly all market channels, product lines, and supporting business segments. Associates and their managers were learning how to conduct much more effective and engaging conversations with members that would identify and clarify their real needs, then know how to comfortably, confidently, and appropriately respond with just the right products and services that could fully satisfy those needs. This behavioral shift was recognized as the critical skill set at the heart of the new operating model. It also represented a very significant change in how associates communicated on an everyday basis with each contact.

Within a few months, several hundred associates and managers had completed the voluntary development experience. The time had come for the organization to begin checking their standard performance metrics to learn of any early indications of business impact from changes in behaviors aligned with the new operating model.

As a part of the Rapid Due Diligence diagnostic process, the researcher conducted a series of discussions with key players regarding the variety of metrics that could be used to gauge the performance of the new operating model and the employee development process. The metrics fell in four broad categories:

- Sales productivity by associate would include both revenue production and policy counts.
- Employee development evaluations of key competencies inherent in the new operating model would include immediate evaluation of the development experience, tests of the mastery levels achieved, after action review discussions following each developmental experience, and collection of behaviorally explicit anecdotal evidence.
- Member satisfaction ratings would be compared with previous member survey data.
  - o This would include specific member point-of-view insights on what is considered critical to quality, plus trigger points for member choices, a derivative of decision sciences and customer choice analytics.
  - o Another option was to trace the specific value driver tree or path of greatest opportunity within their internal reports and then match up that granular detail to the standards of competency in the new operating model, followed by triangulating those data points with explicit learning outcomes from the employee development.
  - o In addition, the researcher recommended the tracing of impact scales and performance scores, following the platform drivers to both key and sub-key drivers to the overall outcomes for the respective business units.
- Employee engagement survey data would be compared with responses from previous surveys to those in the upcoming cycle. While this was considered to be an indirect form of evaluation, the cultural effects could be traced in this parallel method.

The causal loop diagram shown in Figure 10.2 provides a simple view of the key factors at work in this relationship.

The researcher also provided specific process steps for consideration as the organization began to collect data, analyze results, and apply them to future activities and decisions. These recommendations and observations were also drawn from the several waves of Rapid Due Diligence diagnostic discovery.

- Investigate the current availability and condition of the metrics that were outlined in the four broad categories above. This was essential due to the clear preference stated by executive and managerial decision makers to use their own data as proof sources.
- Establish a clear baseline date and then collect the initial data. If at all possible, it was desirable to begin the baseline data collection process even before any further communication of the new operating model or the related employee development began. The intent was to gather data that would not be tainted.

222 Case Studies

FIGURE 10.2 Causal Loop Diagram of Service.

- Establish a single reporting or evaluation template in which the organization would simply and clearly assemble all the related metrics within one compact report. Reliance on visual cues to permit very rapid discernment of impact was suggested. Where possible, it was desirable to use those visual cues, color codes, target signs, deltas, or other symbols or devices that were already familiar to the associates.
- Show the metrics in the sequence of the organization's economic value-producing cycle, loop, or upward spiral of action so the associates can see the progressive improvement and causal relationships within the metrics. The typical path would show employee engagement, to individual skill development and performance, to individual performance expectations achieved and appearing on an individual performance scorecard, to the business unit sales performance scorecard, to the enterprise scorecard, and finally to a return on customer or member satisfaction index, accompanied by revenue production, policy counts, and member retention or loyalty data.
- Incorporate a simple discussion of the selected metrics in each of the employee development sessions. This might include declaration of the metrics that were selected, how the organization is tracking and evaluating results, expectations for performance following the employee development process, a simple explanation of the economic value-producing loop or spiral with a line of sight between individual performance and enterprise results, and revelation of the purpose to gauge the impact of the new operating model and employee development, presumably to affirm the effectiveness of the model and to identify any pinpointed areas for further refinement or continuous improvement.
- As the tracking is conducted periodically, apply business system dynamic analysis techniques to seek to identify any other systemic patterns or causal relationships that are becoming evident in the data among the categories of

metrics, or to uncover the emergence of other hidden factors that are influencing the results.

- Build accumulating evidence into future communications, courseware refinements, and all reinforcement activity.
- Include the metrics within relevant performance expectations in the formal performance management process.
- Use the data to continually refine the operating model, the employee development process, support processes, communications strategies, and strategy reviews.
- Monitor new insights from their own member research function to adjust the metrics and any sub-component alignments. The researcher suggested the detailed documentation of inflection points to avoid potential future confusion or misinterpretation of apparent changes and causal relationships.
- Capture and activate any implications for future talent management activities, such as recruitment, selection, on-boarding, promotions, rewards, recognition, and performance management. Incorporate the findings within their internal organizational university curriculum and marketing of services.
- Capture data that can provide further refinement of their internal return on member definition, member value proposition, or for brand management.
- Analyze the cumulative data from about twelve to eighteen months of experience to discern even more reliable predictors of success in quantifiable terms. Capture even more precise key performance indicator performance expectations for the phases or pipeline within the operating model. Build these findings into the full measurement cycle of activity, such as prospecting, forecasting, advances within phase, conversion and closing ratios, time boundaries, and all measures of sales efficiency and proficiency.

The first round of analysis and evaluation was conducted by the internal sales analysts in its usual thorough fashion, and their work produced a startling discovery. The analysts concluded that the employee development conducted in alignment with the new operating model had produced a statistically significant and positive effect on gross new policy production. Based on their evidence, the analysts stated that there was an immediate and effective new policy production, or sales performance, improvement that began in the same month as the initial employee development occurred.

Further, their findings suggested an immediate and sustained productivity gain of at least four percent for those who had engaged in the development. In other words, using their own data, the organization showed a notable increase in new policies written, beginning in the first month following the employee development process. This was a direct, traceable improvement within the economic value-producing stream of the organization.

While these early data and perspectives of their own expert analysts were quite convincing, the organization's historical culture of slow, gradual acceptance of

224 Case Studies

any change still inhibited the realization of the full value of the shift in operating models. Perhaps the most significant source of organizational reluctance occurred within the middle management ranks. The functional structure consisted of a relatively high number of direct reports; and managers commonly responded that they didn't have the time, or the inclination, to engage in the requisite daily coaching and mentoring of associates to use the newly acquired skills.

Such inhibitors are often deeply hidden within organizations. The Rapid Due Diligence diagnostic process, conducted in this case in a few waves over a longer period, uncovered the systemic business dynamics and deleterious impact of such reluctance, trapped in the long-term success of the organization. New questions were now encouraged. A series of actions that typically demonstrate management involvement and support to direct reports is illustrated in Figure 10.3.

A group of mid-level managers and executives began to rethink the sales management role. They contemplated how to balance the need to perform administrative functions with the required development and performance management normally associated with a classic sales management position, especially in view of both dramatic and subtle changes exhorted in the new operating model.

Once this group learned of the internally provided evidence of the direct improvement in sales revenue and number of new policies, a newly charged managerial impetus pushed for changes. They made what is often considered a very bold move. They restructured the sales manager job descriptions to require at least half of their time on coaching and mentoring direct reports. Furthermore, the number of direct reports was reduced on average from twenty to eight.

Management accepted the compelling, internally produced evidence. They saw the economic impact of the new operating model on one of their key metrics. They were convinced by their own evidence that the new model was on target. They came to realize the value of the new model for everyone, not just their enterprise, but also their associates, and their members.

A number of elements from the Rapid Due Diligence diagnostic process were carefully captured, plotted out, and sensitively shared with influential thought leaders.

Support Absent	Allows Participation	Attends Ceremonies	Encourages Participation by Others	Participates Actively in Sessions	Teaches Skills & Behaviors	Reinforces Skills & Behaviors	Applies Skills in Own Role

Low Support   **High Support**

FIGURE 10.3 Continuum of Management Support.

- The combination of strategic and granular alignment of the internal operating model research data
- Deeper understanding of the organizational culture
- Collaboration with internal expert performance analysts
- Precise and culturally sensitive implementation planning and execution
- Discovery of hidden dynamics within the business and revelation of both intended and unintended secondary and tertiary consequences of systemic processes and choices
- Filtering of spoken and unspoken ambitions

This complex approach was critical to achieving real and credible results. This Rapid Due Diligence diagnostic process and the resulting execution of this broad-based approach were essential to implementing a major shift in operating models.

Discussion Questions

- How could the exploration of innovative applications of digitization be useful in adapting the new operating model?
- How was the Rapid Due Diligence diagnostic process applied to identify specific strategic gaps?
- Why was it essential for the organization to produce its own evidence of any improvements?
- Why was executive and management support especially important in this organization's culture?

Case Study Three: Improving Operational Quality and Efficiency

A military organization was continually seeking to provide the highest quality of equipment at the right time and in the most cost-efficient manner to soldiers in combat. Command-level decisions had been taken to vigilantly pursue a combination of Lean 6s and Six Sigma process improvement initiatives throughout this command. Current results were mixed. The researcher was asked to conduct a series of inquiries and studies, using the Rapid Due Diligence diagnostic process, to determine how to consistently improve and sustain those results.

Many insights were derived from a combination of workforce surveys, studies of the Lean 6s and Six Sigma initiatives, and observations and practical application of leadership competencies such as teamwork, collaboration, change management, complex problem solving, and process management.

This case includes an overview of the Rapid Due Diligence diagnostic process, results, practical tools and techniques, as well as insights gained from the ongoing site activities and evaluation. Specific implications for other organizations undertaking Lean 6s and Six Sigma initiatives are also included.

226 Case Studies

Simultaneous with the global war on terrorism and the activation of soldiers on the ground, there was a firm goal to ultimately support the broad-scale military transformation. Specific objectives in this transformation included:

- Linking strategic goals and objectives directly to create consistency of purpose
- Improving and focusing leadership, management, and technology on critical systems and processes
- Influencing new ways to manage, make fact-based decisions, and change the internal culture
- Aligning metrics and reward systems with the strategic intent

Command-level decisions were taken to create an Enterprise Excellence Federation. This was a holistic approach with tools and techniques intended to:

- Improve and focus leadership, management, and technology on critical systems and processes.
- Infuse a sense of urgency.
- Establish a new way to manage, make fact-based decisions, and change its internal culture.
- Focus first on the people.

The strategic transformation plan for the command focused on people as the key enabler. By focusing first on the people, the objective was to develop the workforce's and management's ability to adapt to change and cope with the stress and demands by fostering the following leadership competencies: leadership, teaming, communications, employee support, strategic thinking, and a positive organizational climate. This focus and application of the six leadership competencies were expected to contribute to four specific goals to transform the organization:

- The people
- Readiness
- Business processes and organizational effectiveness
- Relationship management and customer focus

The tools and techniques within the Enterprise Excellence Federation included the quality management system, the Lean 6s and Six Sigma initiatives, the voice of the customer, and the leadership competencies program. Efforts in all of these areas were launched. These decisions and stated goals represented a significant shift from previous practice and a challenging transformation of the fundamental culture of this military organization.

Since the inception of the leadership competencies program, annual workforce surveys had been conducted at each of the twenty-nine command sites to determine measurable progress in the routine use of thirty behaviors that further

Case Studies **227**

described the six leadership competencies. Comparative reviews were conducted at the headquarters and provided for the command at each separate site.

One particular depot had long been considered a performance leader in the command's community of arsenals, engineering, and program offices. This depot's positive, comparative results from the annual workforce surveys bore further testimony to its attention to the leadership competencies.

This depot had also been actively conducting Lean 6s as a prelude to even more rigorous inclusion of Six Sigma protocol. The preliminary results of the Lean 6s project work were mixed among the number of rapid improvement event project teams. The depot command sought to discover how the integration and diligent application of leadership competencies could improve the results of the Lean 6s and Six Sigma activities.

On the basis of the preliminary results of Lean 6s and its first three years of workforce studies, the command approved a multi-phase, short-range project, using the Rapid Due Diligence diagnostic process. The purpose of the project was to uncover ways to gain even greater benefits from the Lean 6s and Six Sigma activities underway and scheduled at that depot. The scope of work initially included the following two phases:

- Conducting behavioral observations at Lean 6s rapid improvement events conducted by trained project teams
- Designing and delivering pilot training sessions to address specific gaps uncovered during the first discovery phase

The Rapid Due Diligence diagnostic process was designed to secure direct observations of the on-site application of leadership, teamwork, change management, problem solving, and process improvement skills in the Lean 6s working sessions. Detailed findings from those observations were used to design pinpointed training experiences that could produce even better Lean 6s and Six Sigma results that last.

A structured observation process, protocol, communications plan, and observation grid worksheets were prepared to capture behavioral evidence of leadership, teamwork, and process management behaviors as they occurred naturally within the rapid improvement event process. Table 10.2 shows the structured observation grid with the expected competencies, behaviors, and decision rules for classifying the observed incidents.

The research team conferred in advance of the on-site visit to ensure a consistent approach to gathering observation data and assessing its effectiveness. The intent was to conduct direct, structured observations to provide an accurate, rich depth of valid data that could be used to pinpoint specific leadership, teamwork, change management, and process management skills. Routine use of these skills could take the depot to the next level of enterprise excellence in its application of Lean 6s principles and Six Sigma activities.

TABLE 10.2 Lean Six Sigma Rapid Improvement Event Structured Observations Grid

Team Identification: _____
Location: _____
Date/Time: _____

Lean Six Sigma Competency Label	Name Role	Name Role	Name Role	Name Role	Name Role	Name Role	Comments
Recognizing opportunities							
Taking initiative beyond requirements							
Thinking and acting strategically							
Dealing effectively with ambiguity							
Focusing on needs of the customers							
Identifying unspoken needs							
Effective communication							
Involving others							
Practicing team effectiveness							
Planning and organizing projects							
Managing projects for results							
Applying stat. problem solving proficiency							
Gathering relevant data							
Paying attention to detail							
Defining work flow							
Analyzing and interpreting data for meaning							
Applying creativity and innovation							
Discerning distinguishing differences							
Formulating criteria for decision making							
Applying judgment to make decisions							

Setting performance standards of excellence
Sharing information
Demonstrating accountability for results
Embracing change
Monitoring and measuring performance
Evaluating performance
Providing feedback to others
Coaching others
Maintaining and promoting Lean Six Sigma
Driving for results

Rating Decision Rules: + = Positive example; − = Negative example; 0 = Opportunity presented and missed; one mark per observed incident

Team Identification: _____
Location: _____
Date/Time: _____

Leadership Trait Competency Label	Name Role	Name Role	Name Role	Name Role	Name Role	Name Role	Comments
Speak with one voice							
Treat associates as customers							
Set an example by modeling appropriate behavior							
Ensure associates have right tools to get job done							
Consider how their work will impact others							
Apply policy and procedures consistently							

Rating Decision Rules: + = Positive example; − = Negative example; 0 = Opportunity presented and missed; one mark per observed incident

(Continued)

Team Identification: _____

Location: _____

Date/Time: _____

Strategic Thinking Trait Competency Label	Name Role	Name Role	Name Role	Name Role	Name Role	Name Role	*Comments*
Consider the impact on readiness in everything we do							
Focus on internal as well as external customers							
Focus on our future by zeroing in on outcomes we want							
Get feedback on change initiatives from all sources							
Concentrate on the good of all							

Rating Decision Rules: + = Positive example; − = Negative example; 0 = Opportunity presented and missed; one mark per observed incident

Team Identification: _____

Location: _____

Date/Time: _____

Communication Trait Competency Label	Name Role	Name Role	Name Role	Name Role	Name Role	Name Role	*Comments*
Know who our customers and suppliers are							
Communicate with associates openly and honestly							
Share both good news and bad news with associates							

Rating Decision Rules: + = Positive example; − = Negative example; 0 = Opportunity presented and missed; one mark per observed incident

Team Identification: _____

Location: _____

Date/Time: _____

Organizational Climate Trait Competency Label	*Name* *Role*	*Name* *Role*	*Name* *Role*	*Name* *Role*	*Name* *Role*	*Name* *Role*	*Comments*
Effectively plan ahead							
Demonstrate flexible behavior							
Demonstrate a willingness to take risks							
Demonstrate respect and mutual trust toward each other							
Show pride in organization							

Rating Decision Rules: + = Positive example; − = Negative example; 0 = Opportunity presented and missed; one mark per observed incident

Team Identification: _____

Location: _____

Date/Time: _____

Teaming Trait Competency Label	*Name* *Role*	*Name* *Role*	*Name* *Role*	*Name* *Role*	*Name* *Role*	*Name* *Role*	*Comments*
Allow associates to make mistakes and fail							
Support fewer management layers							
Maintain other people's self-esteem							
Involve others in decisions that impact them							
Demonstrate teamwork							
Provide employees resources to accomplish their mission							

Rating Decision Rules: + = Positive example; − = Negative example; 0 = Opportunity presented and missed; one mark per observed incident

(*Continued*)

Team Identification: _____

Location: _____

Date/Time: _____

Employee Support Trait Competency Label	*Name Role*	*Name Role*	*Name Role*	*Name Role*	*Name Role*	*Name Role*	*Comments*
Help create a great place to work							
Help others see the link between individual and corporate goals							
Help associates understand the importance of their work							
Provide clear options for career growth							
Show concern for associates							

Rating Decision Rules: + = Positive example; − = Negative example; 0 = Opportunity presented and missed; one mark per observed incident

Case Studies **233**

The observations were conducted on-site over a week-long period. During that time, a series of Lean 6s rapid improvement events were underway with six project teams. The research team observed their team meetings, wrap-up and brief-out presentations to their leaders, plus portions of a value stream analysis for another depot area.

There were numerous additional opportunities to observe project team activity and to secure an overview of the Lean 6s business system and Six Sigma structure, tools, and techniques. The research team silently observed activity without disruption to the project teams' activities. Limited clarifying questions were later addressed to facilitating team members, team leaders, supervisors, and managers. Anonymity was assured for individual or team data to the degree possible. All relevant behavioral data were noted and labeled. Specific attention was given to the occurrence of positive, negative, or missed opportunities for the application of thirty Lean 6s and Six Sigma competencies, plus an additional thirty behaviors related to the six command leadership competencies.

The findings from this first phase were mixed. There were limited numbers of demonstrations of positive team leadership or group facilitation skills, some openness to change and risk-taking, evidence of leading and guiding project teams to accomplish concrete tasks within a short time, a single incident of sharing a vision of the future state of the process, support offered for fellow team members, and expressions of positive reaction to the explicit upper management declaration of its support for Lean 6s and Six Sigma.

On the other hand, there was little evidence of clear, planned, or executed meeting management and fully participative application of the Lean 6s and Six Sigma tools and techniques. There was evidence of less than full support by supervision. There was little evidence that the project teams knew who their internal and external customers were or any intent to communicate directly with people in other shop areas. There were clear communication gaps between shifts, within the larger work groups, and across functional areas. The roles of process owners, supervisors, team leaders, and team members were unclear and unknown by many. There was repeated evidence of risk aversion and fear of supervisory rejection of new ideas.

Descriptions voluntarily offered by several team leaders and members about the current depot culture provided behavioral examples that were assessed to be non-conducive to the desirable environment for long-term successful application and realization of Lean 6s and Six Sigma results. All project teams struggled with meeting management, communications, and acknowledgment of the needs of customers.

Upon thorough review of the behavioral observation findings, comparison with the workforce survey detailed data, interviews with a cross-section of all levels involved in the Lean 6s and Six Sigma process, and multiple analyses of triangulated data, the research team concluded that it would be unlikely that

234 Case Studies

any material advancement in process improvement or production output could be sustained in the longer term without further human interaction development. The complete set of findings, conclusions, and recommendations was presented in writing and discussed with further detailed commentary with the depot command.

After reviewing the findings from the first phase, the depot command chose to proceed with the second phase, that is, to conduct one or more pilot training sessions to focus on development opportunities discovered in the first phase. The project was further extended to include another review step approximately thirty days after the training to observe and evaluate the application of skills and any improvement in project team activities.

Upon discernment of specific skill development opportunities for improving the human interaction skills from the phase one findings, three pilot training sessions were designed. The developmental design was highly interactive and provided many opportunities for open dialogue on roles, challenges, and practical application of leadership, teamwork, and process management skills to their own Lean 6s and Six Sigma projects. The content included meeting management and group facilitation techniques, change management tools, and project team tools and techniques for project start-up, collaborative participation, keeping project activities on course, and effective communications.

The participants in each of the three pilot sessions were enthusiastically involved and applied the tools and techniques to their own assigned rapid improvement event projects. Formal pilot evaluation data were collected. After-action review discussions were conducted in addition to gathering informal, anecdotal feedback. Specific recommendations for adjusting the developmental design and learning experiences were prepared for any future offerings of these skill applications sessions.

For the third and final phase of the study at the depot, two project teams that had been involved in the phase two training pilot sessions were scheduled to prepare for their Lean 6s rapid improvement event work. A month later, the researcher returned to observe and evaluate the application of the leadership, teamwork, change management, and process improvement skills throughout their respective rapid improvement event activities. Separate discussions were conducted with team members, project team leaders, supervisors, and managers.

In this third phase, the researcher was seeking behavioral evidence and any critical incident data of:

- The personal readiness and active involvement of team leaders and members within the changing environment and their reactions to the impact of the Lean 6s activity in their respective work areas
- The quality of the team meeting process and participation
- Team involvement in idea generation, problem solving, and process improvement activity

With the observations of managers and supervisors, the researcher was seeking behavioral evidence that:

- Provided clarity
- Removed roadblocks to Lean 6s and Six Sigma activities
- Showed any level of active support
- Offered recognition
- Monitored progress
- Engaged in guiding or coaching discussions
- Offered feedback
- Demonstrated communications across boundaries such as shifts or shops

Each of these behavioral categories had been noted as specific, repetitive opportunities missed or deficits in the phase one findings.

The findings from phase three observations and critical incident interviews included considerable evidence of improvement in the quality of the project team meeting process and participation. The frequency and degree of positive application of the leadership, teamwork, and process management skills appeared to be significantly influenced by:

- The scope and nature of the respective rapid improvement events themselves
- The degree of enthusiastic demonstration of team leadership skills by the team leaders
- The role of the Lean 6s facilitator at the team meetings

Greater confidence, skill application, and higher quality participation were displayed by nearly all participants. The quality of input, questions, and pursuit of the Lean 6s and Six Sigma tools and techniques improved significantly. Team leaders, supervisors, and managers repeatedly volunteered that the real potential for lasting results with the Lean 6s and Six Sigma activity is highly dependent upon the leadership, teamwork, change management, and process for activating those initiatives. They stated that using a strong-arm, highly directive approach would get the list of boxes checked; yet they had observed the people demonstrating limited interest in making the recommended changes last.

A comprehensive report of findings, conclusions, and further recommendations was prepared. After detailed presentation and thorough discussion of results at the close of the third phase of the project, the depot command requested a proposal for alternative approaches to integrating the Lean 6s and Six Sigma training and project team activities. This needed to include just-in-time developmental experiences and direct application of leadership, teamwork, change management, and process improvement skills to the assigned projects.

The command later assembled a planning discussion to share information from the three-phase project with a cross-section of depot senior leaders. The agenda

236 Case Studies

was focused to gain their opinion about the relative potential value to the current accelerated production environment, as well as gather input and explore alternative ways to implement the next phase of the leadership competency program, particularly with project teams doing Lean 6s and Six Sigma activities.

With the ongoing global war on terrorism and demand to serve the soldiers in combat, the depot continued to have an urgent focus on production with a significant increase in required performance to schedule, extended work schedules, expanded employment, ramping up the frequency of Lean 6s rapid improvement event projects, the need for full realization and sustenance of results from all Lean 6s and Six Sigma work, plus the need for greater collaboration and teamwork among the full organization as it grew and shifted. All of these major issues were explicitly stated, in addition to the need to secure the benefits of leadership competencies training, tools, and techniques without diminishing the production output and further to provide a cost/benefit impact with both quantitative and qualitative evidence to satisfy all the military oversight questions.

The group discussions reached consensus on the importance of pursuing the following actions:

- Managing a balance of training with performance to schedule requirements
- Focusing first on specific, targeted Lean Six Sigma work and preparing people who are new to their leadership roles
- Condensing the training experience where possible to reduce distractions from production activities
- Helping the depot independently apply an assortment of reinforcement and refresher tools, techniques, and job aids so both leaders and employees could more readily live the leadership competencies on an everyday basis
- Including non-manufacturing, administrative, and support areas in the focus training and reinforcement activities
- Establishing a set of meaningful metrics that gauge progress and business impact, drawing upon the depot's production performance scorecard, quad charts, and Lean 6s scorecard tracking process
- Creating even greater focus, efficiencies, enthusiasm, and lasting, measurable results from all Lean 6s and Six Sigma work, especially targeted value stream areas

Three alternative plans for implementation options were prepared in the schedule and resources to pursue results: minimum, standard, and aggressive. Specific information was prepared to support each of the implementation options in the following areas:

- Business focus
- Implementation planning at both the strategic and tactical level
- Communications planning within the site

Case Studies **237**

- Type of developmental training and number of participants
- Timeline for the next two fiscal years
- Reinforcement techniques
- Evaluation to gauge progress
- Expected impact
- Comparative advantages and disadvantages of each of the three alternatives

A fourth alternative was also developed to combine all three alternatives on a time-and-resource continuum to fit the production schedule and employee effectiveness needs. Despite command level enthusiasm for proceeding with at least the minimum option, suddenly announced changes in the production requirements to meet war demands temporarily suspended the commencement of these plans.

The results from this multi-phase Rapid Due Diligence diagnostic study at one depot were shared with the headquarters command. There was sufficient convincing evidence to stimulate the consideration and approval of a command-wide systemic leadership competency initiative with an expanded, comprehensive menu of services.

A number of primary actions to achieve the targeted cultural transformation were authorized. Fundamentally, the expanded leadership competency initiative was expected to drive the Soldier and Ground System Enterprise vision for attaining cultural transformation by showing direct connections to the central, critical mission of the military organization. Further, the initiative was expected to build advocacy, active propagation, and leadership by example by daily practice of the leadership competencies.

The cultural transformation was being anchored by offering organization-wide learning sessions for executive and mid-level leaders, frontline or work group leaders, frontline associates, and Lean 6s and Six Sigma project team members and leaders. The leadership competencies were integrated and applied to all enterprise initiatives, such as the Quality Management System (QMS), the Capability Maturity Model Integrated (CMMI), the Voice of the Customer (VoC), as well as the Lean 6s and Six Sigma initiatives.

The researcher was asked to communicate directly with the arsenals, depots, and program executive offices to explore and build their understanding of the connections of the leadership competency skills to their respective organizational objectives, accelerated production activity, and explicit workforce needs. Where requested, on-site assessments were conducted to identify strengths, pinpoint developmental gaps, and draw specific connections to local initiatives and working environments. Development activities were offered and conducted to complete or refresh any previous leadership competency work at each site. The just-in-time applications sessions with tools and techniques for initiatives such as Lean 6s and Six Sigma were designed to incorporate recommendations from the pilot sessions.

Comprehensive, systemic implementation plans were created to establish everyday operating practices to model, coach, reinforce, and measure the disciplined

238 Case Studies

application of leadership competencies. Several levels of evaluation were offered to gauge the impact of the leadership competencies training and application for any given site, including:

- Immediate after-action review feedback and improvement discussions
- Evaluation of training environment and participants' experience
- Evaluation of mastery of course content or skill acquisition
- Evaluation of observed behavior change or application of learning outcomes
- Evaluation of the Soldier and Ground Systems Enterprise or site's organizational and business impact
- Quarterly review sessions with site leadership teams
- Evaluation and comparative analyses of the annual leadership competencies or climate survey results

The site leadership team review sessions focused upon:

- Measuring, evaluating, and reinforcing progress
- Securing pinpointed coaching to the leadership team itself
- Sharing best practices from other command sites
- Generating innovative ideas for developing critical mass and more rapidly gaining the full benefits from the leadership competencies combined with other initiatives
- Discovering ways to continually drive improvement
- Communications plans for sharing and recognizing results with all people at their respective sites and across the command as a whole

The expanded, more disciplined, systemic, organization-wide approach to combining leadership competencies with Lean 6s and Six Sigma and other related initiatives got underway. Within six months, there were quantifiable results from the comparison of the annual workforce or climate surveys. The organization's climate survey aggregate score improvements ranged from fifteen to sixty-one percent per site. The leadership competency of communications had had the greatest improvement and highest means at twenty-six of the twenty-nine sites or survey groups. The lowest scores for all sites or groups were evident for two competencies: teaming and employee support.

Detailed analyses and reports for each site were prepared, summarizing the scores, means, and changes among all reporting years for the six leadership competency areas. Specific opportunities for development with any of the supporting thirty behaviors were provided for site command consideration and action, especially in conjunction with Lean 6s and Six Sigma initiatives.

Recommendations were provided to include these behaviors as specific areas of emphasis in any future training, reinforcement activities, coaching and feedback dialogue, as well as both formal and informal performance management

Case Studies **239**

discussions. These behaviors had been assembled earlier within the command as the most significant opportunities for advancing the intended cultural transformation and sustaining lasting results within the Army cultural transformation and Enterprise Excellence Foundation initiative.

The Rapid Due Diligence diagnostic process results and preliminary indicators of improvement in the application of leadership competencies and the related results, behavioral evidence, and stated motivations of project team members, team leaders, supervisors, and managers involved in the Lean 6s and Six Sigma initiative within the command, and especially at the designated depot site, provided encouraging evidence of the potential for gaining significantly greater and longer lasting benefits from these process improvement initiatives.

While further study, analyses, and evaluation of results over a longer term were desirable, these preliminary results bore important implications for other organizations. As noted in previous studies conducted by the researcher, technology-intensive organizations tend to concentrate management attention on the technology itself, selected technical targets, and the business or statistical process control tools and techniques within either Lean principles and/or Six Sigma initiatives. The pressure for immediate results, the urgency to realize process efficiencies, increased quality, or greater production output, and the impatience of investment resources often result in concentration on the technical dimension and limited attention to the impact of a combined technical and human capital model. More effective solutions included broader consideration of technical systems and processes, governance and political structures, transformative changes in behavioral engagement and performance at all levels, plus environmental, regulatory, and market impact.

As a result of this Due Diligence diagnostic process and the results, following are a number of questions that technology-intensive organizations are encouraged to contemplate:

- What's happening within our organization, with the competition or the marketplace, with regulation, or in technology ideation that warrants attention and potentially the infusion of Lean principles and/or Six Sigma initiatives?
- What is the degree of change that needs to be accomplished, and can simple process improvement techniques produce the targeted results?
- What Lean or Six Sigma processes do we already have in place; and how complete are the accompanying plans for communications, change management, plus training in process improvement tools and techniques?
- To what degree have we integrated important leadership, teamwork, change management, and problem solving training or development with the Lean or Six Sigma initiative?
- What plans are in place to capture and evaluate both qualitative and quantitative results and thus measure progress achieved and sustained over time?
- What changes or hurdles within our working environment need to be effectively addressed in order to pursue and sustain Lean or Six Sigma results?

240 Case Studies

- What is the risk of not addressing leadership, teamwork, change management, and problem solving areas in conjunction with our Lean or Six Sigma pursuit?

To summarize the findings from this particular Rapid Due Diligence diagnostic study, there is a high probability that the combination of human behavioral skills and Lean 6s and/or Six Sigma technical process improvement techniques can produce significantly greater benefits. Such results materialized within this military organization, and there is a strong likelihood of the realization of similar results in other organizations.

Discussion Questions

- Why was it important to engage in direct, structured observations in the production environment?
- What variations in the Rapid Due Diligence diagnostic process were applied in this case to secure important observable and measurable results?
- Why was it necessary to create four alternative implementation plans for this organization?
- What other questions would be particularly important to address in a Rapid Due Diligence diagnostic process in technology-intensive organizations?

Case Study Four: Creating a Post-Merger Talent Management Strategy

A very large hospitality organization was in the early stages of setting strategy for the coming business year. A number of additional properties had been acquired as a result of a recently concluded merger. As the executives from all of the properties assembled and began plotting the moves for the future, it became apparent that more attention was required for human resources. The executive with responsibility for human resource management across the entire organization sought the assistance of the researcher in conducting a baseline assessment as an initial step for developing a broader strategy.

The Rapid Due Diligence diagnostic process was applied for two specific purposes:

- To gain a clear understanding of the training and development activity currently in place and required for future business success across all the properties.
- To identify opportunities to build upon what was already in place for the human resources strategy.

The findings of this assessment were intended to serve as the core guide for recruitment, selection, skills assessment, development curriculum, promotion, performance management, retention, and impact measurement of the human resource or talent management strategy in the coming year.

It was particularly important for the assessment process to demonstrate respect for the planning and work that this large organization had already invested in this subject. Therefore, the researcher planned to collaboratively engage with any contacts to:

- Take careful stock of what was known or already in place.
- Gauge how well those elements were working and producing any positive impact.
- Understand the future business context and performance targets.
- Identify the critical competencies (skills, knowledge, abilities, and motivations) required for the business success they were seeking.
- Compare all findings with other best practices, research, and experiences of best-in-class organizations.
- Pinpoint specific opportunities for building on what was already in place and creating a more cohesive, integrated approach to talent management, while at the same time accommodating the unique cultural aspects at the various properties or business units across the entire enterprise.

The schedule for this Rapid Due Diligence diagnostic process was necessarily more compact than usual. The assessment results were required within three weeks.

To prepare for highly focused and effective interviews to be completed onsite or by telephone within a one-week period, the researcher reviewed in-depth several relevant internal documents that provided background on the business and current human resources processes. These documents included:

- Results from the most recent employee survey
- Notes from deliberations among the property executives
- Training and development planning goals
- Current training and development offerings

Focus groups and individual interviews were tightly scheduled. Participants represented multiple levels, functions, and properties in order to secure any differing perspectives on a number of important, related factors and issues. Principal topics included the following areas of inquiry:

- The business situation following the merger
- Guest expectations for distinctive provision of hospitality
- Business metrics used to track success
- Skills, knowledge, abilities, and motivations (competencies) required for business success

242 Case Studies

- Current training and development systems, delivery methodologies, and recommended changes
- Any challenges or other factors that could either propel or impede the attainment of a future talent management strategy
- Other insights related to the current curriculum and talent management

The advance reviews, focus groups, and interviews were conducted on schedule; and the findings and recommendations from the Rapid Due Diligence diagnostic process were presented ahead of schedule. To provide greater depth as background for the findings, all of the interview and focus group commentaries were organized and summarized into the inquiry categories noted above. The information was provided without attribution to preserve anonymity to the degree possible. Some editing was applied to condense the content. Where similar comments had been offered more than once, the frequency of mention was noted parenthetically following the respective statements. The executive who requested the assessment was thankful for this level of specific and granular detail.

In reviewing the detailed comments, the researcher offered several preliminary observations. A sample of those observations includes the following:

- Participants from all properties voiced considerable anxiety about the known staffing plans, and there was fear of a potential talent drain to the benefit of the most desirable properties and to the clear deficit of others.
- A recent reduction in force process continued to have lingering, negative effects on the morale of current employees.
- The organization's talent management processes were primarily supported in manual mode by an outdated tracking system.
- The results of the recent employee engagement survey had some favorable results yet presented many opportunities for improvement when compared with the standards of best-in-class organizations.
- With many hundreds of training courseware offerings across the enterprise, it was clear that there were significant redundancies, inconsistencies, gaps, and differences in both training designs and outcomes.
- There were considerable inefficiencies, unnecessary costs, and unmet needs in the current training and development approach.
- Training had largely focused on what tasks needed to be done, with little or no attention to the behavioral way to do things.
- Learning experiences were often being truncated to accommodate limited schedules.
- The level of skill transference and application was unknown.
- While there was keen interest by many, not everyone could agree about the creation of a core curriculum. There was a strong desire for each local property's training to be customized to accommodate their unique distinctions. This was a lingering post-merger theme.

- The properties had evolved into a somewhat unbecoming pecking order of "haves" and "have-nots" with very little evidence of collaboration or sharing among the training functions.
- People within the training functions expressed being overwhelmed by training demands while simultaneously being anxious about job security and professional stature.
- There was no evidence of career paths, identification of high potential employees, or succession planning anywhere across the organization.
- There were many reports of conscious and stiff resistance at all levels of leadership at the various properties to performance management in nearly every form. The targets of resistance included setting expectations for accountability and results, coaching, development planning tied directly to performance standards, offering constructive feedback, and conducting appraisals and evaluations.
- In addition, there was active refusal to conduct performance evaluations for fear of setting expectations of compensation changes.
- Many property leaders reportedly preferred their current degree of autonomy and would choose not to fully embrace the advantages of a more unified organizational approach to talent management.
- There was no appreciation for the full cost of turnover within the properties.

On the basis of the scope of the Rapid Due Diligence diagnostic process and its analysis, the researcher offered some conclusions for this newly merged hospitality organization. The overarching opportunities were:

- The adoption of a unified, competency-centered talent management system across all properties within the enterprise
- The cultivation of a culture that demonstrates the value of the people to the business
- The disciplined accountability for performance management tied to measurable business results and guest experiences

In pursuing these three opportunities, the researcher observed that this organization could have the potential for igniting a new source of competitive edge for the collective properties within their unique market areas. In particular, it was the opinion of the researcher that the use of a competency-centered approach could have significant affect on the quality of work life, the stature of the organization as an employer, and ultimately on the economic performance of the business. This would encompass behavioral hiring, selection, development of leaders at all levels, everyone's responsibility for guest experiences, the infusion of performance standards and performance management in its fullest definition, plus cultural changes that meld together the business vision, values, and distinctive guest experiences, and the likely positive impact on employee engagement and retention.

244 Case Studies

These conclusions drew upon best-in-class experience and research findings:

- Best-in-class, high performing organizations consciously focus upon creating mutually valuable relationships with their customers (guests) and pay deliberate attention to the ways in which to earn the highest marks by their targeted customers and market segments.
- Attaining consistently high performance requires a comprehensive and systemic view of strategic, cultural, and infrastructural elements that all contribute holistically to organizational attention to customers and delivery of services with both efficiency and effectiveness. This requires disciplined performance management that is directly tied to the customers' experiences and impact on measurable business results.
- These factors combine with the focused provision of the right set of behavioral skills, knowledge, and motivational factors to serve the customers according to specified performance standards.
- A competency-centered approach to talent management can ensure improved recruitment, selection, deployment, focused growth and development, and greater engagement and productivity over the full tenure of employees.
- Great points of leverage exist in equipping all levels of leaders to effectively and routinely set expectations for performance standards, model those standards, coach, reinforce, recognize, monitor, and measure progress.

Based upon the observations and conclusions derived from the Rapid Due Diligence diagnostic process, the researcher proposed a number of recommendations for potential action by this organization. Given the capabilities and strength of players within the organization, the researcher stated with some confidence that the work could be conducted solely by themselves with little to no outside assistance.

An essential first step was the conduct of dialogue among senior leaders and members of the human resource function to share the results of this baseline assessment process. Then, they needed to secure mutual commitment to be fully engaged as leaders and influencers of the talent management strategy. Some actions to be undertaken by this group included:

- Deliberate the value and business needs to move forward promptly with a full commitment to a unified talent management and development strategy.
  - o Estimate the impact of the talent management strategy, including performance management focus, on financial measures, competitive advantage, guest experience and loyalty/referral ratings, ambitions to attain and sustain coveted hospitality ratings, alignment with the overall organizational strategy and property branding, explicit guest value proposition, and full cost of turnover.
  - o Consider how a new structure, roles, responsibilities, performance expectations, and accountability for results can provide further clarity, emphasis, and direct support to the talent management strategy.

Case Studies 245

- o Determine how to implement a talent management software system to most effectively support the immediate needs of organizing the recruitment, applicant tracking, selection, and training processes.
- Consider how a host of research shows that these practices are critical to business performance, productivity, and effectiveness and deliberate their application to this organization.
  - o There is a strong relationship between the availability and readiness of leadership bench strength and financial success.
  - o A study of strategy-to-performance gaps shows that there is an average shortfall in realizable results of thirty-seven percent. A significant contributor to such gaps is the failure to have the right leadership and critical talent in place, people who can also effectively translate the strategy into actionable priorities. Another major contributor is the consistent use of performance management to guide expectations and performance.
  - o The long-term viability of an enterprise requires a continuous flow and abundant pipeline of high-potential performers who can move into leadership roles at all levels throughout the organization.
  - o Organizations that score in the top twenty percent in talent management and leader development have produced an average of twenty-two percent greater total return to shareholders.
  - o The quality of an organization's human capital management is a primary indicator of its success. One study showed a ninety percent increase in shareholder value when organizations focus on human capital management.
  - o Highly talented line or operations managers have been shown to generate between fifty to one hundred fifty percent growth in revenue or profit when compared to the relatively flat performance results contributed by average or low performing managers.
  - o Human capital is considered a valuable source of competitive advantage.
  - o Aligning leadership development efforts with business strategies is critical to driving business impact.
  - o The only unique asset that a business has for gaining a sustained competitive advantage over rivals is its workforce, i.e., the skills and dedication of its employees.
  - o The most admired organizations on the Fortune 500 list have strong leadership development practices with:
    - o Emphasis on ongoing development efforts closely linked to strategic business goals and supported by formal reward programs
    - o Frequent use of competency models as well as a wide variety of developmental programs to select and advance leaders
    - o Low tolerance of inappropriate behavior in order to meet numbers
    - o Emotional intelligence of leaders
  - o Successful leaders create workplace environments that foster performance, pride, and purpose, and do not support low performance at any cost differential.

246 Case Studies

- o In top performing companies, active chief executive officer involvement in leadership development produced performance at the seventy-fifth percentile or higher in total shareholder return.
- o Systematic interventions (training, coaching, and reinforcement) focusing on performance-based human resource development deliver a two to eight multiple return on investment within the first year of application.
- o Of the top twenty-two processes and systems that drive the highest level of impact in an organization, coaching yields the highest impact.

This lengthy list of proof sources from recent human resource research was provided to the sponsoring executive for the express purpose of helping to provide convincing evidence of the value of paying attention to talent management. The researcher was keenly aware that there was significant resistance among the leadership to the core pursuit of any talent management strategy.

In addition, the researcher provided a substantive, detailed human capital cycle document describing six stages, typical key tasks and outcomes within each stage, likely consequences if unsuccessful, and primary issues or questions to address. This integrative strategic human capital alignment framework has appeared as an illustration earlier in Chapter Six and is shown again in Table 10.3 for easy reference.

A number of other recommendations were made for the organization's consideration. These included:

- Refine a set of core competencies for leaders at all levels in all properties and business units. Use this set of competencies as the central driver for recruitment, behavioral interviewing, selection, promotion, development, and performance management.
- Foster greater engagement and stem unwanted turnover through the creation and application of an employee value proposition for inclusion in recruitment, selection, ongoing development, and ultimately career path processes.
  - o Address specifically why bright, ambitious, skilled, and dedicated people would want to invest their careers within this organization and become contributors to premium guest experiences in the respective properties.
  - o Incorporate the employee value proposition and guest experience performance standards into line-of-sight expectations for performance.
  - o Include stories of highly relevant examples on how to apply the employee value proposition and optimize the guest experience to fit the various brands across the enterprise.
  - o Build the employee value proposition into the objectives and actions by all levels of leaders to ensure it is delivered and experienced as intended.
  - o Incorporate the employee value proposition into all talent management policies, processes, systems, and practices.
- Institute an expectation for day-to-day performance management plus regular formal evaluations throughout the enterprise.

TABLE 10.3 Integrated Strategic Human Capital Alignment Framework

Stage	Key Tasks	Outcomes of Stage	Consequences If Unsuccessful	Issues or Questions to Address
Emergence of New Organizational Need, Strategy, or Direction	• Affirm nature of new organizational need (examples: launch of new initiative; change of direction; preparation or response to new internal or external situation) • Secure facts and create compelling case for specific action and outcomes • Set overarching strategy with plan for execution • Establish process for implementation • Define human capital resources required • Specify critical knowledge and talent required for success • Align with employee value proposition • Define outcomes and measures of progress	• Clarity of need and desired outcomes • Clarity of overarching strategy to achieve outcomes • Comprehensive, integrated, systemic approach to strategy execution • Thorough plan with accountabilities for results • Accurate description of required human capital, especially critical knowledge and talent • Organizational commitment to follow through • Determination of how to secure periodic evidence of progress and effectiveness of strategy and programs	• Lower probability of achieving outcomes • Untimely results • Ambiguous description of need • Outcomes may not fit situation • Wasted resources • Insufficiency and low readiness of the people to perform (do not have right people, right skills, right place, right time) • Unlikely improvement in reputation of the agency • Not viewed as attractive place to work and contribute to the public good	• How will we effectively sort competing priorities, points of view, sense of urgency, and limited resources to secure prompt clarity and direction in complex situations? • How will we build shared ownership of an important, realizable strategy? • What strategic options do we need to explore? What criteria will we use? • What risks might we encounter, and how will we mitigate them? • How will we test the strategy to avoid unintended, unfavorable consequences? • How will we determine what human capital resources are truly necessary? • Where do we have strategic vulnerability with critical knowledge and talent?

(Continued)

Stage	Key Tasks	Outcomes of Stage	Consequences If Unsuccessful	Issues or Questions to Address
	• Set communications strategy • Establish feedback loops to monitor situation			• How will we communicate effectively to build broad commitment to the strategy, changes required, and responsibility for results? • How well do our current processes, systems, policies, practices, and culture align with the proposed strategy? • How will we measure success? • How will we recognize people and celebrate success? • How will we set and monitor feedback loops?
Definition of Human Capital Plan	• Define the overarching Human Capital plan to support the new strategy • Define the competencies required for superior performance in the new strategy • Conduct a census or inventory of employee capabilities • Assess or calibrate the current set of competencies and resources	• Clarity on the precise Human Capital needs to support fulfillment of the new strategy • Accurate assessment of current capabilities • Thorough and fair plan to identify Human Capital • Reconciliation of existing talent management, bench strength, and succession planning processes	• Unclear and inaccurate identity of Human Capital needs • Unlikely to have perception of fairness • Not likely to have right people with right skills are ready at the right time and in the right place • Human resources functional support will miss the mark	• How will we accurately define the skills, knowledge, abilities, and motivations required for superior performance in fulfilling this strategy? • How will we organize and conduct a census that captures employee capabilities? • How do the targeted competencies compare with our current capabilities? • How will we pinpoint gaps for developing internally – or for hiring from outside our organization?

- Identify specific gaps in competencies required for success
- Set a comprehensive, fair, and equitable process to align the current resources – or secure additional human capital
- Verify the alignment of processes, systems, policies, practices and culture
- Ensure the Human Capital plan reflects the employee value proposition
- Set communications strategy
- Determine feedback and evaluation process

- Clear communications of the situation, intentions, and plan
- Double-loop feedback stream in place

- How will our job profiles need to change?
- How will we be sure our processes, systems, policies, and practices fit the Human Capital plan?
- How will we ensure fair and equitable consideration for current and outside candidates?
- How will we set performance expectations for all leaders to find, fully engage, develop, and retain the right people who fit the Human Capital plan?
- How will we identify mission critical roles and individuals that require special retention strategies?
- How will we test rewards, recognition, and compensation practices to attract the right talent?
- How will we continually secure double-loop feedback and deploy new findings?
- How will we set an evaluation plan to gauge impact?

(Continued)

Stage	Key Tasks	Outcomes of Stage	Consequences If Unsuccessful	Issues or Questions to Address
Recruitment and Selection	• Clarify recruitment strategy and specific targets • Align all actions with the employee value proposition • Activate talent market that can pull through prime candidates • Build in any cultural transformation ingredients • Prepare details of recruitment and selection plan • Verify process, systems, policies, and practice alignment to ensure fair and equitable opportunities and efficient pipeline of qualified candidates • Prepare all interviewers and decision makers for consistent, fair, cost-effective, high quality process • Document all key steps and findings in a candidate tracking process • Secure double-loop feedback to adjust as needed	• Fair, efficient, and effective recruitment and selection process • Employee value proposition and branding attracts people who fit • Prompt identification of the right people with the right skills, especially critical knowledge and talent • Low-cost placement	• Not very cost-effective process • Risk securing the right people • Delay in organizational readiness to fulfill strategy or programs • Overlook talent in unlikely places • Legal challenges	• How will we ensure we're as effective, efficient, and fair as possible in our recruitment and selection process? • How will we be confident we're selecting the right people – with skills, knowledge, abilities, and motivations that best fit our needs? • How will we communicate our employee value proposition in as appealing and compelling way as possible? • How will we more effectively position our organization's opportunities as compared to others in the external talent market? • How will we activate an efficient, inclusive, pull-through process in an internal talent market? • How will we continually gather and deploy feedback? • How will we ensure we meet human capital deadlines without compromise?

Employee Orientation or On-Boarding				
Employee Orientation or On-Boarding	• Link roles to strategic outcomes and any scorecards or dashboards • Establish specific expectations for roles, responsibilities, and standards of performance • Demonstrate the employee value proposition • Develop a clear, mutual understanding and expectations for fulfilling the organization's mission, vision, values, cultural practices, and measures for performance • Clarify the expectations for every stage of the cycle • Equip new employees with essential, actionable knowledge about the organization, its customers, partners • Institute mentoring and networking connections to accelerate learning	• Effective, efficient, and thorough initiation into the assigned roles and the organization's mission • Clarity on performance expectations, especially the application of critical knowledge and talent to drive results • Heightened employee engagement and validation of employer choice • Clear understanding of the lifecycle process	• Not likely to experience accelerated learning and preparation • Delays in contributions and realizable value to the strategy and mission • New employees experience confusion and disillusionment	• How will we accelerate commitment, learning, and contributions of new employees to the strategy of the organization? • How will we design and deliver a clear sequence of learning that produces understanding, comfort, and confidence in a new organization or role – without confusion or inundation with too much detail? • How will we communicate clear line of sight connections to the strategy and measures of success? • How will we develop a working knowledge of the organization's mission, vision, and values? • How will we effectively communicate essential organizational and customer knowledge? • How will we set up mentors or a social networking system for supporting new employees? • How will we establish systemic attention to an integrating culture? • How will we ensure every step fits the employee value proposition?

(Continued)

Stage	Key Tasks	Outcomes of Stage	Consequences If Unsuccessful	Issues or Questions to Address
	• Position on-boarding as part of an orderly developmental process over time			• How will we verify the degree of employee engagement and support in this early period of employment? • How will we position the on-boarding within the broader development process throughout the lifecycle? • How will we secure feedback on the orientation process – and quickly learn what additional help is needed?
Development of Ongoing Capabilities or Career Growth	• Identify a development process to deepen knowledge and refine skills required for defined career paths and fulfillment of strategies • Ensure enduring fulfillment of the employee value proposition • Conduct periodic assessment of capabilities and growth – compare with changing organizational needs	• Continual preparation and readiness of Human Capital, especially critical knowledge and talent • Continual growth and development of current and new skills • Human Capital capabilities on target with strategic needs • New career growth opportunities are identified efficiently and fairly	• Lower probability of organizational strategies and results being met • Human Capital needs may not be fully met – uncertainty about having the right people, right skills, right place, right time • Reduced employee satisfaction and engagement • Higher voluntary turnover	• How will we build a comprehensive employee development plan – in timely phases – that meets the needs of the organizational and individual career growth plans? • How will we engage in formal and informal performance management discussions, coaching, feedback, reinforcement, and recognition to produce superior performance? • How will we periodically assess and gauge growth? • How will we continually verify employee engagement, satisfaction, and commitment?

	• Provide coaching, feedback, reinforcement, and recognition of growth • Conduct formal and informal performance management • Create a talent market to accelerate growth • Reconcile actions within talent management and succession planning • Identify readiness for new opportunities for advancement • Communicate developmental opportunities and process for participation	• Employees exercise initiative to grow and contribute • Employees experience the employee value proposition as intended – and provide positive referrals	• Best talent leaves first	• How will we build in a retention strategy that's meaningful to the employees and saves organizational resources? • How will we stay apprised of unique generational or professional shifts and requirements? • How will we continually deliver the employee value proposition experience? • How will we establish a pull-through strategy in a talent market? • How will we track system dynamics over time to ensure this stage stays on track? • How will we ensure our critical talent stays and contributes? • How will we avoid redundancies, overlap, and outdating in resources?
Employee Departure	• Engage in periodic review of capabilities and early identification of possible departures for any reason • Assess impact of potential departures on the organization and customers • Identify mission critical knowledge and talent	• Sustainment of organizational knowledge and talent, plus benefits to customers • Orderly, respectful, and dignified closure to employee career • Clarity on rationale for all departures	• Organization loses critical knowledge and talent and suffers business shortfall and failure to perform for customers • Experience does not promote a positive reputation for the organization	• How will we identify or anticipate possible departures of all types? • How will we effectively plan for the transfer of working knowledge from current employees to others? • What are our mission critical skills and knowledge that we need to preserve? How will we easily and effectively create broader coverage?

(Continued)

Stage	Key Tasks	Outcomes of Stage	Consequences If Unsuccessful	Issues or Questions to Address
	that may be at risk – and require broader or transferred coverage • Track employee engagement and other cues of potential departure – take action • Plan for effective transfer or shared knowledge with other designated employees • Recognize contributions of departing employee to mission and vision • Analyze rationale for all turnover – use to improve Human Capital planning at all stages • Seek appropriate, ongoing good will • Communications planning • Seek continual system feedback	• Promotion of a positive reputation for the organization • Follow-through on employee value proposition • Deeper understanding of employee's employment decision analytics	• Failure to keep the employee value proposition promise • Feedback and opportunities may be missed as sources of continual improvement ideas to the Human Capital strategy • Other employees choose to leave	• How will we effectively and efficiently gather useful exit data and use that data in future planning? • How will we prepare people to effectively and respectfully assume the roles of departing employees, irrespective of the reasons? • How will we evaluate how well we are fulfilling our employee value proposition? • How will we reduce voluntary turnover to an acceptable level? • What will we do to promote a positive reputation for the organization? • What kinds of ongoing good will or service relationships can we establish with departing employees? • How will we tap into system feedback to gain early alerts to potential unwanted departures?

Case Studies **255**

- Refine or create communications strategies that promote the business, vision, values, and culture, plus the distinctive qualities of the respective properties.
- Seek a much higher degree of consistency in providing performance information and promoting double-loop feedback.
- Reconcile and refresh all curricula to provide more direct support to the talent management strategy. Streamline and enrich the curricula and delivery process to provide more active, transferable learning while reducing unnecessary redundancies, inefficiencies, and costs. In doing so, several key objectives could be simultaneously accomplished:
  - o Accelerate the learning and performance curve and thereby significantly improve the time-to-proficiency rate in new roles.
  - o Establish an effective, accountable performance management and coaching culture at all levels.
  - o Enable much greater ease of movement into new roles across properties and meanwhile set significant anxiety aside.
  - o Establish the basis for meaningful career growth and developmental paths.
  - o Improve the performance and employee engagement levels while reducing unwanted turnover levels.
  - o Provide more active, transferrable learning and skill application.
  - o Invest in development experiences that effectively and efficiently contribute to business success and positive guest feedback and loyalty.
- Consider restructuring the current array of training professionals across the multiple properties into a centralized cadre or consortium of curricula developers, instructional designers, internal performance researchers, and certified organizational performance trainers who could provide efficient and effective training services to properties across the enterprise. A long list of accompanying details was provided to support this recommendation.

In addition to these recommendations, the researcher provided a draft set of core competencies that could be applied to all employees at all locations, plus an additional set of competencies for their leaders. These competencies were drawn from behavioral analyses of responses in the interviews and focus groups, plus insights from the review of relevant business documents.

The findings, observations, conclusions, and recommendations emanating from this Rapid Due Diligence diagnostic process were well accepted by the sponsoring executive. In fact, the composite set was viewed as a significant jumpstart to the development of the organization's future talent management strategy.

Discussion Questions

- How could the application of the Rapid Due Diligence diagnostic method have been helpful prior to completing the acquisitions?
- Why was the implementation of a unified talent management and development strategy so important to the organization at this time?

256 Case Studies

Case Study Five: Pursuing an Effective Client-Focused Service Strategy

A large, successful financial services organization was seeking even greater efficiency and effectiveness in its financial advisor and client relationships. The researcher was asked to conduct a Rapid Due Diligence diagnostic process to develop observations and any recommendations for how these outcomes might be achieved.

As part of the advance preparation, the organization provided the researcher with a number of relevant documents. These included the current strategic vision, service delivery goals, organization charts, service ratings by outside benchmarking organizations, information about their routine performance management process, and current or planned training for service agents. Online research was also completed to learn further detail from publicly accessible reporting documents.

Interviews were scheduled with a number of employees at multiple levels who were expected to have important perspectives on the current client-focused service strategy. The interviews were focused on four broad areas of open-ended inquiry. Additional probing questions were used to gain further clarity and greater depth of understanding. The four areas are listed below.

- Describe your point of view on client service and its need in this organization.
- What skills and capabilities are needed by you and/or your staff to fulfill your current client service strategy?
- How do you now measure success? How will that need to change?
- What challenges do you expect the organization will encounter as it pursues a more effective client service strategy?

The commentary from each interview was provided to the key contacts without attribution in order to preserve anonymity. Some editing was applied to abbreviate the content. Where similar comments were offered more than once, the frequency was noted. Figure 10.4 displays the elements of the customer service culture change that was underway, recognizing that not all segments were being fully realized.

After review of the detailed commentary from the interviews, as well as the relevant documentation, the researcher provided a number of preliminary observations.

- There was strong agreement that attention to client service was warranted for the current and future success of the business, as well as the satisfaction level of financial advisors.
- The language of "reset" was tested throughout the interviews as one way in which to more fully describe this unique strategic opportunity in the timeline of the business. The label resonated with a high majority of the interviewees.

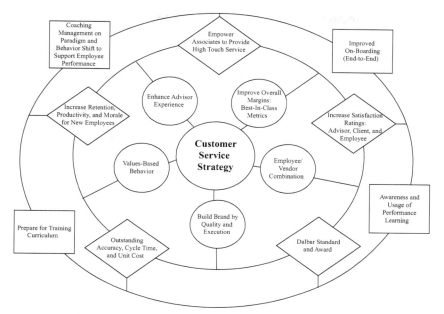

FIGURE 10.4 Customer Service Culture Change.

- There was uncertainty about the exact role or balance of a client service strategy in conjunction with the long-held organizational focus on reducing cost and improving operational efficiency.
- There was expressed concern about the willingness of the organization to make time and resources available to pursue a serious client service strategy.
- In reviewing a number of documents portraying the strategic objectives and priorities for a three-year period, there were many high-level, conceptual labels for service. From an outside observer's point of view, there appeared to be a presence of enticing, attractive labels in the strategy; yet, there were risks of mixed messages when juxtaposed with other language about the role of technology. From the interviews, it was unclear how well leaders and associates understood how to balance the apparent competing areas of focus. Further, without more clarity and line-of-sight connections on performance expectations, the organization would most likely continue on its current service trajectory and not reach the desired pinnacle.
- There was no evidence of a client value proposition that would focus on the competitive attractiveness of this organization to either prospective or current financial advisors or clients.
- While there had previously been significant business process reengineering work undertaken, there apparently had been no extrapolation of an enterprise-wide client relationship process that reflected on the collective experiences of clients and advisors.

258 Case Studies

- There was a growing number of metrics and surveys which focused on different aspects of client service. More discovery work was warranted to determine the degree of accurate reflection of real financial advisor/client needs, alignment, the necessity for all these sources, and how they were used collectively to drive sound decision making, strategy formulation, and execution.
- The performance management process for the coming year had been launched. There was opportunity for more explicit inclusion of client service with behavioral anchors that had been reconciled with the outside benchmark criteria.
- An effective cultural shift from the current focus on operational efficiency to a balance of efficiency and client service would require considerable evidence of conviction, clarity, and active involvement on the part of all leaders at all levels.

On the basis of the initial data collection, preliminary observations, and deeper systemic analysis, the researcher then provided a series of recommendations. These were recommended to be started immediately in parallel in view of what was known or already in place. Then, as a more detailed strategy was developed, the recommendations would need to be refined to fit the final strategy execution plan. A number of recommendations with explanatory or granular detail were provided.

- Convene a service delivery leadership working session to clarify and crystallize the client service strategy. The intent would be to build on what had already been determined or was in place. It would be essential to secure leadership agreement and commitment to at least the following outcomes:
  - o Define the intended role of client service as a strategic business driver for the organization.
  - o Determine the extent to which client service would become a distinctive competitive advantage, from the point of view of the ideal financial advisor.
  - o Define what value this strategy could bring to the organization and the targeted ideal financial advisors.
    - o Clarify an explicit client value proposition that appeals to the ideal financial advisors.
    - o Express clearly why these advisors should choose affiliation with this organization, identifying uniquely distinctive points of differentiation from other choices they might make.
  - o Incorporate this client value proposition into the service delivery goals and priorities for the coming year.
  - o Provide explicit, line-of-sight performance expectations and examples of how to apply the strategy and make everyday decisions that actually deliver the client value proposition.

Case Studies **259**

o Align metrics to the client value proposition to stay on track. Set guidelines for reconciling all existing sources of measurement.
o Describe the organization-wide client relationship process that delivers on the client value proposition and aligns:
  o Critical factors for success
  o Accountabilities for results
  o Leading and lagging performance indicators
  o Critical skills and knowledge required
o Clarify roles and accountabilities for follow-up actions and execution.
o Create key messages for initial communications and a defined culture shift strategy.
o Provide guidance for detailed client service training implementation and planning, answering questions such as how far, how fast, with whom, and who first?
o Confirm how these ingredients integrate into a cohesive, comprehensive, practical, and systemic set to drive real client service performance.
o Identify specific action items for any unfinished items with accountabilities for rigorous follow-through.

- Using the high-level description of the client relationship process, map the current client and financial advisor experiences and transactional processes to uncover potential positive triggers from the client or advisor points of view.
  o Draw upon recent business process reengineering or Six Sigma value stream analyses.
  o Involve service associates, team leaders, and selected financial advisors in the process to avoid making unrealistic assumptions about their respective realities.
  o Look for ways to gain even more efficiency and client service focus within the process.
    o Eliminate any non-value-added activities.
    o Minimize the number of hand-offs.
    o Create clear procedural steps.
    o Set standards of excellence.
    o Create smooth, collaborative, and responsive effort across all functions.
    o Dispatch anticipatory communications internally and with clients and advisors.
    o Reduce time delays, especially between front and back office operations.
    o Align employee accountabilities for measurable results.
    o Improve the reliability, accuracy, and availability of information flowing from current systems.
    o Use tools as effectively as possible.
    o Apply insights from the findings on any positive client triggers.
    o Test changes with internal players, clients, and financial advisors.

260 Case Studies

- Set specific measures that simply, effectively, and best capture critical information on client service, especially those positive client trigger opportunities as defined by financial advisors.
- Examine the multiple measures, surveys, and feedback mechanisms of both advisors and associates to draw clear connections to the point of view of each, plus the goals defined by service delivery leadership in its strategic clarification discussions, noted above.
- Chart any multi-layer points of influence or approval within the client or financial advisor environment or structure.
- Incorporate specific client service goals with explicit behavioral definitions into the performance management process, recognizing that the goals for the coming year were already in the process of being set.
  o Plan for how to easily integrate these new goals.
  o Highlight skills and interactions necessary to produce those positive trigger points to deliver on the client value proposition.
  o Reconcile the definitions for specific levels of performance to client service learning outcomes and appropriate sets of outside benchmark applications and metrics.
  o Include a plan for establishing inter-rater reliability on all these essential metrics.
  o Studies had shown that the full realization of value from a strategic plan is highly dependent upon the alignment and reinforcement of its accompanying performance management system. On average, fourteen percent of the strategy's value is lost without close attention to this area.
- Launch preliminary planning for building the client service capabilities of both leaders and associates. These include the knowledge, skills, abilities, and motivations necessary to deliver the client value proposition and achieve the service delivery goals and priorities.
  o Align the training methodology, adult learning model, and content to create a comprehensive, tightly integrated, results-focused, overarching learning strategy and effective application of new client service skills.
  o Use the findings from the service delivery leadership strategy clarification discussion to conduct working sessions with middle management. This would further develop client service commitment throughout the organization and provide for appropriate modeling, coaching, reinforcing, and measuring progress of key concepts and skills.
  o Set a specific, phased implementation plan for training.
    o Determine who's first, plus how far and how fast to conduct the pace for the initial phase.
    o Suggest identifying two or three potential pilot areas that have a clear need and are both ready and willing to go first.
    o Conduct a detailed evaluation of the initial phase.
    o Try out any tailored training material.

Case Studies **261**

- o Gain early traction in key areas of need which can have a noticeable impact on financial advisors.
- o Accompany any training with a carefully constructed communications campaign.
- o When presenting any training, emphasize why client service is so important to the organization, clients, financial advisors, and to associates.
- o Use stories to crisply illustrate client service in action within the organization.
- o Build direct, line-of-sight connections between individual roles, expectations for performance, and achievement of strategic goals.
- o Make connections with the metrics and any outside benchmarks.
- o Focus on fundamental skills, such as listening, probing to uncover real needs, clarifying information, and dealing with highly emotional situations.
- o Schedule the training sessions with great care to avoid conflict with any mandatory overtime, the tax preparation season, or other initiatives that are already scheduled or underway.
- o Use a premier set of service providers in a dual role of learners and peer mentors.
- o Ensure sufficient time and space within the learning process to acquire the skills and understanding of the client value proposition, client relationship process, and metrics.
- o Prepare the leaders at all levels to model, coach, reinforce, measure, and recognize progress.
- Prepare a detailed coaching and reinforcement plan to ensure application of the new client service skills as intended.
  - o Examine the current coaching role to determine how it can best bring proactive, consistent, practical, cost-effective, and anticipatory assistance to associates in other levels.
  - o Acknowledge that the provision of at least three hours of coaching per month typically produces at least a fifteen to seventeen percent improvement in performance.
  - o Further, without skill reinforcement following the learning experience, people tend to lose eighty-seven percent of what they learn within thirty days.
  - o Finally, when combined with effective coaching, training return on investment improves from an average of twenty-two to eighty-eight percent.
- Create and launch a phased, comprehensive communications strategy.
  - o Prepare a series of messages to be launched before any training activity, during the learning process, and afterward on the job.
  - o Include key messages for clients, financial advisors, functional areas, leaders, and service associates in both front and back office operations.
  - o Embed compatible messages with the insertion of client service goals into the performance management cycle that is already in progress.

262 Case Studies

- o Consider creating a series of communications kits that can be used by a variety of leaders in a host of situations, e.g., thirty-minute highlights, one or two-hour briefings with facilitated discussions, half-day sessions with key concepts, or full-day sessions with selected skill building.
  - o Ensure the key messages are clear, straightforward, include organization-specific examples of performance expectations, and are repeated consistently by people at many leadership levels.
  - o Content should include:
    - o This is what we've learned about the needs of our clients and financial advisors.
    - o This is what we're doing about it.
    - o These are our expectations of you in your roles.
    - o This is how we'll solicit your ideas for continual improvement.
    - o This is why all this is so important.
    - o This is what's in it for the clients, financial advisors, for the organization, for the work group, and for individuals.
    - o This is what you can expect for client service training, coaching, and reinforcement.
    - o This is how we'll measure progress and recognize improvement.
    - o This is how we'll celebrate our success.
- Review and align client service policies and practices.
  - o This includes the explicit pursuit of outside benchmarks and recognition.
  - o Provide explicit and relevant examples for leaders, coaches, and service associates that clearly demonstrate the balance of client service and operational efficiency in everyday situations.
  - o Be clear. This is what you want, and this is what you don't want.
  - o Involve all levels in helping to identify potential misalignments.
- Determine a set of selection criteria for new employees.
  - o These criteria should be drawn from the composite set of competencies (skills, knowledge, abilities, and motivations) that can best deliver the client value proposition and any positive trigger experiences for financial advisors and internal partners.
  - o Use this new set for recruitment, selection, and promotion actions.
- Incorporate client service into the on-boarding process for all employees at all levels to ensure a deeper, personal understanding and acceptance of accountability for the client value proposition, performance expectations, and how this focus contributes to a more complete win for the organization, its clients, financial advisors, and employees.
- Continually verify the fit of the strategy, client value proposition, changing needs of ideal financial advisors, metrics, required skills and capabilities, policies, processes, and practices.
- Engage Lean Six Sigma methodology when and where needed.

While the final strategic decisions and accompanying measurable results from this Rapid Due Diligence diagnostic process are unknown to the researcher, here are a number of sample results from organizations which have pursued a focused, more effective, and efficient client-service strategy.

- Sixteen percent increase in measurable service ratings
- At least a 4.5 rating (on a scale of 1–5) on consistent professionalism
- Twenty-five percent reduction in client complaints
- Fifteen percent increase in first-call resolution of difficulties
- Forty-four percent increase in employees' job satisfaction
- At least a fifty percent improvement in call-handling efficiency
- At least a fifty percent decrease in call escalations
- An increase in client satisfaction scores moving from forty-eight to ninety-one percent

It is reasonable to conclude that at least one or more of such improvements could be achieved with careful formulation and precise execution of a focused client-service strategy. The Rapid Due Diligence diagnostic process and its findings produced a set of recommendations which were specifically customized to fit the needs of this particular organization and its clientele. The intervention moved away from standard patterns and addressed more comprehensive, complex dimensions that combine to produce better results.

Discussion Questions

- What challenges occur when senior executives hold differing priorities?
- What are the potential positive and negative effects of engaging in comparative benchmarking?
- How does an explicit customer value proposition bring aid to a customer-focused service strategy?

Case Study Six: Developing a Corporate University

The Rapid Due Diligence diagnostic process has also been used in clarifying the need and shaping the infrastructure and learning processes within corporate universities. In such cases, typically the executive conversation has focused first on the desire for corporate growth and profitability. In retail-focused organizations, for example, this most often means that retail or store operations initiate the exploration for how such growth can optimally occur.

As noted in earlier chapters, operations often focus initially upon product development, technological advancement, business development processes, and relationships with customers as primary means to generate additional revenue

264 Case Studies

with more efficient cost structures. With the growing realization of the value of human capital assets to the growth and profitability equations, there have been more frequent organic migrations of the executive conversation to the most effective and efficient methods for developing consistent skills and knowledge among employees. Hence, those leaders involved in the learning and development function have been increasingly invited into the process of exploring ways to effectively drive even greater business success. This discussion among operations and learning development often includes topics such as replication of successful market initiatives and responding efficiently to addressing capability gaps.

This is a point where the Rapid Due Diligence diagnostic process can bring significant value. In deeper investigation of the junctures within the organization's business model and relationships with agents, clients, or customers, the Rapid Due Diligence process can reveal the trigger points where specific critical knowledge, skills, abilities, or motivations can bring greater value to the intersection of employees or agents with clients or customers.

The organization may or may not have already gathered significant historical data to place comparative revenue generation values on those intersections. The organization may already have traced precisely the revenue generation stream throughout the execution of its business model. If not, more granular study of that stream, intersections, trigger points that build attraction and loyalty, and skill applications has the capability of unlocking previously unknown opportunities for optimizing the realization of value in the execution process.

Working together with internal analysts, the Rapid Due Diligence diagnostic process researcher can help clarify such trigger points or intersections and how the customer choice process can be more reliably stimulated to produce targeted revenue. Direct contact with customers is desirable to learn of unexpected choice analytics.

In some cases, the organization is not yet convinced that any investment in learning and development on a significant scale can produce a real return. This is another point where the Rapid Due Diligence diagnostic process can be helpful. With deeper investigation into the financial reporting statements, 10-K, 10-Q, website resources such as reports to a targeted financial analyst community, content of presentations by key leaders such as the chief executive and chief financial officers, content of the management discussion and analysis excerpts of financial statements, and even outside sector analysts' or investment analysts' commentary are scoured for clues or insights. These clues are often encased in commentary, for example, about double-digit improvements in revenue streams, new market initiatives, optimizing competitive distinctions or opportunities, multiplying capabilities, seeking greater efficiencies or effectiveness in operations, securing greater payback on invested assets, initiating fresh and compelling experiences for customers, or consistent performance at points-of-contact or intersections with customers.

A compilation and quantification of the value potentially realizable in all such opportunities from specific investment in human capital learning and development can be quite compelling. Where the organization's ambitions are sufficiently large in scale, the investigation can often focus on how to organize a central repository of the learning and development library of resources with the intent to create a one-stop, single point of contact for its leaders and employees at all levels and locations to ideally and easily access learning opportunities. Such an arrangement is often called a corporate university.

With the application of the Rapid Due Diligence diagnostic process, organizations have acquired frameworks for establishing this central learning repository or university-like operation in ways which contribute to the business success specifically described in financial and operations commentaries.

On many occasions, the researcher has also been asked to quickly conduct the Rapid Due Diligence diagnostic process to prepare multi-year business plans for corporate universities. The content has been derived through the in-depth investigation of the business model, study of operations and processes as noted above, calculation of the likely realizable value of investment in human capital management, and recommendation of specific strategies and implementation plans to fit the organization's targeted success.

The business plans have been assembled to include direct statements about how the specific organization's university is being designed to fulfill the definition and mission of effective corporate universities, described as follows:

- A corporate university is an educational entity that is a strategic tool designed to assist its parent organization in achieving its mission by conducting activities that cultivate individual and organizational learning, knowledge, and wisdom.

Such a corporate university will purposefully and directly promote and support the mission, vision, values, and operating platform of the organization. Key elements of the mission for the corporate university will:

- Provide a consistent, high-quality approach to needs-based learning and development in support of critical business priorities across the organization.
- Develop top professionals and leaders who drive organizational growth, profitability, and branding experiences for all customers at all locations.
- Prepare everyone to serve as brand ambassadors, a particularly important pursuit in retail operations.
- Promote a culture that makes the organization a great place to work.
- Provide simple access to learning opportunities for employees that may be widely dispersed.
- Promote purposeful learning by mapping core leadership and employee competencies to business objectives, roles, and learning opportunities.

266 Case Studies

- Offer effective and efficient transfer, application, and reinforcement of learning to achieve targeted results.
- Improve speed to competency or accelerated proficiency for newly hired or promoted employees.
- Serve as an essential tool within the organization's more encompassing talent management lifecycle or system.
- Market and facilitate development and growth on potential career paths across the organization.
- Appeal to all natural, cultural groupings within the workforce.

The real value of any corporate university is measured by the significance of its direct contribution to the long-term growth and viability of the business and its people. The discoveries from the Rapid Due Diligence diagnostic process contribute to the genesis and ongoing relevance of a highly effective corporate university by virtue of the depth of understanding of critical business issues and a clear realization of how the learning system within the university can contribute to sound business solutions and drive toward more comprehensive strategic execution and achievement of targeted results. These revelations often stimulate greater commitment by both operations and learning development leaders who share their mutual determination to deliver both growth opportunity and results to the organization, its people, and customers. A Triple Win ensues.

The results of the Rapid Due Diligence diagnostic process have been organized into formal business plans that include the following elements:

- A university mission and vision that aligns with the organization's mission, vision, values, and operating principles and disciplines
- Specific statements of relevance to the organization's business issues
- A value proposition for the university
- Primary goals for the early years of its operation
- Key strategies and implementation plan recommendations, such as:
  o Key players, roles, and responsibilities
  o Learning management system implementation options
  o Courseware selection criteria
  o Preparation of any learning facilitation staff
  o Communications planning
- Measures of success within the organization
- Financial plan based on the organization's intended investment

To the degree possible, as identified within the Rapid Due Diligence diagnostic process, the elements of the organization's business strategy and growth ambitions can be directly supported, accelerated, and performed with the desired consistency with the acquisition of knowledge and application of the learning experiences planned within the defined university. Direct links can be made between

Case Studies **267**

the business strategies and priorities and identifiable core competencies used to focus content and learning experiences. Any curriculum choices must be continually tested for direct connections to business results.

A strong collaborative relationship between the university and human resources function is considered a best practice. Some organizations have already established models for human capital management which incorporate the typical talent management processes and metrics for assessing performance and continuously improving employee fit and effectiveness. These models often include processes for attracting, orienting, developing, and retaining leaders and employees at all levels and locations.

For comparative purposes, the researcher's integrated strategic human capital alignment framework may be used. Appearing earlier in Chapters Six and Ten, it includes six stages of the cycle, key tasks, desired outcomes, consequences if actions are unsuccessful, and key issues or questions to address.

The consolidation and refinement of learning experiences through this central learning resource implies significant potential for efficiencies and cost management as learning needs are identified and met. As the organization's market footprint grows either domestically and/or internationally, the cost of conducting learning will ideally grow at a reduced comparative slope. Constant vigilance of university operating costs will also directly support any business strategy of improving margins.

A significant best practice among effective corporate universities is the systematic monitoring, identification, and prioritization of current, changing, and future learning needs required to support business strategies and provide solutions to critical business needs. Most often, this objective is accomplished through the service of an executive-level, internal advisory council that is connected to the core operations of the business.

The value proposition for a corporate university is directly traced to the initial intent for its establishment.

- The corporate university provides opportunities for the development, growth, and engagement of leaders and employees, while leveraging capabilities for the benefit of the business and consistently sustaining the unique, best-in-class, captivating and loyalty-producing customer experiences.

Such a value proposition reflects direct connections with findings that effective leaders and employees tend to seek more training, plus information on career goals, and greater clarity on how their roles and actions can drive customer loyalty and targeted business results.

The learning experiences offered through the corporate university will contextually define and provide for realistic applications of the defined competencies to the everyday roles and responsibilities of leaders and employees. Each learning experience will be designed to simultaneously stimulate personal growth and make clear connections to the application of new skills and knowledge to personal contributions to the business and customer experience.

268 Case Studies

Typical goals for the launch and early periods of tending the corporate university can include the following actions:

- To organize for launch by a specific date, which supports yet does not inherently collide with other strategic imperatives.
- To identify current and anticipated critical business issues and clear links to the initial curriculum.
- To embed actionable knowledge about the relationship of leader and employee behaviors and everyday practices to customer experiences and loyalty, such as may have been discovered during the Rapid Due Diligence diagnostic process.
- To map core and leadership competencies to business objectives and create links to learning opportunities to build those competencies.
- To prepare an initial offering of courses, often with specific focus on building talent, capabilities, and the brand experience for customers.
- To prepare designated leaders to become proficient in facilitating, modeling, coaching, and reinforcing selected courseware.
- To explore how to activate a selected learning management system as a one-stop, single point of contact for access to learning opportunities, plus easy and clear navigation for enrollment, course management, course completion, and tracking metrics.
- To identify measures of success that matter most to the business and its decision makers.
- To communicate the capabilities of the university to targeted audiences.
- To develop a centralized, regularly updated, non-redundant, cost effective, and business-aligned repository of all learning information. This would include all facilitator-led learning experiences, any technology-based training, virtual learning, conferences, video and internet/intranet components, and any accompanying performance support tools.
- To identify and respond to drivers and inhibitors for learning and application of new skills and knowledge, including adaptation to a wide variety of learning styles.
- To create links with the talent management system and any recruitment, selection, on-boarding, career path development, performance management, retention, and succession planning activities.
- To test the appeal of the university and offerings to all segments of the employee population.
- To provide for a full span of learning and development activities to support at least the core content, including assessment, knowledge acquisition, and post-learning evaluation.
- To design or enhance processes for coaching, feedback, reinforcement, and appropriate involvement by leaders and supervisors of all employees.
- To gauge any impact upon employee engagement data.

Case Studies **269**

- To install a tracking process to monitor progress and evaluate the measures of success.
- To investigate further development or investment in technology-based learning management processes, systems, and delivery mechanisms.
- To prepare content and facilitators in local languages as needed to serve the complete enterprise and all international operations.
- To establish at least a rudimentary return on invested capital test for the university.
- To investigate the expansion of selected content for other segments of the organization's value chain, specifically suppliers, agents, or customers.
- To include the expansion of measures and analytics to track impact on suppliers, agents, or customers.

The business plan includes the identification of key players for the corporate university, including a core team, day-to-day operating group, advisory council, and facilitation staff. The core team most often is drawn from the existing learning and development functional leaders. In organizational meetings, this core team is expected to confirm the scope and framework for the university. The following elements are discussed and affirmed:

- Mission and vision of the university
- Relevance and connections to the business
- Value proposition
- Business priorities
- Links with the talent management system, operating system, and identified competencies at all levels
- Roles and responsibilities of the key players, including an advisory council
- Initial targeted audiences
- Primary content to be offered in the first year or two of university operations
- Discernment of any further requirement for needs assessment, beyond what was conducted in the Rapid Due Diligence diagnostic process or other internal analyses
- The approach to facilitated learning and selection of leaders to play facilitator roles
- Adaptation of learning experiences to a variety of learning styles and preferences
- The application of any e-learning, virtual learning, webinar, or other technology-based experiences
- The availability and fit of the current learning management system as a repository and administrative choice
- Initial methods for learning evaluation
- Timelines and project phases for the launch and post-launch evaluation
- Budgets and other resources
- Detailed implementation plans with roles, actions, and timelines

270 Case Studies

Four other categories of work require more detailed attention:

- Curriculum and delivery of learning experiences
- Learning management system and administration
- Communications and marketing
- Measurement and evaluation of progress

A number of key points for discussion in each of these categories are provided below.

- Curriculum and delivery of learning experiences
  o Select content for initial offerings.
  o Determine how far, how fast, who's first for what offerings.
  o Determine how the offerings will be conducted, including use of facilitator-led instruction, e-learning, virtual experiences, webinars, or other technology-based learning, administration, and delivery of learning materials.
  o Define all support logistics and management process for offerings and facilitation methods.
  o Adapt training experiences to be effective among a broad range of learning styles and preferences.
  o Confirm existing or potential integration with the learning management system in place or to be acquired.
  o Clarify current needs assessments and links to drive business priorities and targeted results.
  o Identify the need for any additional needs assessment.
  o Map all content links to the business, customer loyalty drivers, roles, values, priorities, career paths, and segments of the talent management system.
  o Select and prepare leaders for facilitation roles.
  o Define the facilitation role to include modeling, coaching, reinforcement, and measuring progress.
  o Design any train-the-trainer process and master trainer preparation.
  o Establish selection criteria for screening existing or future courseware for best fit and avoidance of unnecessary redundancy.
  o Design coaching and feedback loops that align with culturally accepted or encouraged practices.
  o Link the curriculum with current individual or group developmental planning, high potential or successor development.
  o Identify the need for any additional tailoring or customization of existing and future content.
  o Create a learning experience evaluation process tied with measures of success.
  o Confirm any connections with any outside resources or educational institutions.

Case Studies **271**

- Learning management system
  - o Secure a clear description and architectural capability of the current or likely learning management system, any firewalls within or outside the organization and geographically dispersed locations, any limitations, capacity, and organizational willingness to support the initial and future size and activity of the corporate university.
  - o Design a navigation process for registration, enrollment, administration, tracking participation, and measures for success.
  - o Define specific support activity and resources required to meet the targeted university launch date.
  - o Conduct tests and complete adjustments prior to the launch.
  - o Identify risks or limitations encumbering the successful support of the university.
  - o Establish decision criteria and process for assessing the need for another approach to a learning management system.
  - o Create next-best alternatives if the corporate learning management system is not suitable. Examples may include smaller scaled modules of existing human resource information system packages or temporary lease of learning management system capacity from an outside source.
- Communications and marketing
  - o Clarify what communications and marketing strategies work best within the organization's culture and geographic dispersion.
  - o Create university branding.
  - o Craft the overall communications plan.
  - o Confirm and deploy the value proposition for the corporate university.
  - o Describe effective links with business strategies, priorities, values, metrics for success, and the talent management system.
  - o Incorporate ingredients that align with any customer and employee connectivity or intersection findings and recommendations, especially from the Rapid Due Diligence diagnostic process.
  - o Create unique messaging for targeted roles for before, during, and after learning experiences.
  - o Prepare key messages: what it is, why it was created, who will participate in what ways, when, how it will work, and what to expect.
  - o Identify and prepare key people as communicators.
  - o Create elevator messages and applications in current or new communications devices or media choices.
  - o Create any collateral material with university branding.
  - o Design website or screens within the learning management system to create compelling, consistent messaging and easy navigation.
  - o Determine how communications in the first plan year will flow into the next year.

272 Case Studies

- o Create a plan for regularly pulsing the organization for feedback and ideas for continual improvement.
- o Draft how periodic measures of success will be shared and recognized.
- Measurement and evaluation of progress
  - o Determine simple, practical measures that can be easily applied in the first year of the university.
  - o As possible, make direct links with frequently referenced business metrics. For example, in retail, these may include comparable store sales year-over-year, conversion performance, and metrics tied to the performance of the business and product expertise.
  - o Apply performance engineering techniques where possible to trace direct or indirect impact on business results.
  - o Consider whether and how to gather data at any or all of the typical learning evaluation levels:
    - o Level One: Training preparedness, environment, experience, and support
    - o Level Two: Mastery of course content and related skills or knowledge evaluation
    - o Level Three: Behavior change or application of learning outcomes
    - o Level Four: Organization and business impact
    - o Level Five: Business impact in economic terms
    - o Incorporate after action reviews with each learning experience.
  - o Set the frequency of any evaluation process.
  - o Include periodic checks with any new customer loyalty and employee connectivity or intersections, related engagement, and customer loyalty or choice analytic data.
  - o Test coaching and reinforcement techniques and impact on results.
  - o Determine how to interpret any data in ways that are easy for leaders and employees to understand and use for future decision making.
  - o Create a communications plan for targeted audiences about measurement.
    - o What, why, how, who, when, what will be done with results, and expectations for performance
    - o Recognition for superior results
  - o Plan for how to effectively act on evaluation results to continually improve the university experience and business results.
- Operating group
  - o A key factor for the effective launch and ongoing success of the university is the prompt identification of a full-time operating group.
  - o Members of this group will carry primary day-to-day responsibility for managing the business of the university.
  - o Duties may include the following:
    - o Implementing the processes, systems, policies, standards, and practices for the university
    - o Overseeing the delivery of its value proposition

- o Gathering and evaluating the measures of success
- o Monitoring the changing needs of the business, customers, and the employees to ensure the curriculum is as relevant and efficient as possible
- Advisory council
  - o The formation of an advisory council is considered a best practice for corporate universities to provide strategic advice and governance, particularly during the university formation and evaluation stages.
  - o The primary purpose of the advisory council is to identify and prioritize the current and future learning needs required to support the business strategies, goals, and critical business issues.
  - o Questions that are typically addressed by this advisory council include:
    - o What are the key business strategies and critical business issues that can or must be supported by specific learning and application of new skills and knowledge?
    - o What business metrics or key performance indicators will best gauge the impact of the university on these strategies and critical business issues?
    - o How can the council best keep a pulse on changing situations and make recommendations for how the university might respond?
    - o How can council members demonstrate active, hands-on endorsement of the university?
    - o From an executive perspective, what will success look like at six months and twelve months after the launch of the university, then annually thereafter?
    - o As the business grows and expands, what skills and knowledge need to be acquired and practiced to consistently deliver the organization's unique brand and customer experience?
    - o How can the university best support the talent management system?
  - o Such councils often also choose to provide guidance to other issues related to the formation of a corporate university and its day-to-day operating group. These include:
    - o The development of a corporate learning philosophy and related policies, standards, and practices
    - o The consistent design and delivery of learning content and the balance or blend of learning formats, whether facilitator-led and/or technology-based
    - o Funding strategies and budgeting, including accounting or cost-sharing across business units
    - o Communicating the value and expected contribution of the university to business goals
    - o Conducting periodic evaluation and review of the university operations and contributions to the business

274 Case Studies

- o Membership in the advisory council typically focuses upon four ingredients:
  - o Depth of understanding of the business strategies and critical business issues, from either a broader or enterprise-wide point of view, or a key functional area
  - o Organizational credibility and respect for their contributions, capabilities, and demonstrated interest in learning as a strategy for driving business results
  - o Personal motivation and capability to actively serve on an advisory council for at least a period of two years, for the purpose of continuity
  - o Desire and capability to continually watch for emerging critical business issues toward which university learning can be applied

The corporate university business plan also includes much more granular detail, specifically written to fit the needs of the organization, in the areas of courseware selection, preparation of the facilitation staff, customized communications and marketing, recommended potential measures of success, and financial planning.

As a result of the Rapid Due Diligence diagnostic process, specific examples are also crafted to provide preliminary implementation project maps for the university launch, a detailed lift-off implementation plan, sample action plans and risk factors for deploying a learning management system, communications plans with scripts, draft talking points for the university launch announcements, and competency matches with potential content. An example of a corporate university launch announcement appears in Box 10.1.

BOX 10.1 CORPORATE UNIVERSITY LAUNCH ANNOUNCEMENT: KEY TALKING POINTS AND PROCESS

Who's the Audience?	What's the Message?	Who Delivers the Message?	What Method Will be Used?	When is the Message Delivered?
Executives, Managers, Supervisors, Associates (in the initial targeted audience)	Announce the upcoming launch of the Corporate University.	Designated Advisory Council or Core Team Members	Face to face is ideal. Telecom is acceptable. Handout information summaries or FAQs. Conduct website demonstration (if available). Follow-up with an email on all key points.	Week of 8/30 Allow 1 hour

Launch Meeting Agenda:
- What is a corporate university?
- Why has it been formed?
- What is the expected impact?
- Who has been involved?
- Who will be invited to participate?
- How will it work (include any website demonstration)?
- How can associates log on (if a learning management system is operational)?
  - o Viewing choices
  - o Enrollment
  - o Taking courseware
  - o What they'll see as they navigate the site
  - o Instructor-led classroom and follow-up work
  - o Record-keeping
  - o Evaluations
- When will the initial registration be activated?
- What is the role of executives, managers, and supervisors before, during, and after the launch?
- What's in it for them and their associates?
- What is the estimate of time commitment?
- What is our communications plan?
- Questions and discussion

What is our corporate university?
- Our corporate university provides opportunities for the development and growth of our organization's associates and their contribution to the business. It will be a one-stop, single point of contact for all our organization's associates to easily access the full library of learning opportunities at any hour from any place.

Why has it been formed?
- Purpose:
  - o To pursue the development and growth of our organization's associates.
  - o To leverage existing knowledge and experience to grow the business.
  - o To consistently sustain the customer's experience.

What is the expected impact?
- Acquisition and application of skills to drive business results
- Improved engagement results, particularly about career development and growth opportunities
- Faster speed to competency for associates who are newly hired or promoted

(Continued)

276 Case Studies

- Effective adaptation of successful practices
- Single, unified library with up-to-date, relevant content
- Easy, automated registration and administration
- Increased participation and completion of associate development plans
- Contribution to retention and employer of choice rating
- Cost effective training scaled to accommodate our organization's growth

Who has been involved?
- Core project team
- Advisory council
- Facilitators

Who will be invited to participate in the initial launch?
- Specify groups or roles.

How will it work (if available, conduct website demonstration)?
- Announce the website and how to access it.
- Show how associates can log on.
- Point out the features of the website and what associates will see as they navigate the site.
- Show how to view the learning choices.
- Show how to enroll.
- Show how to access and complete the approved or designated online courseware.
- Conduct a brief overview of course learning design and content.
- Show how to sign up for instructor-led classroom training or follow-up skills practice work after online training.
- Describe how records will be maintained and secured.
- Describe the assessment and evaluation tools.
- Describe what to expect of the process and system.
- Define where to address other questions.

When will the initial registration be activated?
- The website will be open for registration on (specific date).

What is the role of executives, managers, and supervisors before, during, and after the launch?
What's in it for them and their associates?
- During the week of September 13: Designated managers and supervisors are asked to announce the launch of our corporate university in their regularly scheduled staff, work group, or individual meetings.
  - o Alternatives can include special meetings or town hall settings, whatever is most effective for your work group.
  - o Host the meeting and co-present the information with members of the core team. Contact (name) to schedule their participation.

- o Cover the same points from this meeting.
- o Provide handouts with summaries or frequently asked questions (FAQs).
- o Conduct a website demonstration.
- o Follow-up with an email on all key points.
- o Distribute any available marketing collateral.
- o Invite questions and engaging discussion to evoke "what's in it for the associates."
- During the week of September 20: Catch up on any remaining individuals or groups.
- During the week of September 20 and 27: Managers and supervisors are asked to talk with each associate, explore interest and application of initial offerings, personal and career benefits and payoffs, offer help in clarifying development targets and registration.
- During the week of September 27: Offer a reminder during regular meetings that the corporate university website will be open for registration on Friday, October 1st. Reference email and voice mail announcements and postings.
- During the week of October 4: Check on who within your work group has registered for what courses, for what schedule, and in what format (online or classroom instruction). Reference emails that give information about remaining open slots.
- During the week of October 25: Be prepared to provide feedback on your associates' experiences to date. What's the buzz? What ideas are out there to improve the experience or communications?
- During the week of November 8: Offer to the core team more feedback and any anecdotal evidence of impact with associates or their contributions on the job. Make announcements at regularly scheduled staff and work group meetings to start thinking about registration for the next quarter.
- During the week of November 15: All or a sample of managers, supervisors, and associates will be asked for feedback on the courseware, communications, what's worked well, what needs improvement, plus receive a preview of what to expect in the next quarter.
- During the week of December 6: Issue reminders about registration for next quarter, opening January 3.
- During January and February: Continue the pattern of communications, coaching, feedback, and reinforcement.

Estimate the time commitment on their part.
- One hour for the announcement of the launch
- Brief, 5-minute reminders during subsequent meetings
- 15–60 minutes follow-up discussion per partner, depending on their interest and need

(Continued)

278 Case Studies

> - One hour feedback sessions with the core team
> - Short follow-up discussions with associates who register and complete courseware
>
> Provide a communication plan and any talking points for them.
> - Feel free to use this document.
>
> Questions and discussion session

All of these findings and recommendations can accelerate the launch of a corporate university that has the capability of delivering significant impact to targeted business results. Just as importantly, the Rapid Due Diligence diagnostic process can pinpoint specific questions or key elements for deeper internal discussion and decision-making prior to making any investment in a corporate university.

Discussion Questions

- Why is it important for a corporate university to be linked to the organization's strategic dimensions?
- How can the findings of the Rapid Due Diligence diagnostic process help build internal commitment to learning and development strategies, including the formation of a corporate university?
- Why are detailed organizational communications plans required for success?
- How can the Rapid Due Diligence diagnostic process bring value to the creation of a corporate university?

Case Study Seven: Stabilizing a Software Development Startup Organization

This Rapid Due Diligence diagnostic process was completed with a software development startup organization. The firm was formed by a venture capitalist and technologist for the development of specific applications service provider software. As the organization grew to twenty people over the following months, insufficient market traction and revenue were being realized from the original business model. A new chief executive officer, experienced in startup and software development situations, was brought on board several months later. The new set of key players concluded that the original business model was not going to produce a sustainable market position. Furthermore, the funding was rapidly depleting.

By its first anniversary, the organization conceived an idea for another new software product platform. Market research confirmed the highly lucrative potential of the proposed product in an unoccupied market niche. The findings also clarified the need for a different marketing and sales approach to the targeted customers. Armed with these insights, the organization made progress on the new business plan, securing an original equipment manufacturer agreement and another round of venture capital funding within six months.

A number of key players were replaced, including a chief software architect, to address the new product platform. Several new software engineers were hired, yet turned over in the following months. Senior management was concerned with the high churn and began to recognize the high cost. Although candidates often declared their knowledge of specific software programs and were subsequently hired, their lack of depth and/or inability to perform was revealed in the course of daily project work. Senior technical people were continually declaring that the product development was on track. Upon closer examination, however, senior management eventually discovered the whole effort was seriously behind product performance and schedule targets. This discovery prompted additional turnover and a keen desire to stop the expensive loss of rare talent.

The chief executive officer also voiced ambitions to grow the organization rapidly and, in an orderly way, to capitalize upon the highly attractive market position of its products and services. With strong encouragement from its investors, the organization was racing to secure a first-to-market position without unnecessarily wasting or squandering its resources.

This researcher was invited to explore the situation, based upon findings and results from similar, previous Rapid Due Diligence diagnostic research. In initial conversations with the chief executive officer and chief financial officer, it was revealed that no one in senior management roles had a clear grasp of the explicit Critical Knowledge Areas© required to realize the proposed product platform. They stated that this lack of clarity had repeatedly impaired their ability to manage the recruitment and product development process. They were uncertain what questions to ask, what unique measures to monitor, and how to accurately gauge their technical progress. They were also unclear whether their classic stage-gate product development process and detached quality assurance practices were organized to optimize outcomes and efficiently derive the best outputs from application of their Critical Knowledge Areas©. They also didn't know how to recruit with sufficient precision to ensure the best staffing for the unusual product platform.

These initial revelations prompted the creation of a comprehensive approach to define critical talent to be applied at an urgent pace. The data collection and analysis included an in-depth inquiry into the business planning documentation and interviews with key officers and subject experts. The purpose was to define critical talent needs that drive the performance of the business. The investigation also pursued potential gaps in the existing strategy, processes, systems, policies, and practices.

Based on the preliminary findings about the business and its strategic approach, the next step required in-depth discussions with key officers and subject experts. This data gathering process sought insights from people who had expertise on:

- The identity of potential critical knowledge that significantly contributes to the business mission, the value proposition with customers, and other key strategic targets

280 Case Studies

- The identity of a potential talent profile of the experience, education, professional credentials, and behaviors that can very effectively activate that knowledge
- Challenges and issues to consider as the organization pursues a more deliberate approach to talent management

Thorough analyses of this combination of findings produced a set of talent definitions that can directly contribute to the way this organization conducts business. Potential measures of business impact were also identified. These day-to-day measures were intended to be baseline data points for future comparison.

The findings of the study included a set of Critical Knowledge Areas©, definition of critical talent, a set of measures for calculating potential Return on Critical Talent, conclusions about the findings, and specific recommendations for applying these findings to the organization's management techniques, strategies, processes, and systems.

The Critical Knowledge Areas© for this software development startup organization included:

- Comprehensive knowledge of the specific product family software architecture, platform, code interfaces, system integrators, and development methodology
- Research, new product development, and quality assurance processes that fit the customers' acceptance criteria in this product family
- In-depth understanding of the current market and future trends for the real-time enterprise and its highly integrated operations, business process software systems, and installed base footprint, plus how to translate those insights into profitable economics for this business type

This organization's critical talent descriptors include the combination of any of these Critical Knowledge Areas©, plus specific educational, work experience, and behaviors that can best drive the targeted performance results. The depth and type of work experience and education were specifically gauged to fit the demanding combination of technical expertise and accelerated development schedule. For example, certain critical talent required a master's degree level of formal education, combined with six to eight years of specific experience while others could be accommodated by a bachelor's degree level with four or more years of targeted experience.

A behavioral analysis of the business situation and desired culture of this software development start-up produced a set of key behaviors that are most likely to effectively stimulate profitable activation of the Critical Knowledge Areas©.

A number of potential measures of influence or Return on Critical Talent were extracted from the research findings. These measures were also tested with selected financial valuation techniques applied to intangible assets. The list includes:

Case Studies **281**

- Meeting or exceeding the customer's technical and critical-to-quality criteria
- Availability of software product availability at the targeted time and proficiency level
- Capability to capture and effectively influence the targeted software market space
- Increase in the efficiency of internal and external processes and transactions
- Increase in return factors such as revenue, operating margin, and investor equity
- Improvement in human performance scorecard metrics such as revenue and operating margin per full-time equivalent employee, turnover, and the direct-to-support employee ratio

A number of specific recommendations for action were generated from further analysis of the findings. These recommendations were included in a detailed written summary and discussed at length with the chief executive officer. The recommendations were focused on how to apply the findings to achieve greater Return on Critical Talent while constructively addressing the immediate, urgent business situation.

- Create a clear, crisp, differentiating customer value proposition that directly targets the greatest critical-to-quality customer factors, focuses the product design and development criteria, drives the market strategy and shapes the emerging market, while serving to prioritize and leverage the organization's talent.
- Examine how the product development and quality assurance processes may need to be combined and adjusted to more directly support the unique customer criteria and Critical Knowledge Area© efficiency and effectiveness.
- Create an employee value proposition that clearly describes and differentiates the firm's employment opportunity and can be effectively used to attract, develop, deploy, and retain critical talent.
- Isolate three to five critical success factors that serve as individual and organizational management focal points to drive for specific performance and verifiable results.
- Practice a high-frequency performance management approach with at least weekly dialogue at all levels to ensure focus.
- Diligently recruit and retain critical talent that will consistently demonstrate the organizational values while urgently delivering concrete business results. Apply an assessment process to more precisely discern the fit and degree of technical capabilities (Critical Knowledge Areas©) of candidates.
- Manage the internal distractions of non-critical activities and issues. Focus organizational energy on product development and customer acquisition to achieve specific, measurable business goals and ensure financial viability.

282 Case Studies

- Create an organizational system where everyone can win. Develop a level, internal playing field for all forms of recognition and reward. Recognize and resolve internal competitive and resource-access tensions that have arisen. Establish baseline compensation and promotion policies and practices to avoid the perception of unfair treatment, unproductive negotiations, hostage behavior, and unbecoming rivalry that undermines teamwork and collaboration among competitive contributors.
- Establish a balanced scorecard for measuring progress and managing performance to focus on the investors, market/customers, operational efficiency, and Return on Critical Talent. Load it with metrics that directly match the customer and employee value propositions. Cascade the scorecard to every employee to create clear direction and stimulate a stronger sense of personal contribution.
- Conduct and continually monitor a census of critical talent, using the new definitions. Map the Critical Knowledge Areas© and critical talent that reside within key strategic processes, functions, and locations.
- Apply the findings to immediate and near-term staffing needs or reassignments to optimally leverage the talent to meet urgent business needs. Immediately target employees who can arrive with the stated critical talent and have a track record of performance in similar circumstances. Given the urgent business situation, there is too much at stake at this time to risk solely developing critical talent on the job.
- Guide project teams and team leaders to maximize the Return on Critical Talent.
- Use the approach to identify and develop current and future leaders.
- Build Return on Critical Talent into the leadership role and performance management systems.
- Determine the optimal bench strength for critical talent at defined stages of organizational growth.
- Incorporate Critical Knowledge Areas© and critical talent within intellectual property definitions, policies, and practices.
- Create practical tools for monitoring progress, interpreting data, making fact-based decisions to the degree possible, while tracking managers' performance for managing critical talent.
- Use the Critical Knowledge Area© and critical talent definitions as specific targets for any retention strategies.
- Establish a process for periodic evaluation of progress on Return on Critical Talent.
- Brief the board of directors and investors on the purpose, importance, and potential impact of Return on Critical Talent, including findings in periodic reviews.

The senior management team pondered the results of the study and took immediate action on several points to gain prompt results. Within six months of the study, a number of positive improvements occurred that senior management

Case Studies **283**

has attributed at least in part to the influence of the Rapid Due diligence diagnostic process:

- Software engineers created an assessment tool for recruitment to discern the technical Critical Knowledge Area© capabilities with greater precision. Recent hires have demonstrated greater capability to create additional product functionality and repair software malfunctions more rapidly.
- The turnover of Critical Talent has been significantly reduced from fifty to five percent.
- Frequent full-staff communications have been instituted. At least weekly discussions with more candid dialogue are held. Collaboration is now expected and modeled among all levels.
- Key sources of organizational discontent, such as the perception of unfair and inequitable treatment of employees, incivility among key players, and unclear role definitions have been constructively addressed. Open discussions of the effect of such issues have led to the creation and application of selected, uniform practices in specific areas.
- Product development has moved from a stall-out condition to produce customer acceptable product performance. Software malfunctions are promptly and cooperatively addressed by product development and quality assurance within its refined, combined process. A greater percentage of product development dates are being met on time.
- The quality of communications and extent of feedback from customers have improved. Technical employees have been working more effectively with sophisticated and discerning prospective customers. Questions and concerns about the organization's capabilities have been addressed constructively with less tension and a demonstrated willingness to reconfigure within guidelines to meet customer needs.
- There have been numerous, explicit, lengthy discussions among senior technical and marketing management players to constructively address their roles and actions to manage organizational talent, combine customer needs and quality requirements within the product development process, secure more reliable forecasts, conduct daily conversations with direct reports within and across boundaries, and promptly address performance issues.

Within one year of the Rapid Due Diligence diagnostic process, additional results were reported; and management credited their increased attention to talent as a key contributing factor:

- Product version 2.0 was released for sale.
- The organization closed another round of venture capital funding with the four existing investors. At that time, the organization reported a current valuation of $32.9 million and an expectation of positive cash flow.
- The customer base at least doubled and grew to number fifty-seven.

284 Case Studies

These findings reinforce the premise that talent management produces desirable results. Organizations that deliver results on their brilliant strategies all have one thing in common: they deliberately engage their people to use the right knowledge, skills, and behaviors at the right time.

Discussion Questions

- Why is the Rapid Due Diligence diagnostic method helpful in the early stages of operating a startup organization?
- Why is it important to identify Critical Knowledge Areas© and how they contribute to the potential Return on Critical Talent in startup organizations?

Case Study Eight: Applying Rapid Due Diligence to Not-for-Profit Organizations

The process steps of the Rapid Due Diligence diagnostic process can be applied with effective results for organizations that are classified as not-for-profit. Understandably, some of the motives and systemic forces may differ within organizations that are often administered by a smaller number of paid employees and largely supported by a host of volunteers. However, there are still many opportunities for improvement in effectiveness and efficiency, especially where assets and resources can be constrained or limited.

In view of well-publicized growing secularization of North American society and the subsequent reduced attraction toward mainstream religious organizations, there are now large numbers of congregations and faith-based, community service not-for-profit organizations that are challenged by diminished resources.

Following is a description of how the Rapid Due Diligence diagnostic process applied to a large congregation. Its elected leadership requested the assistance of the researcher to gain a deeper understanding of how it could adapt to the decline in its membership and assets. Upon preliminary conversation with the leaders, it was clear that the application of the Rapid Due Diligence diagnostic process was appropriate. Because this may be considered an unusual application, considerable detail without identity disclosure is included in this case.

As part of the process, a series of relevant documents were provided to the researcher for deep review and analysis. Because this congregation also managed a private school and early childhood care facility, the Rapid Due Diligence diagnostic process reached across the full spectrum of this not-for-profit enterprise. The initial set of documents included the following:

- The current constitution of the congregation
- Organizational charts for the congregation, its private school, and early childhood care facility
- The most recent job descriptions for all members of staff

Case Studies **285**

- Recent financial reports, including consolidated operating fund statements, balance sheets, and cash flow analyses
- All recent, formal reports about the school, its governance and operations
- Sample newsletters and similar communications devices for the congregation
- Information that could be shared about the process to fill the current vacancy of its senior pastor

Upon review of these documents, the researcher gathered additional resources for further perspectives of the context of this congregation and guidelines available through the other aspects of its denominational relationship. These documents included:

- Trend reports for the congregation, covering assorted statistical data for nearly a decade
- The most current model constitution for congregations of this denomination
- The most recent set of guidelines for congregational audits
- Draft set of roles and responsibilities for congregational council officers
- Missional planning process workbook and tools, also authored by the researcher
- Guidelines on performance planning and review processes of this denomination

When the preparatory investigation of these documents was completed, more intensive interviews and discussions were conducted with senior leaders. All of the detailed findings and observations were assembled in a formal document for use by the senior leaders. A summary of those findings and observations appears below.

- The current constitution of the congregation was not in full alignment, as required, with the most current denominational model constitution and amendments.
  - o Many clarifications were needed, and conflicting language needed revision.
  - o Several duties of the congregation council were omitted and reportedly not fully exercised in the current governance practices.
  - o Several changes needed to be considered to bring council membership, roles, and responsibilities into an improved governance model.
  - o There were hints of over-control that often emanate from an environment of mistrust.
- The congregation, council, and school were suffering from the absence of any form of long-range planning or intentional missional planning. This void was particularly important with the congregation engaged in the call process to secure a new senior pastor.
- The limited amount and routine availability of sufficiently detailed financial statements, forecasts, and analyses were significantly hampering both the timely and effective decision-making at all levels of the organization.

286 Case Studies

- Without the active engagement of a qualified and effective school committee, combined with the authority of the council and congregation, the school did not have sufficient management attention to realize its full potential.
- In the absence of a current set of administrative policies and employee handbook, there was a tendency toward reactionary, irregular, and ad hoc actions.
- There were no records of performance discussions, expectations, planning, objectives, goals setting, feedback, or formal review, except for a few limited notes for some of the school staff.
- Job descriptions were incomplete and outdated.
- There was no evidence of any form of thorough, strategic, community educational needs assessment nor deliberations about the effects of changing demographics, competitive comparisons, and how all such data influence choices about the future rightsizing of capabilities and services, the revenue stream, or tuition strategy for the school.
- A small group, often of related individuals, tended to serve as the core decision-makers governing both the congregation and the school.
- Annual meetings for the congregation did not have a full set of financial statements available as information to guide decision-making.
- A thorough communications strategy was not in place.
- The congregation had a long-term habit of strong, inward focus. This further raised doubt about the level of commitment to realistically and enthusiastically pursue the outward-focusing targets posed by the committee charged with finding a new pastor.

Based upon the findings and observations, the researcher delivered a series of detailed recommendations for consideration by the senior leaders of the congregation, school, and early childhood care facility. A summary appears below.

- The current constitution requires deep review and mandated amendment to bring it into alignment with the required denominational model and to deal effectively with a number of governance, policy, and process issues.
- Specific changes to the structure, membership, terms of service, roles, responsibilities, and authorities of both the congregation council and school governance group are required.
  - o In part, these recommendations were made to remove overlaps, conflicting interests, and introduce better governance.
  - o For example, the school group needed to formulate annual operating and resource plans, conduct community needs assessments, clarify competitive positioning, monitor learning outcomes and requirements for sustaining accreditation, create tuition and revenue stream strategies, identify funding sources, and draft other proposals that require council and congregation review and approval.

- The congregation council needs to adopt routine provision of much more immediate, complete, and detailed financial statements for use in aiding more effective, efficient, agile, and fact-based decision-making. Such statements would also be useful for monitoring progress toward missions and ministries by the council, senior staff, school administration, and the congregation.
- Strategic, missional planning is immediately warranted to set the congregation and school direction for at least the next one to two years.
  - o The results of this planning are necessary to crystallize the work of the process to call a new senior pastor who will be best equipped and enthusiastic in fulfilling the preferred missional direction.
  - o This planning is also necessary to guide immediate development of budgetary assumptions and decision-making.
  - o Another spin-off benefit is the avoidance of unnecessary waste of time, resources, and aimless application of precious volunteers.
- Upon identification of a qualified school oversight committee, this group too needs to engage in strategic planning.
  - o This activity is needed to plan for broader involvement of congregation members, parents, educators, students, and community leaders.
  - o It is necessary to gain an accurate understanding of the market area's educational needs, comparative offerings, and how to best position the school's capabilities.
  - o The data and perspectives would affirm the right size and programming that could be sustainable in the long term and would include detailed revenue stream analysis, tuition strategy, and proper scholarship levels.
  - o The planning would also establish aligned goals and objectives, precise measures of progress on all dimensions, set performance expectations, define critical ratios and other metrics for risk management and trend-watching, guide any marketing and fund development activity, and sustain accreditation.
- Upon election, new congregation council members need to complete an indepth orientation. Such an orientation needs to include specific information on areas such as:
  - o Governing authority
  - o Unique requirements for school governance
  - o Decision-making processes
  - o Roles, responsibilities, and ground rules for behavior
  - o Familiarity with the constitution, policies, and critical procedures
  - o Requirements as an employer
  - o Relationships across the denomination
  - o Local ecumenical partners
  - o Outreach into the community
  - o Servant leadership

288 Case Studies

- o Stewardship
- o Fiduciary responsibilities
- o Methods for building heightened levels of trust and engagement throughout the entire community of the congregation
- All employment practices need to be updated and more thoroughly completed and tracked.
  - o Special attention is required in the annual review of performance, including documented performance planning with goals and objectives that mesh with the long-range and current year plan, setting expectations for performance in both tasks and behaviors, any changes in objectives, performance reviews, giving candid feedback, and preparing developmental plans.
- The congregation and school would benefit greatly from a comprehensive communications strategy to surround all of the recommended actions noted earlier.
  - o Other benefits would include:
    - o Demonstrating a desirable level of transparency
    - o Continually building an environment of mutual trust and respect
    - o Helping all people to operate from informed perspectives
    - o Providing an appealing and energizing communications tools for all corners of the membership and communities
    - o Attracting and engaging broader participation in leadership and volunteer roles
    - o Moving the organization from its current inward focus to one that includes much more attention to the mission and ministry outside its walls

Following the delivery of the documented results of the Rapid Due Diligence diagnostic process and clarifying discussions with senior leaders, the researcher was invited to guide the missional planning process for the current congregation council. Using some of the findings from the Rapid Due Diligence diagnostic process plus the framework for missional planning, originally written by the researcher, a customized agenda was developed for the planning discussions. For purposes of illustration, several exhibits were created to support this missional planning process session. A detailed design of the purpose, objectives, activities, and learning points for a compact, day-long session appears in Table 10.4. The researcher guided the planning process to incorporate constructive movement and involvement by all players.

The planning meeting agenda and supporting charts appear in the series shown in Box 10.2. For purposes of the meeting with many participants, all charts were presented in large sizes and posted on the walls to maintain a focal point for discussion throughout the intense day-long working session.

Among the outcomes of the day-long working session was a set of congregation and leader goals. The samples shown in Table 10.5 were provided as a stimulus for the group's reference during the planning process. The researcher guided

TABLE 10.4 Mission Planning with Congregation Council

Purpose & Objectives
- Engage in initial mission planning for the whole community
- Identify and plan for key areas of mission and ministry
- Affirm our commitment and accountability for results

Time	Topic	Activity	Materials	Learning Points	Notes
9 am	Welcome, Opening Prayer, Purpose & Objectives, Agenda Dwelling in Scripture	Welcome, prayer, purpose & objectives, how it fits work we've already been doing. Overview agenda. Read aloud Eph 3:18–20 and 4:15–16. Pose key Qs, inc.: What is God calling us to be and to do in our community? What changes are needed? Self-organize into pairs, read aloud same Scripture, use deep listening & answer Qs. Report out responses to full group & debrief for insights & central themes.	Large print charts on stand or guiding PowerPoint Chart or PPT with process & Qs to guide work	Set expectations for the day With deep listening, discover new insights into what we are called to be & do	Participants complete prework. Focus on building up the body of Christ; begin process of growing into God's preferred & promised future
10 am	Analyzing Our Environment – or Listening to Our Community Analyzing Our Assets & Capabilities – or Identifying Our Possibilities	Look beyond congregation. Build on findings to date. What community needs are not being met that we can address? Focus on internal culture, heritage, all forms of assets. Key Qs on possibilities for using/leveraging our capabilities.	Chart or PPT with process & Qs Chart or PPT with process & Qs	Gain fresh insights into community; affirmation of previous findings Tell the truth about who we are today & could be in future	Focus on the outside community; self-managed nature breaks Focus inside our congregation.

(Continued)

Time	Topic	Activity	Materials	Learning Points	Notes
10:45 am	Formulating Our Vision & Goals – or Clarifying Aspirations & Goals Continue through working lunch	Populate Strategic Planning Map as full group. Identify key areas of mission & ministry. Introduce worksheet & process. Divide into small groups. Use worksheets for developing goals, key actions, measures, obstacles & mitigating actions.	Chart or PPT with partial Strategic Planning Map; blank key areas of mission & ministry worksheets for all	Practice collaborative & creative networking while beginning, developing, or redefining current mission plans	Complete real plans; all actively engaged; check how these plans respond to our findings from dwelling in Scripture
12:45 pm	Debrief worksheets	Each group summarizes its work. Clarifying Qs, discussion.	Small groups present their worksheets	Build shared vision & ownership of goals	Reality check
1:30 pm	Aligning Our Resources, Fulfilling Our Plan, Gauging Our Progress	Key Qs on resources, reporting, communications; sample Strategy Fulfillment Map; sample scorecards	Chart or PPT; sample map & scorecards	Check our financial and people resources	Another reality check w/tough questions
1:45 pm	Next Steps	Identify accountabilities with Council, Congregation, School Committee; check for personal commitment & follow-up	Chart or PPT with Qs	Clarify personal accountabilities & test individual commitment	More tough questions
2:00 pm	Wrap & Close with Prayer	Seek feedback on the process and outcomes from the day.		Build confidence	Courage to act!

Case Studies **291**

BOX 10.2 MISSION PLANNING CHARTS

(Congregation Name)
Mission Planning
(Date)
Agenda

9 am	Welcome, Purpose, Objectives Dwelling in Scripture
10 am	Analyzing Our Environment, Assets & Capabilities
10:45 am	Formulating Our Vision & Goals Working Lunch
12:45 pm	Debrief
1:30 pm	Aligning Our Resources Fulfilling Our Plan Gauging Our Progress
1:45 pm	Next Steps
2:00 pm	Wrap & Close With Prayer

Purpose & Objectives
- Engage in initial mission planning for the whole community within reach of our congregation
- Identify and plan for key areas of mission & ministry
- Affirm our commitment & accountability for results

Ground Rules
- Open & close with prayer
- Seek God's will & His peace
- Keep to the schedule
- Cellphones off
- Treat each other with respect
- Encourage each member to participate
- One speaker at a time
- Listen attentively – be fully present
- Encourage openness to differing points of view
- Invite new ideas & give them a chance
- Fulfill our commitments

Building Blocks of Trust (AchieveGlobal)
- Focus on the situation, issue, or behavior, not the person
- Maintain the self-confidence & self-esteem of others
- Maintain constructive relationships
- Take initiative to make things better
- Lead by example
- Think beyond the moment

Dwelling in Scripture
Ephesians 3:18–20 & 4:15–16
- Pastor reads Scripture
- Self-organize into pairs

(Continued)

292 Case Studies

- Read aloud same Scripture
- Ask these questions & engage in deep listening
  - o What is God calling us to be and to do in our community?
  - o What changes are needed?
  - o What is the greatest possibility we can envision?
- Prepare to debrief

Analyzing Our Environment
- Looking beyond our congregation
- Building on findings gathered to date
- Applying SOAR (Strengths, Opportunities, Aspirations, Results) with key questions:
  - o What community needs are NOT being addressed?
  - o Underserved? Overlooked?
  - o What additional clarity do we need?
  - o How & where can we help?
  - o Do we need a partnership?
  - o If so, with whom? Why?

Analyzing Our Assets & Capabilities
- Focus on our internal culture, our heritage, operational capabilities, all forms of assets
- Insights from earlier research
- Ask key questions:
  - o What's working here? How do we know? Why are things working well?
  - o How do we typically approach opportunities?
  - o How do we conduct our mission & ministry operationally to optimize results?
  - o How does our heritage manifest itself?
  - o What assets are lying idle? Or contributing less than what is possible?
  - o What is in our midst that we have not recognized as an asset?
  - o How can we use all these assets to achieve greater possibilities?

Formulating Our Vision & Goals
- Ask key questions
  - o What is God up to here?
  - o What is God's purpose for our ministry?
  - o What are we being called to be & do?
  - o What is the greatest possibility we can imagine God doing in or through our congregation?
  - o What changes are required?
  - o What degree of commitment do we share together about God's mission & ministry here?
- Tough questions: Do any apply to us?
  - o Do we choose to ignore challenges?
  - o Do we only tend to look inward?

Right-aligned header: Case Studies **293**

- o Are we focused on maintaining the status quo – or a former image of our congregation?
- o Do we embrace real excitement on any topic or program?
- o Are we calling on the same few people to do the real work?
- o Are we holding back resources for ourselves?
- o Are we reluctant to reach out to genuinely assist the community?
- o Are we just surviving as a church?
- o Do we engage in authentic conflict resolution, reconciliation & healing?
- o Are we unwilling or too exhausted to work hard or follow-through on plans?
- o Are we ready to boldly step forward to fulfill God's plan for our future?

Strategic Planning Map
- Draft content from earlier research

Key Areas of Mission & Ministry
- Identify 3–5 Key Area labels
- Divide Key Areas across small work groups
- Work independently to complete the worksheet
- Prepare to report out at 12:45 pm

Aligning Our Resources
- Importance of complete & regular financial reporting
- Resource stewardship
- Skills & talents of people

Activating Our Plan
- Strategy Fulfillment Map & its application
- Accountability for results

Gauging Our Progress
- Do periodic checks on quantitative, qualitative, and time-bound measures
- Spot the need for any course correction
- Communicate plans, goals & results to all members
- Invite ongoing input & engage in deep listening

Next Steps
- What tasks & accountabilities will we sign up for?
- What are we willing to do & say among ourselves to fulfill God's plan for ministry through our congregation?
- How will we keep ourselves on track?
  - o Comfortably raising issues with other?
  - o Receiving feedback?
- What will we do & say with others?
- How will we know that today's discussions & commitments made any difference?

TABLE 10.5 Congregation and Leader Goals

(Name of Congregation)
(City)
Congregation Goals for (Year)

Item	Goal Description	Timeline	Comments
1	Activate stewardship program to stimulate growth. Increase unified giving by 10%.	January – February (coming year)	Assessment, education, planning, implementation & evaluation process; offer options for giving; Consecration Sunday; planned giving for major property improvements; benevolence commitments
2	Engage more members & visitors with wider variety & more music in inspiring worship experiences.	Full period	Balance of traditional & contemporary; hymn selection; grow music programs; use art & technology
3	Communicate mission & ministry opportunities more fully & raise church profile in the community.	Full period	Improve online presence; giving options; more volunteer opportunities; collaborate with X congregation & local groups; improve property signage
4	Offer more & varied education opportunities for all age groups.	Full period	Pastor-led adult Bible studies; quarterly pre-K to youth studies; recruit & equip teachers; church retreat; adult VBS; book studies
5	Foster a more welcoming, family-friendly environment.	Full period	Enhance hospitality & visitor programs; opportunities for fellowship; redesign/refresh worship & other spaces
6	Expand youth & young adult ministry to attract more participants.	Full period	Evaluate staffing level required; support students from local colleges; food for finals; online presence
7	Leverage area partnerships for more social ministry.	Full period	Explore partnerships; grow current ministries; find more volunteer opportunities
8	Identify & grow more & new leaders or volunteers for mission & ministry.	Full period	In responseful living stewardship, identify and/or volunteer as leaders; education for developing leaders
9			
10			

(Name of Congregation)
(City)
Rostered Leader's Goals for (Year)

Goals for Senior Pastor (Name)

Item	Goal Description	Timeline	Comments	Progress
1	To provide a well done, engaging and thought provoking worship experience.	Full period		
2	To meet every household within 1 year.	Full period	Targeting completion by June.	
3	To meet staff, clarify expectations, and foster healthy working relationships.	Full period	Initial meetings complete by December.	
4	To connect with local colleges.	Full period	Start with music & faith in 1st quarter.	
5	To strengthen stewardship.	Full period	Work with stewardship committee.	
6	To offer adult class on Sunday mornings.	Full period	Commence in November.	
7	To engage with the confirmation class and help with teaching.	On rotation	Beginning in October.	
8	To provide pastoral assistance as needed to members and non-members.	As needed		
9	To actively participate in denominationally sponsored activities.	As opportunities arise	Attend all that are scheduled.	
10				

(Continued)

Goals for Youth Director (Name)

Item	Goal Description	Timeline	Comments	Progress
1	Conduct joint confirmation program with X congregation.	Per schedule		
2	Teach Sunday Bible study for junior/senior high youth.	Full period		
3	Organize & conduct junior/senior high youth events, fundraising & service opportunities:	Per schedule		
	• City event parking • Shrove Tuesday Pancake Dinner • Winter retreat • Summer outing • National, regional, and local youth gatherings • Graduations, sports, recitals • Advent dinner			
4	Conduct individual youth counseling.	As needed		
5				
6				
7				
8				
9				
10				

the participants through a lengthy, small group process to identify key areas of mission and ministry and essential actions, milestones, timelines, metrics, roles, and budgetary resources, plus the potential risks and ways to mitigate the effects of those risks. The worksheet is shown in Table 10.6.

Upon completion of all of the key areas of mission and ministry, the researcher provided a sample strategic fulfillment map with descriptions and timelines to track the work of the small groups. The sample map is shown in Table 10.7.

Another tool provided by the researcher for this group of congregation leaders was a sample, one-page strategic planning map. The intent was to create a compact, one-page summary of the strategic direction, guiding principles, and assumptions for use in their leadership meetings or in communications with larger groups. The sample strategic planning map is shown in Box 10.3.

A final tool provided to the group was a sample strategy fulfillment scorecard that could be used for communicating progress and measurable results. A sample scorecard appears in Table 10.8.

In summary, the Rapid Due Diligence diagnostic process can be easily adapted to apply to the purposes and challenges of not-for-profit organizations. All too often, such organizations are overlooked as legitimate targets for such forms of enlightening discovery and assessment. As a result, their worthy missions and ministries to local communities and beyond unnecessarily suffer without the attention of some techniques that perhaps were originated in for-profit business situations.

TABLE 10.6 Key Areas of Mission and Ministry Worksheet

Key Area of Mission and Ministry Title: _____

Item	Goal Description & Outcome	Key Actions, Milestones, Timelines	Metric	Budget	Players
1					
2					
3					
Alternative or Additional Goals					
4					
5					
SMART Goals: Specific; Measurable; Attainable; Relevant; Time-bound					
Item	Risks/Obstacles/Constraints to Goals & Outcomes		Mitigation Actions		
1					
2					
3					

TABLE 10.7 Strategic Fulfillment Map

Key Areas of Mission & Ministry	Year One						Year Two											
	Jul	Aug	Sept	Oct	Nov	Dec	Jan	Feb	Mar	Apr	May	Jun	Jul	Aug	Sept	Oct	Nov	Dec
Preaching & Worship Leadership		Redesign Sunday bulletin																
			Add variety to the worship experience.															
				Dedicate more resources to our music ministry.														
Teaching		Recruit new Sunday School teachers for quarterly pre-K through adult programs.																
				Conduct short-term adult study opportunity every 6 months.						Conduct adult study opportunity every 6 months.						Ongoing studies.		
									Plan & conduct retreat.									
Evangelism & Mission		Increase name recognition & presence online.																
				Create opportunities to support local college students. Create more family-friendly environment.														
	Maintain youth ministry. Evaluate upon arrival of new senior pastor.																	
			Enhance coffee hour and visitor program.															
Social Ministry				Explore & leverage partnerships: Who's already doing this well?														
	Sustain & grow current ministries .																	
	Communicate volunteer opportunities proactively & intentionally.																	
Stewardship							Increase giving by 10%.											
	Improve communications concerning giving. Conduct education for changing our mindset on stewardship.																	
				Estate-focused planned giving & endowments.														
Resource Stewardship		Mid-yr report		Audit done				Clear & repair windows					Planning & evaluation; mid-yr report					
	Roof repair				Annual report			Freshen landscape										
		Clean sanctuary		Prepare quarterly financial forecasts; communicate status to congregation.														

Box 10.3 Strategic Planning Map

Strategic Planning Map for X-Month Horizon (Dates)

Strategic Direction

(Name of Congregation) will foster a lively, Christ-centered environment that has authentic appeal to draw more youth, young adults, and families into intergenerational and multicultural fellowship and service to others.

Mission Statement

(Name of Congregation) is you and me. We are a people created by God and redeemed by the blood of Jesus Christ. The Holy Spirit empowers us to share God's gifts of forgiveness, love and eternal life. Our mission is rooted in Jesus' command to love one another. Inspired by the Holy Spirit, we reach out to our community, sharing God's free gift of salvation, seeking and welcoming all people into our fellowship.

Guiding Principles

Jesus is Lord   All are welcome   Everyone has a gift   Practice grace   Love changes people

Key Areas of Mission & Ministry

Preaching & Worship Leadership	**Teaching**	**Evangelism & Mission**
• Redesign Sunday bulletin. • Add variety to the worship experience. • Dedicate more resources to our music ministry.	• Recruit new Sunday School teachers. • Conduct short-term adult study opportunity every 6 months. • Conduct a Congregation retreat. • Adult education every Sunday.	• Increase name recognition & presence online. • Create opportunities to support local college students. • Create more family-friendly environment. • Enhance coffee hour & visitor program. • Maintain youth ministry.

Social Ministry	**Stewardship**
• Explore & leverage partnerships: Who's already doing this well? • Sustain & grow current ministries. • Communicate volunteer opportunities proactively & intentionally.	• Increase giving by 10%. • Improve communications concerning giving. • Education for changing our mindset on stewardship. • Estate-focused planned giving & endowments.

Gauging Progress

(Summation of quantitative, qualitative, and time-bound metrics for each key area of mission & ministry)

Resource Stewardship

(People, talents, time, property, funding)

Principal Assumptions

Congregation will achieve its proposed budget. We will have a half-time youth minister. Property requirements will be managed.

300 Case Studies

TABLE 10.8 Strategy Fulfillment Scorecard
Time Horizon: _____

People We Serve	*Operations & Processes*
• Frequency of visits to members' homes • # of meals served to homeless people • # of school supplies and backpacks for children • Frequency & % of visits to homebound and hospitalized • Quality of educational experience for children, youth, and adults • Quality of counseling/caregiving services	• Accuracy of parochial records • Quality of financial recordkeeping processes • Timeliness of quarterly & annual reports • Completeness & accuracy of employee records • Quality of performance management • Timeliness & quality of property maintenance
Financial Sustainability	*People Who Serve*
• Rate of increase in giving per member unit • Completion rate on financial pledges • Growth rate of endowment funds • Healthy cash flow management & balance sheet • Accountability, %, and timeliness of mission support • % allotment for reserves	• Fair market compensation for rostered leaders & staff • Quality mutual ministry support • Timely & balanced performance feedback • Timely acknowledgment of all gifts • Completion of development plans • Recognition for volunteers • Frequency of rotation of volunteers

Discussion Questions

- Why is the Rapid Due Diligence diagnostic method helpful for not-for-profit organizations?
- What are the differences in the investigative research design between for-profit and not-for-profit organizations?
- What are the differences in the recommendations between for-profit and not-for-profit organizations?

Case Study Nine: Pursuing an International Business Development Strategy

A pharmaceutical organization with market reach in Asia Pacific, India, Australia, Europe, and North America was determined to craft a more productive international business development strategy. The intent was to increase market share in existing and future markets and to make the organization a more formidable competitor in its product and market target areas.

The organization's current market spaces were occupied by reputable, very large, and aggressive competitors. Effective business development strategies required a combination of both exceptional product performance plus high levels of service and business relationships with customers. The organization acknowledged that the long-term success and financial viability would be greatly dependent upon the ability of the business development or sales organization and its individual representatives to identify, approach, and successfully sell portfolio solutions into both new and existing customer relationships across the nearly worldwide span of its markets.

The executive group crafted a specific growth strategy to prepare the international business development organization for superior performance. This growth strategy was designed to create and institutionalize a system of best practices embedded within the business development process and apply the underlying behavioral competencies. The combination was expected to increase the productivity, revenue, and overall profitability of the international business development organization. The Rapid Due Diligence diagnostic method was engaged to identify a comprehensive, strategic model to support this strategy.

An initial step in the pursuit of this new business development strategy focused upon introducing the strategy and gaining the support of the international business development executives. A senior officer, the owner of the business issue, announced the new growth strategy, its purpose and importance to the viability of the organization, and the critical timing of preparation for the business development force around the world. This leader invited the participating international executives to learn from each other about their own best practices, share their knowledge about how they effectively conducted business in their market spaces, and embrace a consistent, effective business development process that could produce superior performance and lead to lasting growth for the whole enterprise.

The researcher described the scope of the inquiry, key steps within the diagnostic process, roles, and involvement of the international executives and their respective managers. The participants nominated subject matter experts for both field visits and an intensive working session to identify the comprehensive, strategic model to support the overall new international business development strategy.

Following the period of preparatory investigation, development of the research plan and discovery protocol, the researcher conducted lengthy telephone interviews with senior level subject matter experts representing a number of distant geographic markets, such as Australia, Singapore, India, and several countries in Europe. Additional telephone interviews were then conducted with sales professionals to gain their perspectives on the same set of discovery questions and fields of inquiry. The interview questions were respectful to the unique differences of each geographic area and cultural way of doing business, including the following:

- What are the current and near future prospects for doing business in your market area?
- How would you describe the current relationship with your customer base?
- How are those relationships changing?
- How is your market area and business development environment shifting?

302 Case Studies

- What do business development professionals need to do better in response to these changes?
- What best practices do you use that you would like to recommend to others in the worldwide organization?
- What are any challenges or potential barriers to your business development success?
- What recommendations do you have for pursuing this new business development strategy?

Following these initial numbers of telephone interviews and the creation of additional probing questions within the research design discovery process, the researcher traveled to several countries in Europe to conduct on-site discovery in-person with multiple offices of the organization. Interviews were completed with senior business development directors, managers, account development professionals, and supporting services managers. Additional questions included the following:

- What are all the steps of the business development, delivery, and installation process of the products in your market area?
- What is the current customer relationship, and how is that progressively developed?
- How do you measure customer satisfaction? What tools and techniques are used? What feedback has been received? How have those results been used?
- How does your organization differentiate itself from the competition in your market area?
- How is the marketing and business development strategy translated into territory and key account planning?
- What are your primary, targeted markets and product mix? What is the current level of penetration?
- How do you currently equip business development professionals with the skills and tools to be successful in your markets?
- What process is used by business development managers in orienting, developing, coaching, and measuring the performance of the sales professionals?
- What is the departure rate of business development personnel? What exit rationale is given?
- What recommendations for improvement do you have?

The senior business development manager in each country provided a variety of the most recent and relevant customer survey data, conducted by both internal and external market research sources, collectively encompassing both Europe and Asia Pacific. These data were useful to the researcher in preparation for on-site visits with a variety of customers with different product needs and applications.

The perspectives and data from the combination of interviews of all types, customer visits, and preparatory investigation of all relevant background information were applied by the researcher in crafting an agenda for an intensive working session in Europe with senior level subject matter experts representing several countries and product portfolios. The researcher incorporated a set of analysis and synthesis techniques into the facilitation process to help guide the deliberations of the senior leaders, without introducing biased perspectives. The agenda included the following areas for further exploration and refinement:

- The customers' process for how they make their purchasing decisions
- The current business development process used by each product portfolio
- Isolation of best practices and important opportunities for improvement
- Description of the organization's future strategic, global business development opportunities
- Identification of the core competencies required for both business development professionals and their managers
- Recommendations for effective implementation of the new business development strategy, supporting processes, and competencies for performance

Following deep comparative examination, the senior leaders agreed that their respective customers for each product portfolio practiced a similar decision-making process in pursuing their purchases. The core questions included the following:

- What is the initiating situation or stimulus for the customers?
- Who are the players, and what are their roles?
- What are the primary process steps these players follow in their progressive decision-making process?
- What decision criteria or decision rules are used?
- What factors are considered most valued or critical to the prospects and current customers?

In addition to the detailed process steps, players, and rules, the group identified the following criteria as the most valued and critical to the customers:

- The trust and confidence level in the business development relationship with both the representing sales professional and the organization
- Capability of the business development professional in helping to identify a hidden need
- Level of technical and service support throughout the purchasing process
- Responsiveness to customer questions and needs
- Degree of product innovation
- Compliance with governing regulation
- Product and service pricing

304 Case Studies

The group voiced an opinion that most of the business development professionals tended to function as problem-focused solution providers. The behavior of their respective competitors was unknown but estimated to be the same.

These findings were compared with customer survey data excised from a number of formal research reports, highlighting the requirements for doing business in sequential quantitative factoring. The group discussed at length these findings on customer satisfaction drivers plus opportunities and priorities for improvement in their respective market areas. All of these discussions focused on the necessary ingredients for successfully pursuing the new business development strategy and its commonalities irrespective of geographic location and product portfolio.

The researcher worked with the group to chart the primary business development process steps used to respond to and/or drive their respective customers' purchasing and decision-making process. The group was asked to identify the following, according to their respective product portfolios:

- Primary steps or key activities they currently practice in business development
- Best practices they currently use and that they want to continue
- Opportunities for improvement that they want to design into the new business development strategy and its supporting processes

Having completed an abbreviated description of the current customers' purchasing and decision-making process, plus the current practices within the respective product portfolio business development processes, the attention of the group was shifted to a focus upon the opportunities for the future. The intent was to use such opportunities as the contextual anchor for designing an appropriate business development process that could efficiently and effectively identify, seize, and execute the best business for the worldwide organization.

The group was asked to consider what they knew about the marketing and business development strategy for each portfolio for the near and longer term. Questions focused upon a variety of strategic dimensions, such as the following:

- Customer creation
- Customer expansion or penetration
- Customer protection or insulation from the competition
- Any information about underserved markets
- Any metrics on customer loyalty, beyond what appeared in the currently available customer research data
- Any intended influence on the customers' migration path or patterns during decision-making
- Any business development performance standards or metrics
- Information about competitive strategies and the organization's offensive or defensive moves

Case Studies **305**

- Unique differentiators that could be positioned as distinctive benefits with customers
- Information about how the marketing and business development strategies are translated into subsidiary, regional, territory, or key account planning

The researcher took special note that none of the participants had detailed information on the typical strategic targets listed above. The group did, however, identify a number of significant opportunities, which must remain private.

Upon completion of these collective discussions, the researcher facilitated the group's focus upon creating the future-oriented business development process to support the broader strategy. The group agreed upon a set of assumptions as a starting point. These included the following:

- The business development process will apply to all the product portfolios.
- The process will apply to all international locations.
- The global marketing and business development strategy will be integrated and clear.
- The market potential and gross targets for new products and systems will be provided.
- The international business development organization will routinely provide feedback and market or competitive intelligence from all process steps as needed to internal parts in business development, marketing, and product development.

Following intensive and comparative exploration, the group identified the following eight key process steps for the international business development process to support the overall strategy to all product portfolios:

- Identifying opportunities
- Qualifying opportunities
- Analyzing situations and preparing solutions
- Presenting solutions and resolving customer concerns
- Reaching agreement and closing the business
- Installing or supplying the solutions
- Monitoring performance of those solutions
- Leveraging the success of the relationship and solutions

Specific details were created by the group to add important distinctions by product portfolio for each of the business development process steps. These details included at least the following information:

- Precise language of the organization's goal
- Description of the customer's expectation of each process step

306 Case Studies

- Sequence of key activities to be performed by business development professionals and support staff roles
- Performance standards or key metrics

The group contemplated the compilation of the comprehensive future-oriented business development process as the basis for identifying the specific competencies that business professionals and their managers would need to demonstrate in order to consistently deliver superior performance. The researcher provided definitions and examples of competencies in terms of skills, knowledge, abilities, and motivating factors. The competencies for these respective roles appear in Box 10.4.

BOX 10.4 COMPETENCIES FOR BUSINESS DEVELOPMENT PROFESSIONALS AND MANAGERS

Competencies for Business Development Professionals

The sub-group acknowledged that salespeople and others who have direct contact with customers ideally will possess these competencies.

Skills:
- Sales communications skills, such as:
  - o Asking questions
    - o Listening for full meaning
    - o Influencing or persuading
    - o Negotiating
    - o Asking for the business (closing)
    - o Sales presentation skills
- Planning and organizing time and territory
- Developing effective sales strategies
- Problem solving

Knowledge:
- Scientific background
- Product knowledge
- Territory and customer information
- Competitive intelligence
- Regulatory background

Abilities:
- Extroverted or outgoing personality
- Independence or autonomy
- Applies intuitive sensing
- Takes initiative for positive results
- Competitive

Case Studies **307**

- Accepts responsibility for performance
- Self-confidence and positive outlook
- Resilience and tenacity
- Assertive (as compared with aggressive, abrasive)
- Professional image
- Comfortable receiving feedback

Motivations:
- Team spirit – takes pride in the group's success
- Thrives on achievement and recognition of results
- Driven to succeed
- Seeking continual personal development

Competencies for Business Development Management

The group stated that the competencies for business development management must include a fundamental mastery of the sales skills required of sales professionals in order to establish credibility and be effective in this role.

Skills:
- Communications
  - Asking questions and listening
  - Providing feedback and coaching for development
  - Negotiating
- Devising sales strategies
- Delegating with appropriate follow-up
- Analytical skills
- Multi-lingual capability
- Problem solving
- Establishing priorities and managing resources
- Planning and organizing to address priorities

Knowledge:
- Organizational and political savvy
- Knowledge of the markets and customers
- Financial, business and policy acumen
- Product knowledge
- Legal and regulatory knowledge
- Market and sales strategies and application to local circumstances

Abilities:
- Personal credibility
- Approachability
- Charisma
- Decisiveness

(*Continued*)

308 Case Studies

- Responsibility for achieving success
- Self-confidence
- Creativity
- Pragmatism

Motivations:
- Takes pride in developing the staff
- Desires to serve and satisfy customers
- Thrives on achievement and recognition of positive results
- Driven to succeed
- Seeks continual personal development
- Seeks economic success

The researcher invited the group to comment about how to effectively build and apply the competencies for both business development professionals and their managers. They also provided observations and descriptions of factors that they perceived as critical to the success of the business development organization in pursuing the overall strategy. Those factors are summarized below.

- A comprehensive, systemic, tightly integrated, global approach to the marketing and business development strategy was needed as soon as possible.
  - o This strategy was expected to be a complete business model encompassing the end-to-end customer relationship, from the initial marketing contacts through the full range of business development, and all forms of service provision.
  - o The strategy was also expected to capitalize upon the organization's superior competitive advantages in any product or market categories and enable successful pre-emptive, first-to-market competitive positioning.
- This global approach needed to look beyond the perceived, current North American centric practices. Examples included:
  - o Greater visibility with international pre-marketing activities
  - o A thorough and realistic plan for product launches
  - o Timely provision of marketing collateral, applications studies, and professional publications and references for international markets
  - o Guidance for regions and countries to effectively adapt the corporate marketing and business development strategy to local circumstances and regulations
- Development and propagation of a specific corporate and international image, with comprehensive, consistent, and timely communications and physical presence were needed at targeted worldwide exhibitions and conferences.
- Achievement of greater competitive force through direct, synergistic product portfolio links was needed to address situations that were readily apparent in the organization's image and reputation within the marketplace.

Case Studies **309**

- Marketing and business development strategies were needed to more rapidly and effectively position the organization as top-of-mind with noted, scientific thought leaders in larger customer groups and research organizations. It was noted that the competition had already established a reputation with such influential players.
- The business development organization deserved to be viewed and respected as an equal contributor to the success of the organization. Global unity and stronger sense of community were recommended to produce significant lift.
- Immediate attention to these observations and concerns could make a significant difference to the long-term viability of the organization and all of its operations. Weak attempts or failure could dangerously signal the strategic intentions to the competition, and the organization would suffer mediocre market and economic results at best.

The researcher invited deeper exploration of recommendations for effectively implementing the future-oriented business development process. The principal recommendations included the following:

- An essential factor for the success of the new business development process and overall strategy was the visible buy-in, support, direct, and involved leadership of the executive sponsor, the international directors, marketing management, and business development professionals.
- A number of tools and information resources were needed to most effectively conduct the business development process. These included at least the following:
  - o Up-to-date, accurate, and precise feature and benefit information, with complete and global proof sources
  - o A consistent and reliable customer relationship management database that either improved or replaced the current, scattered and unaligned capabilities
  - o Accurate and verifiable competitive information that could be easily shared and accessible from any place, any time, and dynamically adapt to changes in the market spaces around the world
  - o Email access for business development professionals and managers in all countries, with laptop capability and connections so that everyone could participate real-time with enterprise peers
- Development of a more collaborative marketing and business development functional relationship with evidence of stronger, practical, and mutual focus on results.
- A practical process for the international business development professionals and managers to propagate competitive, market, regulatory, and product intelligence and expertise.
- A template to conduct situation analysis, establish pricing, create proposals, and craft the presentations of solutions to customers.

310 Case Studies

- Conducting skill assessments of the business development professionals as the basis for development and managing performance for superior results.

With the researcher's urging, the group made recommendations on measuring progress and the success of the pursuit of the new business development strategy and supporting processes. Their input list included the following items:

- The senior executive team's response to the outcomes and opinions of this intensive working session
- Establishing a specific project plan with timelines and milestones of accomplishments
- Conducting an inquiry or survey process to determine the impact of the new business development process on the entire international organization and its customers
- Establishing a baseline and periodic evaluation of the feedback and any areas of improvement
- Identifying specific impact or contributions to revenue, profitability, and the rate and rationale for staff departures
- Tracing the impact on the effectiveness of new product launches, cost of business development, and efficiency of close rates for the business
- Noting the degree of acceptance, involvement, and adaptation of these ideas by the North American counterparts, with the international group being recognized as a model for the organization

Upon the conclusion of the intensive working session, and in the final analysis and synthesis of all sources of findings throughout the comprehensive Rapid Due Diligence diagnostic process, the researcher offered further observations, conclusions, and recommendations for action.

- The organization enjoys a positive reputation in its international market space, due in large part to the sincere and diligent efforts of its geographically dispersed business development organization.
- Each contact expressed significant pride in the current accomplishments of the organization, optimism about its future, eagerness to seek out opportunities for continuous improvement, and readiness to lift the organization to an even higher level of performance.
- Upon reflection of the information and perspectives manifest throughout the Rapid Due Diligence diagnostic process, it is clear that the organization can significantly benefit from the creation and prompt implementation of its future-oriented business development process and the accompanying competency profiles for both professionals and managers.
- The researcher found little to no evidence of the application of consistent business development process steps across the international organization.

There was a high degree of freedom for how business development professionals prepared and organized for all customer contacts. Little to no uniformity of approach was evident in the customer contacts. In some, but not all cases, the business development professionals took an active role in these customer visits in identifying and seizing opportunities for further business.

- Nominal training has been offered to business development professionals and managers. The principal focus today is on orientation toward products. There is a variety of very short, one or two-day periods of skills training. There is no training for how to effectively convert an overarching marketing and business development strategy into explicit territory and key account planning.
- Not one business development professional could articulate the organization's strategy. They stated that they had become considerably self-reliant in establishing their own account strategies or any version of a territory plan. There was little evidence of frequent, active coaching for business development strategy and execution. Customer survey and other feedback data were not used to an acceptable degree, given the absence of an active and integrated marketing and business development strategy.
- A variety of locally designed mechanisms are in place to track business development activities. There is no pattern of follow-up to the provision of data. Little evidence was provided on how those data were analyzed to track direct linkages with any overarching business development strategy for market penetration, account protection, or business development effectiveness. Specific performance standards or expectations at various steps or stages in the business development process have not been established. This leaves a gap for coaching and performance management targets.
- Marketing and business development strategies and their sufficiency and clarity for global execution require a fresh evaluation.
- The current manifestation and consistency of the corporate image that is propagated globally, plus the marketplace reaction and response, require examination.
- The newly defined future-oriented business development process needs to be affirmed and launched. All members of the international business development organization need to be engaged to secure commitment to their respective roles and expectations for performance. The process needs to be supported by system tools, an in-depth communications plan, territory and account planning, and performance standards and metrics within a more intentional performance management mindset.
- The competency profiles identified for both business development professionals and managers need to be applied throughout the human resource or talent management system across the organization.
- Definitive business development tools, such as value proposition statements that differentiate the organization from its competition in high-value targeted markets and product categories, are needed.

312 Case Studies

Upon completion of the written report and supporting documentation, the researcher was invited to facilitate an executive team review and discussion of all key findings, observations, conclusions, and recommendations. Sincere gratitude was expressed for the thoroughness of the diagnostic process and the active engagement of so many levels of subject matter experts throughout the worldwide enterprise. According to the senior executives, this highly interactive variation of the Rapid Due Diligence diagnostic method produced significant insights into an already well-established and reputable organization. The approach also invited deep involvement and greater acceptance by a wide range of business development professionals, managers, and executives into the diagnostic results and recommendations.

Over the following months, the organization adopted nearly all of the recommendations and later reported significant engagement of the business development professionals and management in application of the new strategy and its supporting processes, systems, and tools. A number of performance metrics were already moving in consistently positive directions.

Discussion Questions

- Why was it important for the Rapid Due Diligence diagnostic method to include a wide variety of discovery techniques to secure international subject matter expert perspectives, plus the intensive working session?
- Why and how were analysis and synthesis techniques incorporated in the facilitated working session?
- How can the researcher refrain from introducing bias in such a complex diagnostic process?

11
FOR FURTHER CONSIDERATION

Learning Objectives

* To summarize the viability of the Rapid Due Diligence method as a diagnostic process for strategic decision-making.
* To gain ideas for further research and discovery.

Considering the number and selection of true examples in previous chapters, it should now be clear that the Rapid Due Diligence diagnostic method can indeed discover insights and hidden secrets for achieving real results. Furthermore, the process is intended to work without the frequent professional handicap of being expected to seek out selective circumstances that beg for a ready-made solution offered by a sponsoring firm.

In its full form, the Rapid Due Diligence diagnostic process diligently investigates all corners and edges of the presenting issue or business conundrum. Deep analytical consideration is given to all aspects at play, including:

* Technical systems, processes, and products
* All levels of leadership, governance models, organizational structures, and political or geographic undertones
* Market and customer choice analytics and multi-level sources of influence and approval
* Organizational culture, behavioral engagement, performance management, and capability and capacity to adapt to change
* Environmental, regulatory, and societal influences, responsibilities, and degrees of impact

314 For Further Consideration

The diagnostic method includes an active search for fresh, unique, even contradictory perspectives that can often emerge from unexpected sources or unlikely juxtapositions of data. The analysis tests the degree of fit between the espoused business model and how the strategy does or is expected to fulfill the intent of that model. The researcher examines the alignment and line-of-sight connections cascading throughout the organization.

All aspects of strategy execution are reviewed, including especially those arenas that long-term research shows are often the weak spots:

- Performance management (attention to setting clear expectations for performance; providing line-of-sight connections between personal actions and the results on the business; acquiring and applying new skills and knowledge; providing feedback, coaching, reinforcement, and recognition)
- Readiness of resources (human, financial, technical)
- Willingness to make changes necessary to fulfill the strategy (organizational and personal capability and capacity to make required changes, whether subtle or transformative)

Decisions, actions, processes, and practices in motion are filtered through tools for critical thinking, strategic analysis, and system dynamics. For example, causal loop diagramming portrays variables and causal links and influences. Positive and negative polarities can be identified that denote the potential for well-intended action to produce unintended consequences, organizational frustration, strategy exacerbation, or poor results. Path dependency and potential equilibrium issues are considered in all known economic, technical, social, scientific, and physical dimensions. Results are reviewed for amplifications or oscillations, even chronic instability, within known or hidden market force cyclical dynamics.

The process also includes inquiry into any cognitive limitations or the degree of rationality in critical decision-making. This includes testing how leaders solve complex problems and use information to make choices, whether decisions tend to be naïve, rational, or optimal, the presence of habitual or systematic errors, and the routine examination of critical assumptions.

Where major business processes lie at the center of the presenting situation, the Rapid Due Diligence researcher compares the actual effectiveness and efficiency to results that can be achieved with thorough, disciplined application of known process improvement techniques. Analyses include tests for the objective and thorough application of value stream analysis, plus the most up-to-date principles and best practices of Six Sigma, Lean, and 6s. The mechanics, or structure of the process, constitute one dimension. The research also evaluates the degree of behavioral engagement, adaptation to required changes, and actual performance in attending to the rhythm and results of a critical process.

For Further Consideration **315**

The Rapid Due Diligence diagnostic process also focuses on whether the current strategy is assuming a defensive focus upon solely mitigating risks. If so, recommendations will include specific ways to identify opportunities and unlock perhaps even greater potential.

Where greater business development ambitions are sought, the researcher will examine existing customer analytics and seek fresh insights from customers about their perspectives. These findings will include detail on the customer's process for moving from dislike or indifference to loyalty and the precise events or criteria that trigger decisions along the customer choice continuum. Where multiple people or layers of influence and approval exist, these dynamics will be investigated. Then, the business development process and competencies will be tested for degree of fit, alignment, and execution with the findings from customers.

An underlying, strong thread throughout the Rapid Due Diligence diagnostic process is the degree of attention to human capital. As noted in the researcher's Integrated Strategic Human Capital Alignment Framework appearing in the text, there is a multitude of considerations in matching the human capital assets with the strategy and performance of the organization. As appropriate, the Rapid Due Diligence diagnostic method draws upon the question sets accompanying each of the six cycle stages. More granular investigation is launched as needed.

Fortunately, in recent years, more organizations have been becoming equipped with facts and evidence that drive much wiser choices and attention to human capital management. Thorough Rapid Due Diligence diagnostics will help discover how well such cognition has been converted into actual daily practice.

Like any other process or technique, the Rapid Due Diligence diagnostic method deserves deeper inquiry and continuous improvement. A starter list of questions and ideas are framed below for further research and discovery.

- How can the Rapid Due Diligence diagnostic method continue to adapt to organizations that rely on digitization, social media, open systems, instantaneous global access, hyperscaled systems, and multi-layered feedback loops?
- How can the use of technology and enhanced online systems improve the quality and quantity of evidence gathering without introducing unintended system bias or tainted shortcuts?
- How can system dynamics be more comprehensively and reliably traced to produce even greater depth of understanding causality?
- What additional valuation methods, data analytics, creative business models, or other frameworks might be incorporated within the thirty-day time limit to gain greater insights and conduct hypotheses testing of recommendations?
- How can the Rapid Due Diligence diagnostic method become more adaptive to unique organizations and cultures residing anywhere in the world?
- How can new research into behavioral economics, customer choice analytics, generational or cultural differences, and the effects of digitization unleash

316 For Further Consideration

new strategic insights and be captured through the Rapid Due Diligence diagnostic method?

- What new competitive forces or strategic dimensions need to be incorporated within the Rapid Due Diligence diagnostic method?
- What is the potential for improving performance through the application of advanced neuroscience insights into neuroplasticity?

In summary, the Rapid Due Diligence diagnostic process is unlike other classic forms of data collection or assessment. The observations and recommendations can influence the organization's business model, core business strategy, key processes and systems, and relationships with customers, regulators, competitors, and employees.

Proof sources are provided, where possible, as convincing, positive evidence, designed to stimulate application of those recommendations. The final determination to act and move forward lies with the key organizational leaders and final decision-makers.

Selected Bibliography

This list of works and sources was helpful in the writing of this textbook and is provided for those who have an interest in pursuing the subject matter to a further degree.

Aghina, Wouter, Aaron DeSmet, and Kirsten Weerda. "Agility: It Rhymes with Stability." *McKinsey Quarterly* (December 2015).

Bass, Eddie, ed. *Talent Management: Cases and Commentary.* London: Palgrave Macmillan, 2009.

Beck, Don Edward, and Christopher C. Cowan. *Spiral Dynamics: Mastering Values, Leadership, and Change.* Malden, MA: Blackwell Publishing, 2006.

BenMark, Gadi, and Maher Masri. "Cracking the Digital-Shopper Genome." *McKinsey Quarterly* (August 2015).

Birkinshaw, Julian, and Jonas Ridderstrale. "Adhocracy for an Agile Age." *McKinsey Quarterly* (December 2015).

Bollard, Albert, Clark Durant, Matt Tobelmann, and Rohit Sood. "Transforming Expert Organizations." *McKinsey Quarterly* (January 2016).

Boudreau, John W., and Peter M. Ramstad. *Beyond HR: The New Science of Human Capital.* Boston: Harvard Business School Press, 2007.

Bryan, Lowell, J., and Claudia I, Joyce. *Mobilizing Minds: Creating Wealth from Talent in the 21st-Century Organization.* New York: McGraw-Hill, 2007.

Burton, Richard M., and Borge Obel. *Strategic Organizational Diagnosis and Design: The Dynamics of Fit, Third Edition.* New York: Springer Science + Business Media, 2004.

Camp, Justin J. *Venture Capital Due Diligence: A Guide to Making Smart Investment Choices and Increasing Your Portfolio Returns.* New York: John Wiley & Sons, Inc., 2002.

Cappelli, Peter. *Talent on Demand: Managing Talent in an Age of Uncertainty.* Boston: Harvard Business School Press, 2008.

Charan, Ram. *Leadership in the Era of Economic Uncertainty: The New Rules for Getting the Right Things Done in Difficult Times.* New York: McGraw-Hill, 2009.

Christensen, Clayton M. *The Innovator's Dilemma: The Revolutionary Book That Will Change the Way You Do Business.* New York: HarperCollins, 2003.

For Further Consideration **317**

Cokins, Gary. *Performance Management: Integrating Strategy Execution, Methodologies, Risk, and Analytics.* Hoboken, NJ: John Wiley & Sons, Inc., 2009.

Davenport, Thomas H., and Jeanne G. Harris. *Competing on Analytics: The New Science of Winning.* Boston: Harvard Business School Press, 2007.

Davenport, Thomas H., Jeanne G. Harris, and Robert Morison. *Analytics at Work: Smarter Decisions, Better Results.* Boston: Harvard Business Press, 2010.

De Jong, Marc, and Menno van Dijk. "Disrupting Beliefs: A New Approach to Business-Model Innovation." *McKinsey Quarterly* (July 2015).

De Jong, Marc, Nathan Marston, and Erik Roth. "The Eight Essentials of Innovation." *McKinsey Quarterly* (April 2015).

DeSmet, Aaron, Susan Lund, and William Schaninger. "Organizing for the Future." *McKinsey Quarterly* (January 2016).

Desmet, Driek, Ewan Duncan, Jay Scanlan, and Marc Singer. "Six Building Blocks for Creating a High-Performing Digital Enterprise." *McKinsey Quarterly* (September 2015).

Dobbs, Richard, Tim Koller, Sree Ramaswamy, Jonathan Woltzel, James Manyika, Rohit Krishnan, and Nicolo Andreula. "Playing to Win: The New Global Competition for Corporate Profits." *McKinsey Global Institute* (September 2015).

Gluck, Fred, Michael G. Jacobides, and Dan Simpson. "Synthesis, Capabilities, and Overlooked Insights: Next Frontiers for Strategists." *McKinsey Quarterly* (September 2014).

Hamel, Gary. *The Future of Management.* Harvard Business School Press, 2007.

Johnson, Mark W. *Seizing the White Space: Business Model Innovation for Growth and Renewal.* Boston: Harvard Business Press, 2010.

Joyce, Paul. *Strategic Management in the Public Sector.* Abingdon, UK: Routledge, 2015.

Kaplan, Robert S., and David P. Norton. *Alignment: Using the Balanced Scorecard to Create Corporate Synergies.* Boston: Harvard Business School Press, 2006.

Keiningham, Timothy L., Terry G. Vavra, Lerzan Aksoy, and Henri Wallard. *Loyalty Myths: Hyped Strategies That Will Put You Out of Business—and Proven Tactics That Really Work.* Hoboken, NJ: John Wiley & Sons, Inc., 2005.

Kilian, Jennifer, Hugo Sarrazin, and Hyo Yeon. "Building a Design-Driven Culture." *McKinsey Quarterly* (September 2015).

Koller, Tim, Marc Goldhart, and David Wessels. *Valuation: Meaning and Managing the Value of Companies, Fifth Edition.* Hoboken, NJ: John Wiley & Sons, Inc., 2010.

Lund, Susan, James Manyika, and Kelsey Robinson. "Managing Talent in a Digital Age." *McKinsey Quarterly* (March 2016).

McFarland, Keith. *Bounce: The Art of Turning Tough Times into Triumph.* New York: Crown Business, 2009.

Midler, Christopher, Guy Minquet, and Monique Vervalke, eds. *Working on Innovation.* New York: Routledge, 2010.

Osterwalder, Alexander, and Yves Pigneur. *Business Model Generation.* Hoboken, NJ: John Wiley & Sons, Inc., 2010.

Pfeffer, Jeffrey. *What Were They Thinking? Unconventional Wisdom about Management.* Boston: Harvard Business School Press, 2007.

Rianchi, Raffaella, Gergely Gacsal, and Daniel Svoboda. "Overcoming Obstacles to Digital Customer Care." *McKinsey Quarterly* (August 2015).

Richards, Tuck, Kate Smaje, and Vik Schoni. "'Transformer in Chief': The New Chief Digital Officer." *McKinsey Quarterly* (September 2015).

Schmitt, Bernd H. *Customer Experience Management: A Revolutionary Approach to Connecting With Your Customers.* Hoboken, NJ: John Wiley & Sons, Inc., 2003.

Skarzynski, Peter, and Rowan Gibson. *Innovation to the Core: A Blueprint for Transforming the Way Your Company Innovates.* Boston: Harvard Business Press, 2008.

318 For Further Consideration

Storey, John, Patrick M. Wright, and Dave Ulrich, eds. *The Routledge Companion to Strategic Human Resource Management*. London: Routledge, 2009.

Thompsen, Joyce A. *Achieving a Triple Win: Human Capital Management of the Employee Lifecycle*. London: Routledge, 2010.

Tichy, Noel M., and Warren G. Bennis. *Judgment: How Winning Leaders Make Great Calls*. New York: Penguin Group, 2007.

Trompenaars, Fons. *Riding the Whirlwind: Connecting People and Organisations in a Culture of Innovation*. Oxford: The Infinite Ideas Company Limited, 2007.

Trompenaars, Fons, and Charles Hampden-Turner. *Riding the Waves of Culture: Understanding Diversity in Global Business, Second Edition*. New York: McGraw-Hill, 1998.

Ulrich, Dave, and Wayne Brockbank. *The HR Value Proposition*. Boston: Harvard Business School Press, 2005.

Vaimon, Vlad, and Charles M. Vance, eds. *Smart Talent Management: Building Knowledge Assets for Competitive Advantage*. Cheltenham, UK: Edward Elgar Publishing Limited, 2008.

Van Dooren, Wouter, Geert Bouckaert, and John Halligan. *Performance Management in the Public Sector, Second Edition*. Abingdon, UK: Routledge, 2015.

INDEX

accountability, virtual project teams 149
acquisitions, cultural fit 113–115
actions, comparing 190–191
advisory councils, corporate universities 273
agendas, slide decks for Rapid Due Diligence discussion 187
aligning: objectives with business 85; strategic dimensions 212
alignment and fit among strategic dimensions 60–83; questions for analysis 61–64
amplifications in key processes 141–142
analysis and observation development 54–55; barriers to strategy execution 82–83; capabilities and capacity to perform and achieve targets 90–94; capability and capacity for change 107–113; categories of 59–60; cultural fit within mergers and acquisitions 113–115; data management 55–59; effective and efficient operations 127–128; employee value proposition 94–97; execution of strategies to achieve targeted results 81–90; high-quality measurement and evaluation methods 72–73; innovative product development 124–127; Integrated Strategic Human Capital Alignment Framework 97–106; measurable targets 73–74; questions 61–64; tracing economic value-producing paths 115–123; tracking impact of learning strategies 75–80
analysis operation 57–59

anonymity 44
applied social science research, Rapid Due Diligence 12–13; applying Rapid Due Diligence to not-for-profit organizations, case studies 208, 284–300; charts 291–293; congregation and leader goals 294–296; mission planning with congregation council 289–290; tracing strategic dimensions 284–300
appraisals, performance management 88–89
awareness building, organizational capacity for change integration 110

barriers to strategy execution 82–83
behavioral economics, synthesis and formulation of recommendations 156
bias, guidelines for reducing 14
bias-free stance for researchers 44
boxes: building organizational capacity for change integration 108–113; competencies for business development professionals and managers 306–308; conducting a variety of discovery techniques 46; corporate university launch announcement: key talking points and process 274–278; customer site visits 50; development of an employee value proposition 96–97; discovery techniques in production operations 48–49; document review notes 32; document review summary 33; draft investigative research design

320 Index

26–27; effects of hidden disagreement 140; example of integrating differing geographic cultures 143–144; examples of scope inquiry 28; external research comparison 161–163; improving operational quality and efficiency 128; insights on customer preferences 119–121; mapping strategic drivers to sales performance metrics 70–72; measuring effectiveness and impact of learning strategies 75–80; mission planning charts 291–293; multinational business development process 122; partial set of sample recommendations 176; sample interview guide 37–39; sample of multiple discovery methods 36; sample of preliminary observations 160–161; seeking product development improvements 125–127; strategic planning map 299

business development management, competencies 307–308

business development process 216

business development professionals, competencies 306–308

business focus, implementation options 167

business models: creating 115–116; examining 73

business plans, corporate universities 265–274

case studies: applying Rapid Due Diligence to not-for-profit organizations 208, 284–300; creating post-merger talent management strategies 204; developing a corporate university 205–206, 263–278; effective client-focused service strategies 204–205, 256–263; improving Lean Six Sigma Rapid Improvement Event Structured Observations Grid 228–232; improving operational quality and efficiency 203–204, 225–240; international business development strategies 300–312; post-merger talent management strategies 240–255; pursuing international business development strategies 209–210; seeking an enterprise-wide approach to sales 201–202, 211–218; shifting operating models 202–203, 218–225; stabilizing software development startup organizations 207–208, 278–284

case study methodology 12–14

categories of analysis and observation development 59–60

causal loop diagramming 222; synthesis and formulation of recommendations 137–138

change, capability and capacity for 107–113

change assessment, organizational capacity for change integration 111

change capability 107, 199

change curriculums, creation of 112–113

change initiatives, interfering factors 107

characteristics of researchers, Rapid Due Diligence 13–14

charts: for comparing courses of action 190–191; mission planning with congregation council 291–293; sample implementation charts 188–190; sample RACI chart 193

client-focused service strategies, case studies 204–205, 256–263

closing, Rapid Due Diligence diagnostic process 199–200

coaching, performance management 87–88

code list for analysis operations 55–56

coding for drawing conclusions, analysis operation: reading data for analysis 58–59

cognitive and behavioral limitations, synthesis and formulation of recommendations 138–140

collaboration, leadership 150–151

communication: corporate universities 271; face-to-face communication 146–147; virtual project teams 146

communication plans 194–197

communications planning, tactical level 169

communities, building 147–148

comparative benchmarking 80–81

comparing: courses of action 190–191; diagnostics methods 7–9

compensatory changes, performance management 89

competencies: for business development management 307–308; for business development professionals 306–307; individual performance objectives 86–87; leadership 229, 238

conclusions: synthesis and formulation of recommendations 158–165; Triple Win 163–164

conducting a variety of discovery techniques 46
constructing questions 34–36
continuum of management support 224
continuum of strategic fit 62
coordination, leadership 150–151
corporate universities: developing 205–206; case studies 263–278; goals 268–269
Critical Knowledge Areas© 90–94; software development startup organizations 280–281; tables 93–94
critical talent 90–94
cultural fit: integrating differing geographic cultures 143–144; leadership 144–145; mergers and acquisitions 113–115
curriculum, corporate universities 270
customer experience, trigger points 118–119
customer preferences 119–121
customer service culture change 257
customer service expectations 165
customer site visits 50
customers, scope of inquiry 23

data management: analysis and observation development 55–59; on-site discovery 51–52
decision analysis processes, examining 156–158
decision-making, need for diagnostics 1–4
deductive researchers 159
delivery of process results 180–200; comparing courses of action 190–191; employee turnover 191–192; implementation project maps, presenting 188–189; project maps 183–186; sample communication plans 194–197; written reports 181–182
developing: corporate universities, case studies 205–206, 263–278; employee value proposition 96–97
diagnostic stages of Rapid Due Diligence 9–11
diagnostics 1; in decision-making 1–4
diagnostics methods, comparing 7–9
diagramming, causal loop diagramming 137–138, 221–222
direct observations, on-site discovery 47–50
disagreements, effects of hidden disagreement 140

discovery, on-site discovery see on-site discovery
discovery methods 34–36
discovery techniques in production operations 48–49
document review notes 32
document review summary 33
documentation: preparatory investigation 31–34; scope of inquiry 23–24
draft investigative research and diagnostic design 25–27
drivers of: loyalty 164; performance 118

economic value: drivers of 70–71; tracing economic value-producing paths 115–123
efficiency: improving 127–128, 203–204; case studies 225–240
employee turnover 191–192
employee value proposition 94–97; development of 96–97
employees, scope of inquiry 23
employment brand 94
engagement 109
Enterprise Excellence Federation 226
enterprise-wide approaches to sales, case studies 201–202
enterprise-wide business development process 123; case studies 211–218
execution 109
execution strategies: achieving targeted results 81–90; organizational capacity for change integration 112–113
executive summaries 182–183; slide decks for Rapid Due Diligence discussion 187
executives, scope of inquiry 22
expectations for performance 199
expected impact, implementation options 173
external research comparison, synthesis and formulation of recommendations 161–163

face-to-face communication 146–147
fairness, performance management 147
feedback loops, synthesis and formulation of recommendations 136–137
flow network diagrams 64, 67
focused management attention, talent 91
frameworks, Integrated Strategic Human Capital Alignment Framework 97–106

322 Index

geographic cultures: integrating 143–144; trust 147

geographic dispersion, synthesis and formulation of recommendations 142–154; leadership *see* leadership

goals: congregation and leader goals 294–296; corporate universities 268–269

guidelines for researchers of Rapid Due Diligence 14

handoffs 149

hidden disagreements, effects of 140

high-quality measurement and evaluation methods 72–73

hostility in interviews 44

human capital, Integrated Strategic Human Capital Alignment Framework 97–106, 246–254

implementation options: expected impact 173; participants 170; preparing recommendations for action 167–175; progress evaluation 172; training identification 170

implementation planning: strategic level 167; tactical level 168

implementation project maps 183–186; presenting 188–190

improvements: operational quality and efficiency 128; to product development 125–127

improving operational quality and efficiency 203–204; case studies 225–240

individual performance objectives 85–86

inductive researchers 159

inhibitors 224

initiative, leadership 148

in-person interviews 34

integrated strategic focus and potential for impact 65

Integrated Strategic Human Capital Alignment Framework 97–106, 246–254

integrating, differing geographic cultures 143–144

international business development strategies: case studies 300–312; pursuing 209–210

interview content and analysis notations, on-site discovery 56

interviews 43–46; panel interviews 49–50; sample interview guides 37–39; telephone interviews 46

investigation research design, Rapid Due Diligence 13

investigative protocols, preparatory investigation 34–39

iterative feedback loops, synthesis and formulation of recommendations 136–137

key contacts, scope of inquiry 20–23

key processes, oscillations and amplifications 141–142

knowledge, Critical Knowledge Areas© 90–94

launch announcements, corporate universities 274–278

leadership: accountability 149; communication, virtual project teams 146; coordination and collaboration 150–151; discovery tool: leadership from a distance 151–154; geographic cultures 144–145; initiative 148; performance management 149–150; vision 148–149

leadership competencies 229, 238

Lean 6s: improving operational quality and efficiency, case studies 227; rapid improvement event structured observations grid 228–232

learning management systems, corporate universities 271

learning strategies, tracking impact of 75–80

Likert-type scale of responses 35

limitations, cognitive and behavioral limitations 138–140

list of commonly used ratios 69

longitudinal research 81

loyalty, value of 118

loyalty drivers 164

mail surveys 35

mapping strategic drivers to sales performance metrics 70–72

mapping techniques 68

maps: implementation project maps 188–190; project maps *see* project maps; strategic fulfillment map 298; strategic planning map 299

marketing, corporate universities 271

matrix intersections 198

measurable targets 73–74

measurement of progress, corporate universities 272

measuring effectiveness and impact of learning strategies 75–80

mergers, cultural fit 113–115

metrics to gauge performance of new operating model 221

middle managers, scope of inquiry 22

mission planning charts 291–293

mission planning with congregation council 289–290

multinational business development process 122

multi-phase approach to building organizational capacity for change 109–113

mutual accountability 149

not-for-profit organizations, applying Rapid Due Diligence to 208, 284–300; applying Rapid Due Diligence to not-for-profit organizations, case studies 208, 284–300; charts 291–293; congregation and leader goals 294–296; mission planning with congregation council 289–290; tracing strategic dimensions 284–300

objectives, aligning to business 85

observations, synthesis and formulation of recommendations 158–165; preliminary observations 160–161

online questionnaires 35

online surveys 35, 51

on-site discovery 42; conducting a variety of discovery techniques 46; customer site visits 50; data management 51–52; direct observations 47–50; discovery techniques in production operations 48–49; interview content and analysis notations 56; interviews 43–46; online surveys 51; panel interview content and analysis notations 57; players involved 42

open-end survey questions 36

operating groups, corporate universities 272–273

operating models, shifting 202–203; case studies 218–225

operational quality, improving 128, 203–204; case studies 225–240

operations, effective and efficient operations 127–128

organizational capacity for change integration 108–113

organizations, strategic dimensions of organizations 31, 60–61

oscillations in key processes 141–142

outside-in approach to customers 165

owners of situations, scope of inquiry 20

panel interview content and analysis notations, on-site discovery 57

panel interviews 49–50

partial set of sample recommendations 176

participants, implementation options (delivery of process results) 170

performance, drivers of 118

performance management 82–85; appraisals 88–89; coaching 87–88; compensatory changes 88–89; competencies 86–87; expectations 199; individual performance objectives 85–86; leadership 149–150

performance metrics 71–72

personal interviews 34

personal scorecards 71–72

players involved: analysis and observation development 54; delivery of process results 180; preparatory investigation 30; scope of inquiry 19–23; on-site discovery 42; synthesis and formulation of recommendations 135

post-merger talent management strategies: case studies 240–255; creating 204

preparing recommendations for action 165–177

preparatory investigation 30; documentation 31–34; investigative protocols 34–39; refined investigative research design 40

presenting implementation project maps 188

principal researcher, scope of inquiry 22

principal themes 160

product development 124–127

progress evaluation, implementation options 172

project maps 183–186; presenting 188; samples 186; template 185

protocols, investigative protocols 34–39

questions: analysis and observation development 61–64; constructing 35–36; synthesis and formulation of recommendations 155; decision analysis processes 156–158

324 Index

RACI chart 191, 193

Rapid Due Diligence 1, 7; analysis and observation development *see* analysis and observation development; applied social science research 12–13; characteristics of researchers 13–14; closing diagnostic process 199–200; delivery of process results *see* delivery of process results; diagnostic process 313–316; investigation research design 13; preparatory investigation *see* preparatory investigation; scope of inquiry *see* scope of inquiry; on-site discovery *see* on-site discovery; stages of 9–11; synthesis and formulation of recommendations *see* synthesis and formulation of recommendations; Triple Win 8–9

ratios, list of commonly used ratios 69

Real Options Value (ROV) 92

recommendations: partial set of sample recommendations 176; preparing for action 165–177

reducing bias 14

references 164

refined investigative research design, preparatory investigation 40

reports, structure of 181–182

representatives of the market, scope of inquiry 22–23

research, external research comparison 161–163

researchers: bias-free stance 44; characteristics of (Rapid Due Diligence) 13–14; guidelines for 14; preparatory investigation 31–32; principal researchers, scope of inquiry 21–22; scope of inquiry 23

results 109

RoM (Return on Merger) 113

ROV (Real Options Value) 92

sales managerial skill critical to productivity and effectiveness 165

sales performance metrics, mapping strategic drivers to 70–72

sales performance scorecard 71

sample communication plans 194–197

sample implementation charts 188–190

sample interview guides 37–39

sample of multiple discovery methods 36

sample project maps 186

SARI (Situation-Action-Result-Impact) 80

scope of inquiry 19, 28; documentation 23–24; draft investigative research and diagnostic design 25–27; players involved 19–21

scorecards 71–72; strategic fulfillment scorecard 300

shifting operating models 218–225; case studies 202–203

situation worksheet with strategic thinking questions 66

Situation-Action-Result-Impact (SARI) 80

Six Sigma 232; *see also* Lean 6s

slide deck for Rapid Due Diligence discussion 187

software development startup organizations, stabilizing 207–208, 278–284

sources of Rapid Due Diligence evidence 26

stabilizing software development startup organizations 207–208, 278–284

stages of Rapid Due Diligence 9–11

strategic dimensions 212

strategic dimensions of organizations 31, 60–61

strategic fulfillment map 298

strategic fulfillment scorecard 300

strategic level, implementation planning 167

strategic planning map 299

strategies: client-focused service strategies 204–205, 256–263; execution strategies, achieving targeted results 81–90; international business development strategies 209–210, 300–312; post-merger talent management strategies 204, 240–255; strategy execution, barriers to 82–83

strategy execution 109, 165; barriers to 82–83

subject matter experts, direct observations 47

summaries 182–183; slide deck for Rapid Due Diligence discussion 187

surveys 35, 51

synthesis and formulation of recommendations 135–136; behavioral economics 156; casual loop diagramming 137–138; cognitive and behavioral limitations 138–140; examining decision analysis processes 156–158; geographic dispersion

142–154; iterative feedback loops 136–137; new strategies 154–156; observations and conclusions 158–165; oscillations and amplifications in key processes 141–142; preparing recommendations for action 165–177; system dynamics 136
system dynamics, synthesis and formulation of recommendations 136

tables: analysis operation: coding for drawing conclusions 58–59; analysis operation: reading data for analysis 57–58; business development process 216; code list for analysis operations 55–56; components of measurable targets 73–74; congregation and leader goals 294–296; discovery tool: leadership from a distance 151–154; elements contributing to an employee value proposition 95; enterprise-wide business development process 123; factor interfering with change initiatives 107; implementation options 167–175; integrated strategic focus and potential for impact 65; Integrated Strategic Human Capital Alignment Framework 99–106; Integrated Strategic Human Capital Alignment framework 247–254; key areas of mission and ministry worksheets 297; Lean Six Sigma Rapid Improvement Event Structured Observations Grid 228–232; list of commonly used ratios 69; managing matrix intersections 198; mission planning with congregation council 289–290; mutual expectations for performance with major customers 199; potential cost of employee turnover 192; potential Critical Knowledge Areas© 93; potential critical talent profile to effectively activate Critical Knowledge Areas© 93–94; principal themes from commentary 160; project map template 185; sample communication plans 194–197; sample competencies by job family 86–87; sample implementation chart 188–190; sample project map 186; sample RACI chart 193; on-site

discovery: interview content and analysis notations 56; on-site discovery: panel interview content and analysis notations 57; situation worksheet with strategic thinking questions 66; strategic dimensions of organizations 31, 60–61; strategic fulfillment map 298; strategic fulfillment scorecard 300
tactical level: communications planning 169; implementation planning 168
talent, critical talent 90–94
talking points, corporate universities 274–278
targeted results, achieving through execution strategies 81–90
targets, capabilities and capacity to achieve 90–94
telephone interviews 46
telephone surveys 35
template, project maps 185
themes 159–160
tracing economic value-producing paths 115–123
tracking impact of, learning strategies 75–80
training identification, implementation options 170
trigger points, customer experience 118–119
Triple Win 8; conclusions 163–164
trust 147

valid business reason (VBR) 113
value driver visualization 91
value drivers 73–74
value erosion 82, 90
value of loyalty 118
value trees 91
VBR (valid business reason) 113
virtual project teams see also leadership; building communities 147–148; communication 146; coordination and collaboration 150–151; geographic cultures 145; mutual accountability 149; performance management 149–150
vision, leadership 148

written reports, structure of 181–182